Servants of the Poor

Servants of the Poor

TEACHERS AND MOBILITY
IN IRELAND AND IRISH AMERICA

Janet Nolan

UNIVERSITY OF NOTRE DAME PRESS
NOTRE DAME, INDIANA

Manufactured in the United States of America

Library of Congress Cataloging-in-Publication Data
Nolan, Janet.
 Servants of the poor : teachers and mobility in Ireland and Irish America /
Janet Nolan.
  p. cm.
 Includes bibliographical references and index.
 ISBN 0-268-03659-4 (cloth : alk. paper)
 ISBN 0-268-03660-8 (pbk. : alk. paper)
  1. Women teachers—United States—History. 2. Irish American women—
Education (Higher)—United States—History. 3. Irish American
women—Social conditions—United States—History. 4. Women—Education—
Ireland—History. 5. Social mobility—Ireland—History. 6. Social mobility—
United States—History. I. Title.

LB2837.N65 2004
371.1'0089162—dc22
2004018914

∞ *This book is printed on acid-free paper.*

To William Francis Nolan

and the late

Janet Moakley Nolan,

Servants of the Poor

CONTENTS

Preface   ix
Acknowledgments   xiii

Introduction: Servants of the Poor   1

Chapter 1
Irish Education: The Best Intentions   9

Chapter 2
Irish Schools: Windows of Opportunity   25

Chapter 3
"Boston Schools for Boston Girls!"   43

Chapter 4
San Francisco: Pioneers in the Classroom   65

Chapter 5
Chicago: Paradigm Shift   81

Chapter 6
The End of a Golden Age   103

Chapter 7
"The One Thing They Can't Take Away"   121

Notes   139
Bibliography   167
Index   185

One of my surprises when I was writing my first book, *Ourselves Alone: Women's Emigration from Ireland, 1885–1920* (Lexington: University Press of Kentucky, 1989), which documented the unusual emigration pattern of young, unmarried women leaving Ireland for the United States in the late nineteenth and early twentieth centuries, was the discovery that my paternal grandmother, Mary Ann Donovan, was one of the women I was writing about. Born on St. Patrick's Day, Mary Ann was a pupil-teacher at her local national school before leaving her home in Skibbereen, County Cork, for Boston at the age of sixteen in 1888. Sadly, since I had been born far away from her home in Lynn, Massachusetts, I do not remember meeting her until a few years before her death in 1960. I was too young then to know how important her life story would be to my future work, and I never quizzed her about her long and remarkable life. Nevertheless, the seventh of her nine children, my father William, and her youngest child, my late Aunt Helen, both public school teachers, later shared with me their memories of Mary Ann's tales of Skibbereen, her migration to America, and her own and her children's adjustment to American life. Like me, millions of other Irish Americans can also point to a parent, aunt, grandmother, or great aunt who left Ireland or who taught in an urban public school. It seems that much of America has been populated by the women I think of as "my girls"!

Both of my parents, in fact, were public school teachers. William Francis Nolan and Janet Moakley Nolan graduated from Salem Teachers College in Salem, Massachusetts, in 1935. My father was born in 1912 in Lynn, Massachusetts, an industrial city of over 100,000 situated a few miles north of Boston along the Atlantic coast. Founded in 1629, a year earlier than Boston, Lynn retained its own separate identity and was never a satellite of the

Bay State's capital. Throughout its history, Lynn had one of the largest school systems in the commonwealth.

As a 1929 graduate of Lynn's English High School, my father spent the years immediately afterwards seeking work in the depths of the Depression. Since his Cork-born father Harry and several of his older brothers already worked at the General Electric plant near their West Lynn home, my father waited by its factory door each morning hoping to get hired for the day by a passing foreman. Unlike his father (who died in 1930) and his older brothers Johnny, Harry, and Joe, who were already on the job before the Depression, my father stood for days on end in a line of other unemployed men without ever getting the nod for a job. One day, his now-widowed mother suggested that he take a post-graduate college-prep year at Lynn's English High School to qualify him for entrance into Salem Teachers College, where he enrolled in 1931. In 1935, he would be the first in his family to graduate from a four-year college, and the only one of Mary Ann Donovan and Harry Nolan's six sons to do so.

My destiny was assured when my father met another Salem freshman from Lexington, Massachusetts, Janet Moakley, although the Depression prevented my future parents from marrying until 1941. Nevertheless, both found teaching jobs after leaving college, my father in Lynn at the Cobbet "Ungraded," a school for those unable to learn at the pace of regular school classrooms, and my mother in Watertown, Massachusetts, where she taught large numbers of Armenian children whose parents and grandparents had fled the Turks. Only after the death of her mother, Mary Ellen (Ella) Martin Moakley, were the two able to marry. Had my mother, who supported her widowed mother, gotten married before Ella's death, she would have lost her teaching job, as laws preventing wives from keeping their school positions were enacted during the dark years of the Depression. My father's salary alone would not have supported three people even though he was the highest paid member of his Salem graduation class, earning a salary of $1,700 a year. My mother, voted the "most popular" girl by her Salem classmates, was paid $1,000 a year in her first job. Both knew they were lucky to have salaries in those difficult economic times.

My parents' modestly-paid teaching jobs changed the economic prospects of their families. My mother was born in 1914, the youngest of three sisters. Her eldest sister Louise was a married mother by the time my mother graduated from Salem Teachers College, and her other sister, Laura, had also left the family household by then. As the youngest daughter, my mother supported herself and her widowed mother Ella with her teaching salary.

Ella's father, William Martin, had been born in Waterford, Ireland, on Christmas Day in 1854. He died at sea in December 1885, going down with his Gloucester, Massachusetts, fishing schooner "Hyperion" off the Georges Banks.* Left alone with an infant daughter, Ella's now-widowed mother, Annie Power Martin, took a housekeeping job on Boston's Beacon Hill. Eventually she remarried and gave birth to Ella's half sister, Anna McInerney. With tuition funds sent by relatives in Belfast, Ireland, Ella graduated from Boston's Burdett Business School in the early 1900s. Anna became a teacher in the Revere, Massachusetts, schools after graduating from the Bridgewater, Massachusetts, Normal School in 1917.

My father's job at the Cobbet Ungraded, plus his summer WPA-sponsored playground instructorships, allowed him to contribute enough to the family income to allow his oldest brothers Johnny and Harry to marry and leave their mother's household. His other older brothers eventually followed suit: Jim left home to be a newspaper reporter and Joe set up housekeeping with his new wife Margaret, a native of County Mayo. Nevertheless, even at the end of the 1930s, two of Mary Ann's six sons and all three of her daughters lived at home.

By 1935, my mother and Ella were living in Cambridge, Massachusetts, not far from my mother's Watertown classroom. Her salary allowed her to support Ella until Ella's death in the spring of 1941. After Ella died, and a decade after they had first met, my parents married in Cambridge on June 27, 1941, and my mother resigned from her Watertown classroom. By that time, my father's youngest sister, Helen, had also graduated from Salem Teachers College and was teaching in Lynn. Her salary, along with that of her older sister Kathleen, a bookkeeper, supported their mother until Kathleen's death in 1954 and Mary Ann's in 1960. Another older sister, Mary, also graduated from Salem Teachers College, but later left the classroom to marry. Helen left teaching and married only after their mother Mary Ann died.

Like all women teaching in Massachusetts in the 1930s and 1940s, my mother had to leave her teaching job when she married. She spent the war

---

* "William Martin, master, leaves widow and one child, Another Gloucester Vessel Given Up With Her Crew of Twelve Men," *The Hyperion* (Gloucester, Mass.), 29 January 1886.

years crossing the United States with her husband, now a naval officer. Their first child, Brian, was born in Minneapolis. I was their second child, born in San Francisco after the war. In the meantime, the marriage bar preventing wives from keeping their teaching jobs had been successfully challenged in the Massachusetts Supreme Court by another Lynn schoolteacher. By the time my family returned to Massachusetts from North Carolina in the mid-1950s, therefore, both my parents could return to teaching. My mother's teaching career was again interrupted, however—this time by her third pregnancy. Although married women no longer permanently lost their class-room jobs, motherhood in those years required women teachers to take a two-year unpaid leave of absence after giving birth. My mother used this enforced period of retirement to raise her last child, Nancy, and to earn a master's degree from Boston University, as my father had before her in 1940. She then returned to teaching.

Like our grandmothers, aunts, and parents, my sister and I also repre-sent a pattern among the children and grandchildren of Irish women in the United States. Our paternal grandmother Mary Ann Donovan had been a pupil-teacher in the national school in her native Skibbereen before leav-ing for Massachusetts, and our American-born maternal grandmother Ella Martin had a post–high school business degree in an era when very few Americans, male or female, reached the eighth grade. Furthermore, both our grandmothers had daughters with college degrees teaching in the Bos-ton area.

I followed in the footsteps of my grandmothers, aunts, and parents by becoming a public school teacher in Delaware and Massachusetts. As new careers opened up for qualified women in the 1970s, I left teaching for graduate school, eventually earning a doctorate in history. My sister also benefitted from the changed opportunities for women. By the time she was in her early twenties, she held a law degree and membership in the Mas-sachusetts bar and now teaches in Washington state, where she lives with her family. My brother Brian never wanted to be a teacher like his parents and sisters. Without the Depression to contend with, he was able to earn far more as a business executive than as a public school teacher. Nevertheless, several of Ella and Mary Ann's granddaughters today are teachers. The edu-cational legacy passed down to us by our grandmothers can be found in countless other Irish-American families as well.

ACKNOWLEDGMENTS

This study builds on previously published work of mine, and on the scholarship of others, particularly Grainne Blair, Joanna Bourke, Mary Hickman, Suellen Hoy, Charles Fanning, David Fitzpatrick, Lawrence McCaffrey, Deirdre Mageean, Maureen Murphy, Grace Neville, and Ellen Skerrett. It also draws on Irish, Northern Irish, and American archival materials including national school enrollment figures, school textbooks and readers, and the deliberations of Irish National Commissioners of Education and their counterparts on the school boards of Boston, Chicago, and San Francisco. In addition, school personnel directories in each American city under study here helped determine the numbers of Irish Americans teaching in their public schools. The staffs at the National Library of Ireland, the National Archives of Ireland, the Public Record Office of Northern Ireland, and the San Francisco History Center were tireless in their willingness to find and, in many cases, help lift the sometimes very heavy files I consulted. Ellen Skerrett and Suellen Hoy also deserve special thanks for sharing the fruits of their tireless work in Chicago-area archives with me.

My own family history stems from the oral and written memories of Ella Martin Moakley's daughters: my mother Janet Moakley Nolan and my aunt Laura Moakley Harvey; Ella's granddaughter Isabelle (Wissie) Harvey Wilkinson and her greatniece Anne (Nancy) Power Parsons; and by Mary Ann Donovan Nolan's children, Helen Nolan Need and William Francis Nolan. William Nolan's 309-page "Memoirs to My Family," written in 1979, has proven to be an exceptionally valuable source.

This book is also enriched by the eye-witness testimonies, written and oral, of other individual Irish Americans, seen here for the first time. These personal testimonies demonstrate the connection between education and

Irish-American mobility in ways that no other sources can. My work is especially indebted to the Irish-born Chicagoan Delia McNeela Tully, and to Chicago teachers Eileen Burke, Mary Ann Clancy, Alice Dargan Clark, Marie O'Donnell Cody, Elizabeth Conlon, Joan Costello, Karen Crotty, Peg Cunningham, Chris Doran, Joan Enright, Ann Garrity, Patricia Hanlon, Margaret Hawkins, Kay Hester, Mary Hogan, Mary Hornung, Eugene Jeratis, Alice O'Malley Keane, Eleanor Mueller King, Daniel King, William King, Joanne Bufferin Konrath, Joyce Kopecky, Mary Theresa Gilger Korrison, Cathleen Walsh Laduzinsky, Helen Lyons, Judith McGovern, Maureen McMahon, Ann McNally, Veronica Meyer, Edward Mueller, Dudley Nee, Loretta Nolan, Tom O'Brien, Betty Hastings O'Connor, Eileen O'Malley, Mary Pat O'Malley, Lorraine Page, Eileen Peterson, Annemarie McNeela Ricker, Dorothy Lally Ross, Irene Tully Ryan, Lenore Ryan, Mary Pat Ryan, Maureen Sheehan Schmit, Helen Sullivan, Aileen Tansy, Edward Tobin, Ann Touhy, Dorothy Hastings Valeo, Julia Mulvaney Walsh, Kate Walsh, Margaret Sullivan Walsh, and Honore O'Connell Whelen. Special thanks are due to Chicago teachers Joan Crean O'Leary and her husband John for their cheerful and tireless assistance and support, and to Mary Foerner for her generosity with the history and photographs of her family's many generations of Chicago teachers.

The family photographs, newspaper clippings, and family lore given me by two grandsons of Boston school leader Julia Harrington Duff—John F. Duff, M.D., and the Honorable Brian B. Duff—also grace this work. My understanding of Irish San Francisco was likewise enlivened by historian and archivist Catherine Ann Curry's family history and by the family memories of James Carey, Mary Cavanaugh, Mary Frances and Patricia Ann Crowley, Maurine Dolson, Caren Cotter Ellis, Judith McGovern, Urania Michaela Moran, Eileen Murphy, Neilus O'Sullivan, and Patricia Walsh. I am also in debt to Aife Murray and to San Francisco History Room archivist Tom Carey at the San Francisco Public Library. The late Patrick J. Dowling and his wife Maureen provided me with unforgettable hospitality and a warm introduction to Irish San Francisco.

Several research grants supported the archival work that underpins this book, including a summer stipend from the National Endowment for the Humanities, a research award from the Irish American Cultural Institute, travel awards from the British Council and the Ulster-American Folk Park in County Tyrone, Ireland, and leaves of absence, research support, and summer stipends from Loyola University Chicago and its Center for Ethics. I am also grateful for the help given me by the Loyola University Chicago History Department's Sylvia Rdzak and Lillian Hardison. Without such support, this book could not have been completed. I also wish to thank historians Thomas Hachey, Ruth-Ann Harris, the late Donald Jordan, Polly Welts Kaufman, Patricia Kelleher, Emmet Larkin, John Lyons, Timothy Meagher, James Murphy, Maureen Murphy, Grace Neville, Alan O'Day, Robert Scally, James Walsh, and the Irish Studies faculties of St. Mary's University in Winona, Minnesota, and Boston College. Discussions with scholars Patricia and John Barnett, Grainne Blair, James Doan, James Donnelly, Sandra Elliott, Michael Gillespie, Michael Glazier, Karyn Holm, Sophie Sweetman McConnell, Kathleen Quinn, Mary Reichardt, and James Rogers have also enriched this work. I am also grateful to the editors and staff at the University of Notre Dame Press.

Introduction

Servants of the Poor

The immigration museum on Ellis Island in New York Harbor presents a fascinating although sanitized picture of the arrival, processing, and eventual assimilation of the millions of immigrants who arrived in the United States between the 1890s and the 1950s. Apart from the charming statue of Annie Moore, the Irish girl who accidently became the first immigrant to disembark at Ellis Island when it opened in 1892, however, the museum displays relatively little about Irish immigration. Or so it seems at first glance. In fact, a closer examination of the museum's photographic exhibits reveals that the Irish are indeed well-represented at Ellis Island, but not as greenhorn immigrants. Instead of being bewildered foreigners, there is a strong Irish presence among the immigration officers, nurses, social workers, and teachers employed on the island. Indeed, the Irish were among the first Americans newcomers met. Among these Irish Americans, women were a sizeable presence.[1] The photographs at Ellis Island, therefore, help illustrate an important point about the Irish experience in America: by the late nineteenth century, large numbers of the American Irish had entered the lower middle class of civil service, health care, and teaching. Furthermore, in an era when social mobility was measured almost solely in male terms, Irish-American women were often the leaders in their group's ascent.

The mobility of the daughters of Irish America was tied to their educational attainments, attainments realized in an era when educating women was reserved for the upper class few among native-born Americans. Yet even as their elite contemporaries enrolled in the newly established Seven Sisters, Irish-American women flocked to four-year academic high schools, followed by one or more years of normal school training. As a result of their time in the classroom, by the first decade of the twentieth century, these women had become one of the largest single ethnic groups among public elementary school teachers in Providence and Boston, and fully a third of the teachers in New York and Chicago. By 1910, women with identifiably Irish last names were an astounding 49 percent of San Francisco's primary and grammar school teachers.[2]

The roots of this female-driven mobility can be connected to the distinctive configurations of Irish immigration to the United States in the late nineteenth and early twentieth centuries. Beginning in the 1850s, in the aftermath of the Famine, and continuing until the 1920s, when world war and restriction permanently altered American immigration, in many years women outnumbered men among those leaving Ireland. Unlike other European immigration at the time, where men usually outnumbered women and females almost always traveled as wives and daughters in male-led families, most Irish women arriving in the United States were young, unmarried, and traveling independently of husbands or fathers.[3]

The anomalies of Irish emigration patterns reveal the growing marginalization of women in Irish life after the Famine. As Ireland recovered from the loss of at least two million people in the space of the six years between 1845 and 1850, the transformation of its heavily agricultural economy from subsistence tillage to market pasturage was completed. Land consolidation and the restriction of marriage to one son and one daughter per family were now commonplace throughout the country. Furthermore, jobs for women in Irish cities outside Belfast, never plentiful, did not increase rapidly enough to absorb the excess unmarried dependent female population in the hinterlands. Women's unemployment was so severe by the late nineteenth century, various government-sponsored strategies were put in place in hopes of getting women back into paying work.[4]

While the Famine also altered the parameters of men's lives, the new world of post-Famine Ireland could accommodate men more easily than women, especially among the growing unmarried population. The bachelor retained a public role in rural communities based on his greater ability to find paid work and a social life outside the confines of the family cottage. "Old boys" could find release from their day-to-day isolation on the farm in the village pubs, race tracks, and livestock fairs. Single women, on the other hand, lost whatever public roles their society had once given them. Most could no longer expect to marry and reproduce or find paid farm work, especially since formerly female jobs like dairying were being taken over by men displaced from the fields by the changeover to pasturage. Furthermore, unlike their brothers, women enjoyed few social outlets outside the home. As the Victorian middle-class ideal of the "Angel in the House" replaced the earlier vision of women as economic co-producers in a family's struggle for survival, the spinster toiling without recompense within the confines of a mother's or sister-in-law's cottage became more and more common.[5] As the nineteenth century merged with the twentieth, hundreds of thousands of unmarried women without prospects at home chose to emigrate instead. Displaced as they were, few ever returned to Ireland.[6]

The Irish national schools, the first system of state-supported education in the United Kingdom, were an important training ground for emigration. By the last quarter of the nineteenth century, national schools could be found throughout Ireland, including the south and west, the areas most resistant to change after the Famine but also the regions with the highest female emigration after 1880. Armed with the literacy and numeracy learned in national school classrooms, Irish women gravitated to cities in the United States, where most found jobs as servants of the rich, whose need for household help expanded rapidly after the Civil War. These servants eventually married and reproduced, and sent their daughters to school in preparation for entrance into the professions open to women at the turn of the last century, especially teaching.[7] As a result, the daughters of mothers educated in Irish schools entered white-collar work at least a generation before most of their brothers, and by 1910 were the largest single ethnic group among teachers in American cities with large Irish populations. While mothers had earned livings as servants of the rich, their daughters earned salaries as servants of the poor in the overcrowded classrooms of urban America's public schools.

Despite its ambiguous status among the middle classes in Ireland and the United States, teaching was held in high esteem by the Irish servants whose American-born daughters flocked into public school teaching. These daughters held significant social and economic importance within their families as well as in their home communities. Irish-American teachers were also instrumental in spreading Irish cultural values and giving these values respectability in the wider culture in ways their working-class brothers could not. Indeed, the "Americanization" of the public school curriculum in the early twentieth century could perhaps more accurately be called a "Hibernicization" in light of the influx of so many Irish Americans into public school teaching in those years. Nor were these teachers mere conduits of their supervisors' conservative values. Instead, Irish teachers on both sides of the Atlantic challenged the educational establishment by leading the uphill fight to gain higher pay, better working conditions, and greater professional autonomy for all teachers.

Irish America's remarkable female-driven group mobility has been overlooked. Almost no study sees the connection between the mass entrance of Irish-American women into public school teaching at the turn of the twentieth century and the growing respectability and prosperity of the Irish in America in those years. Since Irish-American teachers achieved the highest levels of education available to women of their time and class, their success indicates that Irish adjustment to life in urban America was considerably more rapid than most scholarship on the subject has previously suggested.[8] Equally important, no study yet makes the connection between the educational experiences of the mothers before they left Ireland and the professional achievements of their daughters in American public schools, a connection that yields valuable insight into the symbiotic relationship between the classroom and women's mobility, both geographically and socially. In addition, no one has yet compared the worlds of Irish teachers with their counterparts in the United States. Moreover, most histories of both Irish and American education continue to look at the schools through the eyes of male officialdom or from the vantage point of statistical analyses based on aggregate numbers of pupils and teachers.[9] The voices of individual teachers and pupils are rarely heard, and the importance of teachers in the transformation of public education on both sides of the Atlantic is not fully recognized.[10]

A reexamination of what is known about the impact of public education on Ireland and the United States in the late nineteenth and early twentieth centuries is, therefore, overdue. Such a reexamination will also demonstrate the integral role of educated women in Irish and Irish-American mobility. Furthermore, since recent histories of the Irish in the United States have stressed the need to look at regional factors in assessing the Irish adjustment to American life, a comparison of the public schools in Boston, San

Francisco, and Chicago, three regional hubs with high concentrations of Irish Americans in their teaching forces by the turn of the last century, will provide insight into patterns of Irish-American mobility on the national level.[11]

This trans-Atlantic study of the Irish experience in the United States adds to the growing recognition among scholars of the importance of women in the Irish immigrant experience and of the Irish roots of Irish-America. The years between the 1880s, when large-scale female emigration from an Ireland dotted with national schools began in earnest, and the 1920s, when large-scale emigration from Ireland to America had fallen off, also mark a watershed era in American education. These are the years that saw large numbers of American-born daughters of Irish mothers enter teaching in the nation's urban classrooms. By the 1920s, the "golden age" of Irish-American teachers was on the wane, however, as teachers' four decades–long fight to gain economic and professional recognition faced significant reversals.

In these pages, the emphasis will be on the immigrant generation and their teacher daughters in three cities: Boston, San Francisco, and Chicago in the half century or so surrounding the turn of the twentieth century. Too long ignored in most chronicles of the Irish experience in America, these women were fundamental to the origin and growth of that experience. By documenting the entrance of Irish Americans into public school teaching in three American cities at the turn of the last century, this study will also show how this influx was tied intimately to the Irish classroom experiences of girls destined to emigrate. In this way, education in Ireland will be connected to the role of the immigrant generation in the upward mobility of their American-born children in the late nineteenth and early twentieth centuries.

The three cities being studied here were chosen for several reasons. First, each had large Irish populations, both immigrant and American-born, by the late nineteenth century. Second, by the turn of the twentieth century, Irish women were the largest single ethnic group among public school teachers in all three cities, and these numbers illustrate the impact of women's education on Irish mobility. Third, all three cities were regional centers—Boston in New England, Chicago in the Midwest, and San Francisco in the Far West—and each had an impact on life beyond their city limits. Thus, the influence of Irish-American educational mobility extended beyond the confines of city limits. Fourth, a comparison of the experience of Irish-American teachers from east to west will modify the thesis that the Irish were far more successful as they moved out of the cities along the eastern seaboard, especially Boston, to the perhaps more fluid frontiers of Chicago and San Francisco.[12] Finally, these three cities have special meaning for me since I was born in San Francisco, grew up near Boston, and now work in Chicago. The history of Irish-American teachers also resonates with me since both my parents and I were once public school teachers.

In fact, as we have seen, my family's history mirrors that of many Irish-American families whose mobility depended as much on the ambitions of daughters as of sons. Irish-born women and their American daughters expected to work, and becoming a school teacher was seen by many as the best work possible for women of their time and class. Despite its notoriously bad pay, teaching offered educated women, and by the 1930s increasing numbers of men, white-collar status and a chance to ply their learning in the public world. It also offered married women convenient working hours that interfered minimally with their family duties.

Servants of the Poor expands on the theme introduced in *Ourselves Alone* by continuing the examination of the unprecedented public roles educated women in Irish America seized by themselves, alone. Their achievements remain a source of inspiration not only for their own children, but for all who seek to assume full citizenship in modern democracies for themselves and to expand that democracy to new generations through their work in the classroom.

Like *Ourselves Alone*, *Servants of the Poor* focuses on the majority experience. Although women religious in both Ireland and the United States were significant in helping create women's professional mobility, the majority of Irish and Irish-American teachers were lay women teaching in state-supported schools on both sides of the Atlantic. Furthermore, while the majority of Chicago's Irish-American public school teaching force at the turn of the last century were indeed educated in Church-run schools, this experience was not the norm in either Boston or San Francisco where most Irish Catholics attended public schools. The reasons for this difference will be discussed in this text.

In addition to family histories, photographs of individual teachers and their schools enrich this text. These photographs provide unique insights into the nature of teaching as an agency of mobility in Ireland and Irish America at the turn of the twentieth century, in much the same way as do the photographs displayed in the Immigration Museum on Ellis Island. In fact, the photographs included here belie the widely-held stereotype of the old maid schoolteacher dressed in a dowdy shirtwaist with hair confined in an untidy bun at the back of her head. Instead, the women shown here are fashionably coiffed and elegantly and elaborately dressed in silks, velvets, and lace. Three sport not only the latest fashions, but also handsome husbands! Even the newly arrived immigrants destined to be servants of the rich and perhaps mothers of teachers appear to have put careful thought into their appearance as they embarked on their new lives in America.

The displays in the Ellis Island Immigration Museum, then, inadvertently document a mostly untold story: the entrance of large numbers of Irish-Americans, both lay and religious, into the professions open to them at the turn of the last century, especially teaching. In order to remedy this oversight in the history of Ireland and the United States, the chapters that follow seek to demonstrate the importance of educational aspiration in Irish and Irish-American group mobility. The trailblazing experiences of Irish teachers on both sides of the Atlantic enriched the lives of their families and communities and set a precedent for achievement for all those who came after them. Ultimately, however, their upward mobility was circumscribed. Despite their educational and professional achievements, Irish-American teachers remained servants, as my father has remarked, not of the rich like their immigrant mothers, but of the poor in the classrooms of America's public schools.

CHAPTER I

Irish Education

The Best Intentions

In May 1844, a year before the potato blight devastated Ireland's subsistence crop, Thomas Healy applied to the Commissioners of National Education in Dublin for the admission of the school in Castlegregory, County Kerry, to the national system. According to Healy's application, the school's two rooms were each thirty feet by twenty feet in size and held eighty-six boys and forty-six girls. Healy expected these numbers to increase by thirty boys and forty girls when the school joined the national system. The eighteen-year-old girls' teacher, Catherine Connor, earned a salary of eight pounds a year, partially paid by "the scholars" under her care. Connor, a Kerry native, had been educated at the Dingle Convent Model National School, where she earned a "testimonial" from the Mother Superior. Her colleague Thomas Jim, the forty-four-year-old boys' school teacher, had not graduated from a model school, and although he had been teaching in Castlegregory since 1842, his credentials were inadequate under the new teacher qualifications set by the commissioners in Dublin. Nevertheless, Healy told the commissioners, Jim had been "examined repeatedly by the Superintendents" and was competent to remain in his post.[1]

Castlegregory's school became part of a national system of primary education inaugurated by the Commission for National Education in Ireland in 1831 to replace the hodgepodge of educational opportunities for the Irish poor then in place. Education would not only save the Irish from themselves, school officials believed, it would also save Ireland's union with Great Britain from dissolution. According to the commissioners, if the schools succeeded in their mission, the growing squalor of the Irish countryside and its inhabitants would disappear, and a new literate, numerate, and employable working class would emerge. To meet these ends, the commissioners approved a nonsectarian curriculum in 1833 designed to foster new habits of order, cleanliness, and fluency in the English language among Irish school-age children. Perhaps because they were less worrisome than the Irish, the English and Scottish poor had to wait until the 1870s—two generations later—before they too could receive the benefits of this state-funded primary education.

"Easy Lessons"

The curriculum, designed by the then commission chairman, Church of Ireland archbishop, and former Oxford University professor of political economy Richard Whately, was based on the theory that a laissez-faire capitalism regulated only by Adam Smith's "invisible hand" and David Ricardo's "iron law of wages" was an unchanging universal law of nature. Believing that instruction in political economy based on these "laws" would change the profligate personal behavior of the Irish poor, in 1835 Whately published an edited version of his *Introductory lectures in political economy* under the title *Easy lessons on money matters for the use of young people* and placed his primer in the hands of all Irish schoolchildren aged eight and up.[2]

Youthful readers of Whately's text learned that wages, work hours, and social position were based on eternal economic laws. In a free-market economy, poverty was the fault of individual character flaws and early and improvident marriages that produced children who could not be supported. Class envy was thus fruitless and wrong-headed. After all, the rich provided the jobs and wages the poor needed for survival. Self-help, based on work discipline and sober habits, would prevent failure and guarantee a secure life in a benevolent and prosperous world. Frugality and humility on the part of the Irish poor would insure their economic survival. Like Whately, most Catholic clergy also saw the schools as mechanisms for social control rather than social mobility. On this issue, at least, Ireland's sectarian divide was overcome.[3]

The Irish themselves had always held education in high esteem. Even before the national system was put in place in the 1830s, in fact, "hedge" schools provided lessons in literacy and numeracy to the children of the Roman Catholic poor in Ireland. Perched under roadside greenery or in cabins lent for the purpose, hedge-school classes were sometimes secret, meeting in defiance of the Penal Code's ban on Catholic and Irish education in the century and a half after Cromwell's conquest.

Hedge schools were also a popular adjustment to the abolition of clerical education in the Penal era, when Irish priests were forced underground or abroad. Itinerant lay schoolmasters (and the occasional schoolmistress) traveled the countryside instead, plying their often imperfect knowledge of Latin and Greek mixed with Irish language and lore to the children of Catholic Ireland. Beneath the master's stern gaze, students puzzled out Greek and Roman texts as well as romances printed in the cheap chapbooks that flooded the countryside in the late eighteenth century. The glories of a lost Celtic world were also integral to the schoolmaster's lessons. This often haphazard introduction to literacy and history was augmented by lessons in mathematics. In fact, numeracy was as highly prized as literacy, so that land holdings could be measured with precision.[4]

The schoolmaster in a rural community held almost as high a status as the landlord and priest, even though some masters were "failed" priests themselves and were marked as much by their vices as their erudition. Literate in the English language, schoolmasters were usually fluent in Irish also, the mother tongue of two million out of the almost seven million total population in 1821.[5] They thus served as vital liaisons between the "hidden" world of Irish-speaking communities and the English-speaking outside world.

Beginning in the 1780s, Protestant reformers in Ireland established a network of church-funded schools designed to compete with the itinerant hedge-school master. When the law forbidding Catholic education was lifted in 1785, rapidly growing numbers of Catholic teaching orders counteracted this Protestant initiative by founding their own schools throughout the country. Although the 1801 Act of Union prompted the government to look into creating a national system of nondenominational primary education in Ireland, sectarianism in Irish education still prevailed, as only Protestant schools received government support until the 1820s.[6]

Despite the de facto religious bias inherent in state support for education, according to one count, Parliamentary concern with Irish schooling resulted in fourteen reports on education in Ireland between 1806 and 1812 alone.[7] In 1812, the government concluded that private sectarian education in Ireland should be replaced by a countrywide system of publicly funded nondenominational education open to all social classes and overseen by a Commission for National Education. By 1814, Dublin's Society for Promoting the Education of the Poor in Ireland, also known as the Kildare Place Society because of its Dublin street address, acting on the commission's recommendations, drew up what it believed to be a nonsectarian curriculum designed to teach basic literacy, numeracy, orderliness, and hygiene to the Irish poor. In 1816, the government provided the society with funding for the creation of a Kildare Place Model School in Dublin to provide teacher training for what all concerned hoped would become a national system of primary education.[8]

Unlike the hedge schools, which sought to inculcate an appreciation of the lost worlds of classical antiquity and Celtic Ireland in students, the Kildare Place curriculum was based on English models emphasizing basic literacy, numeracy, and time and work discipline.[9] The Society hoped that the new habits of mind and body, coupled with heavy doses of Scripture, would do what the Penal Laws had not: pacify the Irish and transform them into dutiful subjects of a united kingdom. Catholics rejected the society's Protestant evangelicalism, however; and education in Ireland remained a highly sectarian affair after 1812, despite the government's initiatives.[10]

Parliament remained committed to the idea of nondenominational primary education in Ireland, nonetheless, seeing Ireland as the ideal laboratory for Britain's first forays into state-funded schools; and between 1824 and 1828, nine more government reports struggled over the best way to extend a national system of nonsectarian education throughout the country. Acting on the recommendations in these reports, the government took control of the Kildare Place Society's model schools in 1831 and appointed a religiously representative Board of Commissioners of National Education to oversee the schools. While the three Church of Ireland, two Roman Catholic, one Presbyterian, and one Unitarian on the commission represented each of Ireland's main religious groups, the two Roman Catholic members who represented over 80 percent of the population in 1831 were easily outvoted by the board's Protestant majority. Nevertheless, the diversified Commission of National Education in Ireland was a promising new attempt at sharing power among the country's religious groups.[11] Under the commission's direction, the privately funded sectarian schools of an earlier era were replaced by a new system of taxpayer-funded nonsectarian national schools. Henceforward, the training of the Irish young—both Catholic and Protestant—would no longer be in the hands of self-employed hedge-school masters, charitable Protestants, or Catholic religious. It was now in the hands of the state.

From the beginning, however, local bishops rather than lay officials were the chief school patrons in their dioceses; parish priests or local ministers served as the school managers; and few classrooms accommodated a religiously diverse student population. At the local level, trustees like Castlegregory's Thomas Healy petitioned the national commission for permission to build a school, usually on land donated for the purpose by either the church or a landlord. Clerical school managers had virtually complete power in hiring and firing teachers, and almost always hired teachers who professed the same religion as their own. As a result, de facto, the schools were denominational, even if, de jure, they were not.[12]

Popular Demand

By 1891, Castlegregory's school accommodated fifty girls and fifty boys in each of its two rooms, causing serious overcrowding. In fact, attendance at the school had dramatically risen since 1850, when the commissioners learned that the school building of famine-ravaged Castlegregory had deteriorated into a "thatched [stone] house, attached to the master's dwelling . . . , sixteen feet by thirteen feet," with "one room [and] six desks." By that time, teachers Catherine Connor and Thomas Jim had disappeared from the school record and had been replaced by a new master, parish clerk John Towns, age thirty-five, assisted by his wife. Attendance in the school had dramatically decreased in the six years since Manager Healy had written his optimistic predictions of rapid growth. By 1850, in fact, Castlegregory managed to send only thirty-four male and female students to school altogether, and only an average of eight of these children were in class on any given day. Despite the school's decline, District Inspector John Dee reported, "One hour each day [is devoted to] the Scriptures" and the school could accommodate up to sixty students from a parish population of around 3,500, "all of whom are of the poorer class." Furthermore, Dee insisted, "all the Protestants and many of the Roman Catholics will attend."[13] Although Dee's hopes never came to fruition, in 1891 the school's manager asked the commissioners for a twenty-pound emergency fund to build back-less benches known as "galleries" to contain the student overflow, a request the commissioners refused.[14]

Castlegregory's school faced another crisis that year, causing school manager Reverend Browne to write to the commissioners in March 1891 that during a recent storm, "more violent here than in any other part of the country, one of the large windows of the schoolhouse was blown in" and the roof was damaged. The commissioners remained untouched by Castle-gregory's trials, however. Despite the serious damage done to the school-house, the school's students had to wait more than five months and the school manager had to file reams of additional paperwork before the money for the repairs arrived in September.[15]

As Castlegregory's vicissitudes indicate, the national school system attracted more students than it could accommodate despite overall popula-tion decrease, and, after the Famine, schoolhouses were built in every cor-ner of the country to meet the growing demand for classroom space. Be-tween 1851 and 1901, in fact, the number of national schools in Ireland rose from 4,547 to 8,692, even though population fell from 6.6 million to 4.5 million in the same years. While the number of national schools fell to 8,289 in 1911, decreases in the number of schools failed to match the loss of 100,000 in total population in the decade after 1901. Instead, school enroll-ments rose from 15.15 to 16.05 percent of the total population between 1901 and 1911, even though overall population levels fell from 4.5 to 4.4 million in those same years. Attendance among national school pupils also peaked in 1911, reaching 603,059 students in school for over one hundred days. Catholics were 491,988 of this total.[16]

The positive impact of growing school attendance can be measured in the rise in literacy. By 1911, almost ninety percent of the population could read and write, according to the census for that year—a sharp increase from the slightly over half of the 1851 population who had been able to do so. While illiteracy rates were low by 1911, however, they were unevenly dis-tributed, ranging from Connaught's high of 15.2 percent of the population to Leinster's low of 6.8 percent. Catholics had higher illiteracy rates than Protestants, with 11.3 percent of Catholics in 1911 unable to read or write in English. Protestant illiteracy rates fluctuated from a Methodist low of 1.3 percent to an Episcopal high of 4.2 percent.[17]

Girls were more apt than boys to attend state-supported primary schools, although their numbers fell sharply in the much smaller overall enrollment totals for fee-based secondary schools. In 1911, for instance, while girls outnumbered boys in Irish primary schools by 335,694 to 325,458, boys outnumbered girls by 2,218 to 280 among secondary school students. Despite the female minority among secondary school students, however, the number of girls attending secondary schools had risen from ninety-one to 280 between 1901 and 1911.[18]

These increases in school attendance in the first decade of the twentieth century can perhaps be attributed partly to the enforcement of the compulsory attendance law of 1892, which required all parents to send their school-age children (defined as those between six and fourteen) to school for 75 percent of the 220 days of the school year. Nevertheless, contemporaries pointed to the inadequacies in enforcing the law, which can be seen in Belfast school-attendance officer John Kelly's 1896 report of his visits to the homes of the city's female truants. One girl was absent from school for all but one day in June of that year because she was home "minding child[,] mother at work." Others were absent because they were "helping at home," "minding house[,] mother at work," "helping mother at work," or "[k]ept at home[,] mother not well." It seems from these reports that girls missed school only if they were not allowed to go because they were required at home. Boys, Kelly noted, were more apt to miss school on purpose, as they "will not go to school" or were "sent to school—did not go."[19]

Keeping students who were needed at home or at work in school for the full academic year was an ever-present challenge for school officials. According to the educational pamphleteer Frederick Ryan, for instance, only 4 percent of the eligible students were in class for more than 200 days in 1910. Although Ryan pointed out that poor parents were paying for their children's national school classrooms at least indirectly through the taxes on sugar and tobacco, they couldn't "see why a child's school attendance will help him or her earn money." Ryan believed that compulsion itself robbed parents of their free will, making them hostile to sending their children to school. Furthermore, the law had too many loopholes. For instance, children living more than two miles from a school were excused from attending. Moreover, the law allowed for "the necessary operations of husbandry and the ingathering of crops or in the fisheries." As a result, many rural parents kept their children out of school for "immediate profit" rather than investing in the long-range benefits of primary education outlined by the commissioners: "The formation of character, the training of good habits, and the development of intelligence [which] far exceed in permanent value" any lessons learned in the fields and barns of Ireland. Farm children were not the only absentees, however. Dublin's poor, Ryan pointed out, huddled together in overcrowded tenement rooms, depended on chance for a living. Keeping track of this floating population's school attendance was impossible.[20] Despite the low incidence of school participation among Ireland's poorest, however, more and more Irish children were sitting in national school classrooms by the late nineteenth century.

Nonsectarianism and Needlework

Until the turn of the twentieth century, Irish teachers based their lessons on former Marlborough Street Model School principal P. W. Joyce's *A Handbook of School Management and Methods of Teaching*. Stressing the importance of teaching form, not content, and of confining any creativity in reading and writing lessons to the minority of students in the upper grades only, Joyce discussed such topics as "The Human Mind in Relation to Education: The Intellect, the Emotions, the Will," and "Method . . . Inductive and Deductive Teaching." The *Handbook* also included chapters on the teaching of spelling, handwriting, composition, grammar, arithmetic, and geography, and on "Discipline and Order" and the "Time Tables," which outlined the tasks to be accomplished during each hour of the school day. By 1897, the *Handbook* had been through seventeen printings.[21]

Teachers of the youngest pupils also studied Thomas Urry Young's more liberal 1856 *Teachers' Manual for Infant Schools and Preparatory Classes*. Young criticized the existing curriculum for being dull, and he sympathized with the "little sufferers" forced to endure it. Instead, he instructed, "good manners, cleanliness, [and] obedience" were the "key values to be taught in the schools," while the "things to avoid" were "pride, tyranny . . . [and] cruelty to animals." Furthermore, teachers should base their lessons on one of the "modes of intellectual instruction," such as "intuitive teaching," which he believed was the "first and most important mode [as] children grow in awareness of their environments." Intuitive teaching, he continued, should then be followed by "comparisons of two things observed, pictures and verbal descriptions, questioning, ellipses [where children filled in the blanks], and imitation in writing, drawing, music[,] recitation and spelling." Above all, teachers were to impress upon their pupils the need to "come on time in the morning, with clean hands, face, and clothes."[22]

Teaching history, especially that of Ireland, was particularly to be avoided lest it lead to the appearance of covert religious and/or nationalist indoctrination in school classrooms.[23] *The Children's History Book* used in the schools, for example, was merely an administrative record book for keeping track of each pupil's vital statistics—not an introduction to Ireland's past.[24]

Nevertheless, as early as the 1850s, nonsectarian approaches to teaching the history of Ireland were proposed. Young's *Teacher's Manual*, for instance, instructed teachers to hang a map of Ireland in their classrooms and tell their pupils that "Ireland is one of the countries in Europe." They were then to ask the children sitting before them, "Are you Irish?" and to tell them, "Yes, you are called so because you were born in Ireland, and because your parents are Irish." Students then learned that they lived on an island "300 miles long and 170 miles across that would take five weeks to walk the length of at a rate of ten miles a day with Sundays off." Europeans were whites, they were told, who were, "generally speaking, like those of our own country; that is, fair complexioned, with lips and cheeks tinged with red, an oval face, straight nose, small mouth and chin, and high forehead; some have blue eyes; some dark hair and eyes." Young's Irish clearly approximated the Victorian physical ideal, in fact. On the other hand, Laplander women were "no taller than an Irish girl of ten years old."[25]

Throughout the nineteenth century, spelling, not history, reigned as the queen of the primary school curriculum. Educational authorities believed literacy, both reading and writing, could best be taught by mastering spelling. Memorizing the alphabet was a student's first task, followed by learning the spellings of ever more letter-rich words. After mastering these spellings, pupils advanced to reading simple sentences. Writing was also learned by rote as students copied models of perfect penmanship over and over in their copybooks.

The most common school copybooks were those of the educational philanthropist Vere Foster. Foster's texts presented the child with examples of exquisite cursive writing along with the instruction to copy each page in the book six times. Students then copied, in their best penmanship, such aphorisms as "Amendment is the best proof of repentance" or "A moment of time is a monument of mercy." Although they were also cautioned that "A word once uttered can never be recalled" and that "Blessings are on the head of the just," they were reminded to "Correct yourself what you blame on others," lest any become overly smug. Advice such as "Do not let pleasure interfere with business," "Few love those who love none but themselves," and "Habit is the kindest friend or cruelest foe" were likewise engraved in the minds of the Irish young, alongside a warning to the lazy that "Idleness is the parent of want and shame." Farmers' children were warned that if they were to "Plough in winter, [they] shall beg in summer." Restless copiers were instructed to "Quench the spark, or you may dread the fire" and to recognize that "Whatever is worth doing is worth doing well." In the same copybook, students also duplicated a long list of English—not Irish—names, arranged in alphabetical order.[26] Perfect reproductions of the model writing was the goal, not creative thought.

Drawing lessons were also centered on copying models, not innovation. In Foster's *Drawing Book,* students were led through a series of model pictures followed by a blank page for them to make their copies. Some models were domestic commonplaces—a wooden bucket, an iron frying pan, a jug beside a bench, a broom. Throughout, rural themes predominated, and students copied pictures of thatched-roof country cottages, wooden pumps, hay cribs, mountains, and lakes. A city street scene was also included.[27]

When students had mastered basic spelling and copying, they were expected to begin reading an approved series of school texts of increasing degrees of sophistication. Long gone were the tales of rapparee derring-do that had made the chapbooks used in hedge schools so compulsively readable for earlier generations. In their place, national school students were given texts of impeccable religious neutrality and political orthodoxy. Both the *Reading Book for the Use of Female Schools,* introduced by the commissioners in the 1830s, and the *Girls' Reading Book,* which replaced it thirty years later, were designed to be nondenominational conveyers of "information peculiarly adapted to the character and pursuits of females in the middle and humble ranks of life," preparing them for a future of housewifery or of domestic service, the single largest female employment for women at the time.[28]

Classroom lessons in housewifery were reinforced by the 1862 edition of the *Reading Book for the Use of Female Schools,* which, in addition to over two hundred poems, contained such essays as "On Authority Over Children," "On Attending the Sick," "Duties of a Housemaid," and "How to Furnish a House." Girls reading this collection also learned about a wider world in "Chinese Customs," "The Canadian Indians," and the "Manufacture of Pins and Needles." This commissioner-approved text contained nothing on Ireland, however, except perhaps inadvertently in an essay titled "On Equality," where readers learned that there "was no such thing [as] an equality of property or condition . . . nor was there ever such a thing in any country since the world began." Instead, the essay continued, "the inequality of property and condition, which some silly or bad people are so fond of declaiming against . . . must, from the nature of things, exist to the end of [the world]."[29] Apparently, Whately's free market was not expected to bring wealth to all.

An 1897 edition of the *National Readers* offered instructive essays with similar themes to those published in texts more than thirty years before: the "garden" of Glendalough, the plaiting of straw, the dangers of alcohol, the oddities of Australia, and the growing of potatoes. The vocabulary used in the reader was sophisticated, and students were expected to read, pronounce, define, and use such words as "resplendent," "amphitheatre," and "precipice" correctly in sentences. The subject matter, on the other hand, was often dry. The straw plaiting essay, for instance, showed pupils how the once highly skilled handcraft of plaiting straw for bonnets had succumbed to mechanical factory production. In "Alcohol," they learned that, since the first sip of alcohol was universally disliked, human beings were not meant to drink liquor.[30]

Advanced students could study *Biographical Sketches of Eminent British Poets,* a compilation of the lives of sixty-three male poets such as "the father of English poetry," Geoffrey Chaucer. The only poet in this collection with ties to Ireland was Edmund Spenser, who, readers were told, was the author of "'The Fairie Queen,' the most brilliant and popular of his works," and the secretary to Ireland's Lord Lieutenant in the late sixteenth century, who, "as a reward for his faithful service, [was] presented . . . by his sovereign . . . with a grant of land in Ireland, consisting of 3,028 acres, in the County of Cork, out of the forfeited estates of the Earl of Desmond," with the stipulation that he was, "obliged to become resident on the lands." They also read that the "great value" of Spenser's highly negative 1596 essay, "A View of the State of Ireland," was its "authentic and curious picture of national manners and circumstances."[31]

In another advanced text, *Epitome of Geographical Knowledge,* only four pages out of the total 602 were devoted to Ireland. Readers of these few pages were told that Dublin's "Sackville Street is perhaps one of the finest streets in Europe . . . ornamented with the Post Office, a noble Ionic building, and a pillar erected to the memory of Lord Nelson." Despite these imperial glories, readers were also informed that "the oldest parts of the town are in striking contrast with the elegance of the newer portions of it, much of it having a dilapidated appearance, with many indications of wretchedness among the inhabitants."[32]

Perhaps because no one feared the political implications of girls' lessons in housewifery, the domestic arts became even more important in the curriculum at the end of the nineteenth century when cookery and laundering classes were added to the needlework classes already in place in girls' schools. Sewing, cooking, and washing lessons served the commissioners' grand design to uplift Irish life within the home, while also providing women with a means of earning a living outside it. Accordingly, the commissioners predicted that the girls who took these classes would be able to "mak[e] their own clothes and . . . render useful assistance in their families in the ordinary home industries."[33]

From the beginning, the commissioners believed that "a practical knowledge of Plain Needlework is, probably, one of the most important acquirements for females, especially for the class attending the National Schools of Ireland." Needlework remained so important to the commissioners, in fact, that their 1903 edition of the *Rules and Regulations* for teachers stipulated that "A female candidate for the office of Teacher will not be recognised either as Principal or Assistant unless she is competent not only to conduct the *ordinary* business of a school, but also to give instruction in Needlework, Knitting, Cutting-Out, and Dressmaking."[34] In 1914, the commissioners further stipulated that "Girls who have reached the age of eleven years should . . . attend the classes in cookery and laundry-work," and they could receive certificates of merit in "domestic economy—cookery, laundry, needle-work, knitting, cutting-out, and hygiene as well as in reading, letter writing, household arithmetic, and other subjects."[35]

Consequently, one manual instructed teachers to have their students practice hemming and seaming before moving on to gathering and tucking. Once these tasks were mastered, buttonhole making, mending, knitting, and platting were added, followed by muslin work, open work, lace work, and worsted work. "Cutting-out" lessons focused on clothes for everyday wear such as shirts, chemises, wrappers, frocks, flannel petticoats, and "boys dresses." Furthermore, the commissioners required all female teachers "to be familiar with this manual, and to give instruction in it to the pupils daily, and to submit from time to time to the Inspectors specimens of needlework executed in accordance with [the manual's] directions." To further under- score the importance of needlework instruction, women teachers were re- minded that "At the annual examinations all Female Teachers will be liable to be examined in the Manual."[36]

Domestic arts classes taught basic skills. Although girls were taught "the full directions for learning to sew, to knit, and to cut out, and . . . the application of this knowledge in making up and mending apparel," the commissioners observed that "fancy work has been omitted." Even after 1889, when dressmaking instruction was added to the needlework cur- riculum, the commissioners still "hoped that every girl of ordinary ability in the advanced classes of National Schools will be able to cut out and make up neatly and tastefully, a *plain* dress."[37] After all, the commissioners re- marked, "the practical knowledge of needle-work, with its appendages of cutting-out and repairing . . . must be always regarded as very useful to fe- males generally and particularly to those of the humblest classes, whether applied to domestic purposes, or as a mode of procuring remunerative em- ployment."[38]

Even basic skills like cutting-out required a high degree of mathemati- cal ability and a good sense of spatial relationships, as the measurements taken from a three-dimensional human body had to be transformed into a two-dimensional paper or cloth pattern. Intricate patterns for the linings of Victorian Irish clothing also had to be calibrated to fit inside complicated outer layers. Altering patterns for "stout persons" was another important part of the cutting-out skill.[39] If the extraordinary sample pieces preserved in the Public Record Office of Northern Ireland in Belfast are any indication of the mastery exhibited by needlework students a century ago, the national schools had indeed fulfilled their mission to teach seamstress skills.[40]

Cookery lessons were as demanding as those for needlework. A student notebook from the late nineteenth century records recipes ranging from potato soup, scrap bread pudding, baking powder (made with six ounces of rice flour mixed with four ounces of cream of tartar and two ounces of bread soda), baked custard, boiled beans and cabbage, lemonade, gruel, whey, and scones.[41] In a County Cavan school in 1912, teacher Isabella Johnston's cookery class syllabus included recipes for both plain and fancy foods like "boiled bacon and cabbage, steamed custard and fruit, potato soup and fried bacon, fried herrings, suet pudding," along with one for the home remedy "linseed poultice." Four years later, scones were dropped from the menu in favor of apple tarts. In addition to preparing food from recipes, Johnston's cookery students also learned to clean stoves and fireplaces, dispose of refuse, and prepare and serve breakfast.[42] Girls destined for domestic service in middle- and upper-class homes were well prepared for their work.

Laundering classes were another curriculum feature for national school girls, and like those in needlework and cookery, these classes in fine washing and ironing reflected the goal of school authorities to improve Irish housekeeping as well as to train girls destined for service. Girls taking classes in laundering were therefore expected to master the "cleaning and care of baths, basins, irons, etc. . . . removing stains, i.e. iron mould, milk, tea, coffee, mildew[, and] sewing on tapes [and] ironing sheets." They also had to learn techniques for "washing, boiling, bleaching white clothes" and making starch. Fancy pressing was a prized skill, and girls learned to iron silks, muslin, a lady's blouse, collars, flannels, and stockings before leaving the schoolroom.[43]

The national commissioners' emphasis on practical needlework, and by the late nineteenth century, on cooking and laundering classes in the schools was reinforced by popular magazines of the time like the *Irish Homestead,* which told its readers that "Housewifery is recognized here as a profession in itself, needing to be trained for, like any other profession, and [it is] the greatest of national assets in a world which now universally acknowledges the home as a social unit."[44]

Unintended Consequences

By 1856, Castlegregory had sufficiently recovered from the worst of the Famine's devastation to apply to the Dublin commissioners for a salary for the part-time twenty-five-year-old needlework mistress Ellen Flynn. District Inspector James Brown counted fifty-three female pupils in Castlegregory's school that year, "thirty-five of whom take needlework class." Mistress Flynn, he reported, taught "dress and shirtmaking, drapes, caps, marking . . . knitting sampler work, [and] netting . . . every day except Saturday, from twelve to two."[45] The school's full-time female assistant teacher was Joanna Crowley. A decade later, in 1865, Joanna Crowley had been promoted to the rank of principal teacher. Female enrollments had risen to ninety-nine, high enough to warrant District Inspector Denis Driscoll to recommend hiring an assistant, Mary Flaherty, to help Crowley and the new needlework mistress, Ellen Casey, educate the large number of girls now in attendance.[46]

A subsistence crisis again ravaged western Ireland in the late 1870s, and Castlegregory's school faced another setback. In August 1876, when Joanna Crowley's salary stood at only twenty-five pounds a year, she was admonished by the district inspector "to see that proper attn is given to the subject [of needlework], else [the mistress's] fees will be forfeited." A year later, in 1877, the inspector continued to find the "needlework [still] very unsa[tisfactory]"; and in 1879 he recommended that "better discipline . . . be observed." In July 1880, the school was put on the "Suspended List." By August 1880, however, it was restored to the active list, having been "satisfactorily rebuilt and refurnished."[47]

When Joanna Crowley reached retirement age in November 1892, she gave up "possession of the school." In December she received a pension of twenty-five pounds a year, equal to her highest salary during her active career.[48] Crowley's son Michael and his wife Honoria were now Castlegregory's teachers. Although Michael's teaching in the boys' school was criticized by school inspectors "on the numerous and serious defects in the proficiency exhibited by [his] pupils at Results Examinations" in 1897, Honoria's teaching in the girls' school was praised by "the different Inspectors who visited the school," according to Father Browne, the school manager. The following year, Browne reported that the girls in Mrs. Crowley's class "are on the whole carefully instructed. Needlework, singing and drawing throughout show considerable merit." According to Browne, after Inspector Little visited Mrs. Crowley's class in 1911, Little observed that "Proficiency is satisfactory [and the] girls write very good composition exercises."[49]

In June 1913, Honoria Crowley retired from the Castlegregory Female National School with a pension of thirty-four pounds a year. Two years before her retirement, in 1911, Browne had written to the commissioners that he "should like to give an appointment to [Mrs. Crowley's] daughter [Miss Hannah Crowley] in the school on the occasion of her retirement. Unfortunately, the daughter will not be qualified for two years more. She has been at a Convent Intermediate School for two years [where she] obtained . . . prizes. She intends to enter a training college next year. . . . Personally, Mrs. Crowley has been an excellent . . . example [and] a wonderful influence over the pupils of her school."[50] The commissioners approved Browne's request and in 1913 Honoria Crowley's daughter Hannah became Castlegregory's new girls' school teacher.

Born on O'Leary's Island off the Kerry coast in 1899, Nora O'Leary Crean was one of the girls who retained vivid memories of her six years in Castlegregory's national school even after she left for America in 1923 at the age of twenty-four. Her Irish-speaking mother Johanna had learned the rudiments of the English language from her husband while they sat together around their kitchen fire. Despite her own lack of formal schooling, Johanna urged Nora to remember that education was the one thing no one could ever take away from her, and, beginning in 1907, Johanna sent Nora to the mainland so she could attend Castlegregory's school. Although she could return to her off-shore home only on weekends when the tide was right, Nora loved her teacher Honoria Crowley and did well in her classes. For the rest of her life, Nora remembered admiring Mrs. Crowley's elegant clothes and graceful figure at Sunday Mass. Even more importantly, Nora never forgot how Mrs. Crowley introduced her to the possibilities open to an educated woman, a lesson she repeated regularly to the girls in her classroom, and a lesson Nora passed down to her own daughter, Chicago public school teacher Joan Crean O'Leary.[51]

The national schools had a profound impact on their pupils, and the lessons girls learned in school taught them to husband their resources and earn their own livings. Ironically, instead of creating thrifty workers satisfied with their lot in life, Ireland's classrooms unintentionally opened a window of opportunity for young women. "The National Schools have replaced the crowbar," Kerry Bishop Moriarty observed as early as 1868. "Educated youths who have had the maps of the world before their eyes for years are not likely to sit down for a life in a patch of potato garden."[52]

Indeed, throughout the late nineteenth and early twentieth centuries, hundreds of thousands of young women like Nora O'Leary, armed with the literacy, numeracy, and domestic skills learned in Ireland's national schools, left Ireland for the United States. After their arrival, former national school girls like Nora used their training to get jobs as servants of the rich, plying their cooking, sewing, laundering, and fancy ironing abilities for pay. In the careful handwriting they had once practiced in Vere Foster copybooks, they used their letter-writing skills to send remittances and news to families still in Ireland. After marrying in America, they managed their own households and sent their children, especially their daughters, to school to become teachers like Nora's Mrs. Crowley.

CHAPTER 2

Irish Schools

Windows of Opportunity

In the spring of 1886, Aghaloora, County Cavan, Girls' National School teacher Margaret Smyth refused to turn in her school key after being dismissed from her post for physically fighting with Mathew Comisky, her male counterpart in the boys' classroom next to hers.[1] According to local school manager Terence Brady, when Smyth's replacement, Suzanne Wilson, arrived to collect the key, Smyth's sister pulled the newcomer's hair as Smyth "forcibly [held] possession of the school." While Wilson was being attacked by Smyth's sister, Brady watched "a crowd headed by Miss Smyth's brothers with a flag c[o]me . . . to take the boys from my school if I would not put out Miss Wilson. . . ."

Smyth's relationship with Mathew Comisky had never been good, and Comisky already faced charges of intimidating schoolchildren, drunkenness, and assault before Smyth lost all patience with him. Comisky's reputation was so bad, in fact, the local taxpayers supported Smyth in her battle with him. "We the undersigned," local farmer Daniel Kiernan and thirteen other signatories wrote to the Commissioners of National Education in April 1887, "consider it necessary for us to appeal a second time to the gentlemen of the National Board. . . . We reported Master Comisky last February for his bad conduct [and] it is not in the power of any person inside or outside of the County Cavan to give Master Comisky a good character. . . ." In fact, the letter continued, Margaret Smyth had been driven to distraction by the outrageous conduct of her male counterpart. "Master Comisky permitted his scholars to knock [down] part of the wall between the Male School room and the Female School room and he would allow his scholars to spend their time throwing stones and gallons of water into the female school. . . . A few days ago, he threw a coal out of the fire into the Female School and struck a little girl in the face . . . which nearly was the cause of depriving her of her eyesight for life." Furthermore, Kiernan told the commissioners, "There is also a summons against him for assaulting another young girl. . . ." Kiernan concluded by reminding the commissioners that "respectable Farmers withdrew their children from his school . . . [and we want] to put an end to such scandalous proceedings which is [sic] a disgrace in any Civilized District."

Comisky replied to these accusations in his own letter to the commissioners. Answering the charge that he had allowed his students to break through the wall separating his classroom from Smyth's, Comisky excused the action, telling Dublin that "The partition between the fire places of the two schoolrooms is only the thickness of a brick." In fact, he reported, "The scholars in Miss Smyth's school broke our partition on several occasions. They often threw stones and burning turf onto the boards of my school, and on one occasion they threw one so violently as to cut a boy's head with a stone." Despite this harassment, Comisky informed his employers that he had "repeatedly mended the hole myself with mortar and stones. . . ." Smyth's students did not agree with Comisky's version of events, however. One of them, nine-year-old Maria McCabe, maintained instead that she had seen "stones and coals thrown out of the [boys'] school often but I never saw any thrown back."

Convinced that Miss Smyth had legitimate reasons for her refusal to surrender her classroom, Kiernan and other local farmers urged the commissioners to "grant [the school] key to Margaret Smith [sic] who commenced to teach in [Aghaloora] in . . . April 1886 and has since conducted the school to the satisfaction of the said inhabitants." In this, Kiernan was reasserting traditional local control over the schools in the face of outside authority. Insisting that if "any [teacher] vacancy occurs . . . a native of the . . . townland if fairly qualified should be appointed as Teacher in preference to any outsider," Kiernan also reminded the commissioners that "the inhabitants maintained the privilege of appointing teachers . . . for the past thirty years and in 1886 a vacancy occurred in the Female School Room and a native . . . named Margaret Smith got possession by the sanction of most of the inhabitants . . . and the said Margaret Smith has since conducted the school to our satisfaction."

Despite the strong local support for Smyth, School Manager Brady informed the commissioners that the charges against Mathew Comisky were untrue and had been trumped up by the friends of Smyth because Comisky had chosen Wilson rather than Smyth to be Aghaloora's female teacher. Wilson, Brady contended, "outranked Miss Smyth in [the] competitive teachers' examination," coming in first, while Smyth failed the arithmetic qualifying test and was the fourth out of the four candidates for the post. School District Inspector F. Eardley had also strongly disapproved of Smyth's candidacy. In his September 28, 1886, report, Eardley noted that "Miss Margaret Smyth, 18, R[oman] C[atholic], *not* competent, [nonetheless] took possession of the school on May 4, 1886, in opposition to the manager. . . ."

The saga of Margaret Smyth's brief sojourn in the Aghaloora Female National School illustrates Dublin's steady usurpation of local school autonomy. The commissioners spearheaded this change by issuing a series of ever-stricter standards for teacher training and hiring. Smyth was eventually evicted from the Aghaloora school and forced to turn over her key to Suzanne Wilson, Manager Brady's favored candidate. By the 1880s, in fact, more-qualified candidates like Wilson were taking teaching posts from less-prepared local favorites like Smyth. Smyth's short-lived teaching career marked the end of an era of local control over hiring teachers.

To enhance their authority on the local level, the commissioners also appointed district inspectors charged with visiting all classrooms between two and three times a year. Decreeing that, "classes shall be at all times open to the Inspectors . . . , who will report . . . as to the character and efficiency of the instruction," Dublin overrode local taxpayers like Daniel Kiernan and his Aghaloora neighbors' influence over school policy and teacher appointments.[2]

Despite the difficulties faced by Aghaloora teacher Margaret Smyth, pupils like Castlegregory's Nora O'Leary looked up to their own classroom teachers. As schoolgirls like Nora faced fewer chances for marriage or a cash income in post-Famine Ireland, the national school increasingly served as a training ground for emigration, equipping girls with the necessary skills to seek their fortunes outside the country.[3] In fact, by the late nineteenth century and continuing into the twentieth, young, unmarried former national school pupils like Nora were a majority among those leaving Ireland for cities in the United States, the most popular emigrant destination in those years.[4] Designed to keep the Irish young at home, the schools provided windows of opportunity offering students a wider worldview, a worldview that served those who emigrated extremely well.

The national school curriculum provided skills for emigration inadvertently, but since all lessons were taught in English, schoolchildren were introduced to the world outside Ireland at an early age. Although Irish was the sole language of a large minority in the country at the time of the schools' inception in the 1830s, school authorities forbade the teaching of the Irish language until 1878, by which time most Irish had abandoned their native tongue in favor of English. Furthermore, since no Irish-language training classes for teachers existed until 1897, the rare school lesson in Irish did little to revive fluency. In fact, although one quarter of the over eight thousand national schools were teaching the Irish language within regular school hours by the early twentieth century, the introduction of the Irish language into classrooms had come too late to stem the tide of English-language use among schoolchildren.[5]

By providing an eyewitness view of daily life in Irish schools, district inspectors' reports provide some insight into the actual state of language instruction in the classroom, including an occasional success. According to Inspector J. J. O'Neill's observations of the classes of Miss McCarthy, Miss Tuomey, and Sr. Ambrose in County Dublin in October 1909, for instance, "The Irish teaching . . . is in the hands of very young teachers [who] are, however, native speakers of the language . . . and have . . . followed progressive lines in teaching."[6] Nevertheless, by 1911 only 13.3 percent of the total population still spoke Irish.[7] (This figure includes 3.5 percent in Leinster, 6.1 percent in Ulster, 22.1 percent in Munster, and 35.5 percent in Connaught.) Even after independence, when new government policies required that all teachers be fluent in Irish and all school lessons be conducted in that language, language enthusiasts were ultimately forced to acknowledge that English was the mother-tongue of all but a shrinking minority in Ireland. English, not Irish, was the language of emigrants.

Foreign-language classes in the schools fared no better than those in Irish. After an April 1910 visit, Inspectors R. C. B. Kerin and T. Rea reported that a teacher in County Monaghan, "is not properly qualified as a teacher of French [and] the class is extremely dull." In another classroom in the same school, Kerin and Rea noted that "The Preparatory . . . German is taken by Miss Clarke, who has insufficient qualifications and knows little of method." After all, the inspectors concluded, "German could be made interesting even for beginners."[8] In a Tipperary school, the inspectors found "Only one girl took Latin. She is the last survivor from the former state of things, when the school had to take Latin as a subject. . . . The languages are now Irish and French."[9] It seems that English was the language of choice among both teachers and pupils in Irish schools.

Until the early twentieth century, authorities also forbade lessons in Irish history or even geography, in order to prevent any chance of nurturing independence in the classroom. The history of Great Britain and its empire was substituted in their place.[10] Only in 1900, when the reform-minded commissioner W. J. M. Starkie authorized the distribution of the pro-establishment Irish history text by former Marlborough Street Training School principal P. W. Joyce, did Irish history become part of the school curriculum for the first time. After the 1916 Rising, however, Starkie withdrew Joyce's mild text from the classroom, once again declaring any teaching of Irish history at all as too dangerous a subject for the national schools.[11]

Starkie's short-lived Irish-history teaching initiatives seemed to have had very little impact on students who remained well-versed in the English, not the Irish, past. When District Inspector C. E. Wright observed a history class in Queen's County [Laois] in May 1910, for instance, he "questioned the class on the events of Queen Anne's reign [and] the girls were delighted to give in answer a list of Marlborough's victories, with dates." Although he was disappointed that one girl "had never heard (or so it seemed) of Milton, Cromwell, or the Battle of Trafalgar," he was pleased to find that when he tested the class "on the early history of England, [I] never received such an intelligent account of Britons, Angles, Danes, and Normans. They knew the original settlement of the Angles and Saxons: a rare bit of knowledge. . . . Their only weakness was in Irish history," Wright concluded, although they were, "better on the geography of Ireland." Furthermore, the two lowest classes in the school "knew their English History and Geography courses excellently, [but] the portion prescribed of the History of Ireland was not known at all as well." Wright found the state of Irish history to be even worse in Protestant schools, "where teachers and children dislike the tone of the school book."[12]

Lessons in literary studies apparently fared no better than those of history, geography, or foreign language. In a Louth school in April 1910, for instance, Inspectors Kerin and Rea were amazed to find, "two girls [who] told [us] that Oliver Twist and Oliver Cromwell were two famous names in Irish literature in the eighteenth century."[13] After their March 1910 visit to a County Carlow school, Inspectors Wright and Ensor offered the observation that "Country-bred girls are not well read, and sometimes lack intelligence. . . ."[14] Inspectors O'Neill and Rea apparently agreed, observing that in an Antrim classroom that same month, "Little or nothing is known of general literature. . . ."[15] Sometimes, inspectors placed the blame for students' low level of literary appreciation squarely on the shoulders of teachers. In February 1910, Inspectors Wright and Ensor reported that a County Tipperary teacher "took a lesson on one of Steele's Essays. She read the essay to them sentence by sentence, and then asked questions on the meaning of the phrases. There was no merit in her way of teaching."[16] Nevertheless, despite sometimes poor instruction methods, by learning about a wider world beyond their native shores, national school pupils were inadvertently being prepared to become successful expatriots.

"Perpetual Espionage"

While the schools were windows of opportunity for their pupils, they were a more problematic means of mobility for their teachers. As in the cases of the uninspiring Tipperary teacher and in the competition between the less-qualified but popular local favorite Margaret Smyth and her more qualified rival in Aghaloora, teacher training and oversight were perennial issues of debate among educational authorities from the beginning of the national system in the 1830s. Throughout this debate, the commissioners sought ways to curtail teacher autonomy, especially in cases like that of Smyth, where the local favorite had scored badly on qualifying examinations.

Originally, the training of teachers in Irish schools was patterned on Andrew Bell and Joseph Lancaster's monitorial system pioneered in England in the 1790s. Designed to provide nondenominational education for the poor, each Lancastrian school was to be run by an adult "model" teacher assisted in the classroom by her most promising senior pupils, or monitors. Monitors, who were often the same age as their charges, kept order in the classroom. On the basis of their classroom experience, monitors could eventually become teachers themselves.[17]

By the late 1830s, the monitorial system was under fire, however, accused of producing inadequately trained teachers; so a new method of

teacher preparation was introduced, that of the "pupil-teacher." Henceforward, the most intelligent pupils were apprenticed at the age of thirteen for
five years in their own schools. During their apprenticeships, pupil-teachers
taught younger children during school hours and received further instruction themselves after school. At the age of eighteen, female pupil-teachers
were required to pass an entrance examination for the Marlborough Street
Model School in Dublin, which offered two three-month courses of instruction for would-be teachers each year. There, teacher-trainees studied the
"theory and practice of teaching," along with instruction in "plain needlework, . . . the art of cutting out and making up articles of female wearing
apparel; . . . [and] the arts of domestic economy, such as cottage cookery,
washing, ironing, mangling, and other useful branches of household management."[18] Only graduates were granted teacher certification. By 1900,
there were three teacher training colleges for Catholic women in Ireland,
and the training course now lasted for two years. Uncertified teachers who
lacked this preparation earned lower salaries than their certified colleagues
until they themselves completed a one-year training course after teaching
for three years.[19]

The commissioners hoped that teacher training would improve with
the advent of formal preparation classes at the Marlborough Street School,
but many teachers remained uncertified, forcing Dublin to implement more
stringent methods to upgrade teacher education.[20] In 1862, the "Revised
Code" for schools in England made the results earned by pupils on an annual examination in the three Rs the criterion for teacher salaries for the
next year. This innovation, known as "payment-by-results," was adopted in
Irish schools in 1872. Meant to motivate teachers to excel in the classroom,
the results system made little noticeable improvement in overall teacher competence, although observers remarked on the improvement in student handwriting, spelling, and arithmetic as teachers drilled for results on examinations. Eventually, in the late 1890s, the payment-by-results system was
jettisoned.[21]

In the midst of the ongoing debates about their qualifications, teachers
were expected to master a strictly structured curriculum. According to the
commissioners, "ordinary subjects" for classroom instruction included English ("reading, spelling, writing, composition, and grammar"), geography,
history, arithmetic, singing, drawing, needlework, laundry work, physical
drill, manual instruction, elementary science, and cookery. Lessons in hygiene and temperance were also part of a teacher's repertoire.[22]

Teachers were further enjoined to focus on "reading, spelling, prose, and poetry," as well as citizenship and the "general outline of the history of Great Britain and Ireland." Writing classes practiced penmanship, composition, and grammar, while geography classes pored over maps of Europe and the Empire. Arithmetic lessons gave instruction in money, weights, measures, and "mental arithmetic," which in the upper grades included decimals, averages, and square roots. Drawing and singing classes rounded out the school day. "Physical Drill" consisted of calisthenics and marching classes and girls' "deportment during games."[23]

"Cookery and laundry-work," the commissioners instructed, "form part of the ordinary school programme for girls enrolled in the fifth and higher standards (and all girls over age eleven)," and women teachers were expected to have mastered these skills themselves. Teachers taught their first-year students the "cleaning and care of the kitchen stove [and/or] fireplace," along with "disposal of refuse [and] the simple treatment of cuts and burns." "Practical Cookery" was practiced by preparing tea and cocoa, porridge and gruel, poached eggs and toast, fried bacon and fish, cabbage, and potato soup. Second-year students learned how to create daily and weekly household schedules, set a dinner table, and keep "simple" household accounts. Laundering instruction taught girls how to clean and otherwise care for tubs, irons, and clotheslines, as well as the chemistry of cleaning materials like soap, soda, borax, and starch. Removing stains and fancy ironing completed the curriculum. The daughters of farm families were also taught the importance of personal as well as household cleanliness. Needlework stood above all in the hierarchy of domestic instruction, and an hour of each school day was devoted to classes ranging from knitting for beginners to dressmaking for advanced pupils. Domestic education classes were so important to the commissioners, in fact, that they offered schools five-shilling premiums for each girl who attended at least half of them each year.[24]

Teachers were not only responsible for the quality of their classroom lessons, however. They were also evaluated on the upkeep of the classrooms themselves. In fact, National Education Commission guidelines instructed inspectors to evaluate the physical as well as the intellectual conditions in the classes they visited, stating that a teacher's responsibilities included keeping schools "properly furnished, lighted, cleaned . . . and dusted every day. . . ." Oversight of the "internal whitewashing or distempering the walls at least once a year and washing out the rooms with carbolic soap, or other disinfectant, at least three times a year" fell on teacher's shoulders also.[25] Teachers were also assessed on the basis of the availability and condition of such classroom furnishings as clocks, maps, blackboards, and books. The condition of outdoor toilets, the notorious "out offices," was another constant concern to classroom observers.

The tone of an inspection report varied with the school, the teacher, and, of course, the inspector; and schools like Castlegregory's earned and lost their reputations over time. In February 1907, for instance, Inspector Louis S. Daly observed classes in another Kerry school, Caherciveen's National School Number 2. "[The] teacher ought to superintend pupils at play," he suggested, since, "The playground is rather muddy and the dividing wall is beginning to give. . . ." Furthermore, "the [out] offices ought to be cleaned out." In January 1908, Daly revisited the school and reported that "The pupils of this little school are bright and nicely mannered [but] the teaching of arithmetic ought to be sounder. . . . Unless these defects . . . are removed it will be impossible that the school can retain the grading now assigned. . . ." Daly finished his report by cautioning the teacher to "endeavour to avoid undue loss of time . . . at one lesson today twelve minutes was lost while the teacher distributed copies, sharpened pencils for Drawing, etc., while all the time a class of infants stood on the floor idle." Moreover, Daly observed that "some of the [school's] woodwork wants painting. The clock should be out [and] in working order. There is no globe."[26]

On October 20, 1908, Inspector J. V. Doody visited Caherciveen's school and reported that, "the decline in attendance has been followed by a decline in general proficiency. . . ." Furthermore, "The walls require limewashing and [the] woodwork painting. . . . Maps of the British Islands . . . and a globe are required." Eventually a map arrived but, as Inspector D. Lehane noted in his report dated September 12, 1910, "a map of the British Isles [has] been provided but . . . not suspended in the school room." Inspector Kane visited a year later, on October 18, 1911, and reported that while "the tone of the school is good . . . there is [still] no globe." The school lacked even more basic amenities. According to Inspector Doody, the school's "out offices" were missing a door. In May 1917, Caherciveen's school received its last inspection, and the annoyed tone of Inspector E. T. Darmon's entry suggested a sad fate for a school that had steadily lost students over the past several years. "*At least* three days notice of all closings should be sent to the Inspectors," he testily reported after showing up for an inspection at the empty school.[27]

In addition to the all-seeing district inspectors, local school managers watched teachers closely. In 1895, former teacher W. Erskine summed up teacher antipathy to this tight regulation in a pamphlet that called the largely clerical school managers "an interfering lot" who, along with the inspectors, saddled teachers with two masters. "Cases are turning up every week," Erskine told his readers, "of the injustice which teachers suffer from cruel, tyrannical managers, and [teachers] have no redress." To support his accusation, Erskine gave the example of a female assistant teacher given three months' notice to quit her job because she "had not been an enthusiastic participant in working for the [school manager's wife's charity] bazaars, [or] collecting money for the church" or performing "other extraneous duties." Despite such obvious wrongs, teachers "are ashamed to parade their degradation and they are afraid to rebel lest it should prevent them from getting another situation." According to Erskine, taking a teaching job in a national school subjected the teacher to a system of "perpetual espionage."[28]

The scrutiny teachers faced both inside and outside the classroom that had so outraged Erskine stemmed from the national commissioners' periodically updated *Rules and Regulations* for teachers. The 1869 edition of the commissioners' rules, for instance, stipulated that teachers "be persons of Christian sentiment, of calm temper, and discretion; . . . [obedient] to the law and [loyal] to their sovereign." Required to promote "by precept and example, *Cleanliness, Neatness, and Decency,*" teachers were to be exemplars of "the great rule of regularity and order—A TIME AND PLACE FOR EVERYTHING, AND EVERYTHING IN ITS PROPER TIME AND PLACE." Furthermore, despite their low wages, teachers were not to moonlight on other jobs, especially in pubs. They were also to avoid all public political gatherings in order to "abstain from controversy," and they were forbidden to attend all fairs and markets.[29] Isolated as they were from these popular community events, teacher rectitude would therefore be unassailable. Almost a half century later, the commissioners' 1914 edition of the *Rules and Regulations* continued to forbid teachers to moonlight "in any job that will interfere with their teaching" or to "assist in or run pubs or even to live in a house owned by a pub keeper," or to "attend political meetings or run for Parliament. . . ." Voting, the only political activity left open to them was, of course, limited to male teachers alone. The same rule book required teachers to "sign in and out under the principal's supervision every day."[30]

If a teacher failed to keep her classroom clean or violated the rules in any other way, "The manager shall have the *absolute* [emphasis added] power to determine the . . . employment [of a teacher] at any time, without previous notice, on payment . . . to the teacher of three months' . . . salary. . . . The manager shall also have the power to determine [a teacher's] employment, without previous notice, for misconduct . . . [if the] manager shall obtain [the approval of] the Commissioners of National Education . . . the teacher shall not be entitled to any compensation."[31]

Teachers could also lose their jobs by breaking the commissioners' rules against living over a pub, joining political groups, or running for office. Dismissal was not supposed to be arbitrary, however. A teacher had to be given "fair warning" and due process before she could be fired, and the report of a solitary inspector alone was not sufficient to get a teacher ousted from her job. Furthermore, a teacher was allowed to write directly to the commissioners if she had a complaint about an inspector or manager.[32]

By the late nineteenth century, getting a teaching job was as difficult as keeping one, and winning a promotion was no easier. Teachers had to be between the ages of eighteen and thirty-five at the time of their first hiring, and all teachers were on probation during their first years on the job. Principal teachers topped the teaching hierarchy, followed by two ranks of probationary assistant teachers. Each teacher rank was subdivided into three divisions, and promotion from one division to the next depended on an individual's training, seniority, service, and "general attainments."[33] A teacher's ability to attract students and keep them coming to school was perhaps the single most important factor in her gaining a promotion and an increase in salary, however. Nevertheless, no matter how large her class, no teacher could move up to the next grade until she had spent a minimum of three years in her current position. Furthermore, the commissioners insisted that "The successful teaching of cookery has an important bearing on the award of increments of salaries and the promotion of teachers."[34]

In order to reach the highest teaching rank, therefore, a young woman had to win appointment as a pupil-teacher, graduate from the training-school course, win a first appointment as a probationary assistant teacher, and work her way up through the subdivisions of each teaching rank. Since no teacher could move to the next highest rank in less than three years, a woman hired at age eighteen at the entry rank of junior assistant teacher would be at least thirty-six before she reached the lowest division of the highest teaching rank, that of principal teacher. Since only teachers with "higher ability" could win promotions, and these abilities were largely determined by inspector reports, many women were considerably older than thirty-six before they attained the highest teaching rank, if they reached it at all.

In addition to the rigorous promotion system, teacher ability could also be recognized by money "gratuities," paid on a half-yearly basis at the end of March and again at the end of September. "Ordinary" national school teachers could earn these premiums for "Order, Neatness, and Cleanliness." If a school manager or a district inspector knew, however, "of any just cause for withholding the Premium from the Teacher," he was, "to return the receipt [authorizing the payment] unsigned, and state his reasons for so doing."[35]

"Good Service," or supplemental salaries, could also be earned by teachers who maintained an average daily attendance of at least thirty-five pupils and who had amassed at least eight years of service. Nevertheless, "No teacher [is] eligible for such Supplemental Salary who shall have been . . . fined for misconduct or neglect of duty, or on whose school a decidedly unfavorable report shall have been made within the preceding three years. . . ." Supplements were also not paid to a teacher "who shall not have shown . . . *throughout [her] whole career,* to have been attentive and painstaking, and mindful of all details of school-keeping."[36]

"Ottoman Tyranny"

Individual inspectors and managers wielded considerable influence over teacher job security and promotion. One notorious inspector, W. H. Welply, was even accused of deliberately making hostile reports so that particular teachers were denied promotions. After Welply visited principal teacher Mary Morris's Kerry classroom in August 1907, for instance, he damned her with faint criticism when he reported to the commissioners that "Miss Morris will do well to study . . . the part I have marked—p.9—in Notes for Teachers . . . carefully and apply the suggestions contained in them." Furthermore, Welply criticized Morris for poor record keeping. "Miss Morris," he wrote, should, "without delay . . . enter any other [reports in] arrears in [her] books."[37]

In 1911, Welply was transferred to the Tipperary school district, and teachers there accused him of deliberately trying to "reduce" all teacher evaluations. In an August 1912 speech that was later published, a Tipperary teacher named Mansfield publicly objected to Welply's tactics. News of the dissent reached the commissioners in Dublin and they fired Mansfield in October of that year. With their manager's approval, however, Mansfield and his wife, an assistant teacher at the same school as her husband, continued in their posts without pay. When a Dublin newspaper, under the head-line "Ottoman Tyranny in the Education Office . . . ," reported Mansfield's dismissal, the commissioners, perhaps fearing further negative publicity, re-instated him with pay in November 1915.[38]

Although the existence of husbands and wives drawing combined salaries caused resentment among local taxpayers in many school districts, spousal teaching teams like the Mansfields were fairly common, especially in rural areas, since marriage was not a bar to a woman's teaching career until 1933.[39] The Mansfields are also indicative of another trend in relation-ships among teachers, that of the significant differences in the salaries paid to male and female teachers. In the Mansfields' case, the husband was a principal teacher, earning a far higher salary than his assistant teacher wife. At every teaching rank and at every grade level, in fact, male teachers earned considerably more than their female colleagues, even if training levels, rank, and length of service were equal. In 1914, for instance, the maximum an-nual salary for the highest-paid female teacher was 151 pounds, while top-ranked male teachers received 185 pounds for the same year's work. Male and female teachers were paid four times annually, on the 15th of January, April, July, and October, although the commissioners reserved the right to reduce a teacher's salary at any time "on account of inefficiency or other sufficient cause."[40]

As teacher training and hiring practices became more rigorous in the course of the late nineteenth and early twentieth centuries, however, women teachers began to demand more economic and political equity with their male colleagues. Female teachers joined their male colleagues at the first Irish Na-tional Teachers Organization Congress (INTO) held in Dublin in August 1868; however, women teachers had to wait until 1907 to win the right to sit on INTO's executive council.[41] Nevertheless, in a period when women's suffrage remained a distant goal and nationalist politics largely ignored the possibility of a gender dimension in the quest for Irish independence, INTO offered women teachers a public voice and an organized counterforce to their growing regulation by Dublin-based school bureaucrats.

No teacher, male or female, had job security when INTO was founded in the late 1860s. School managers could fire them at will and without notice by simply refusing to continue to pay their salaries. In 1879, however, teachers were granted the right to at least three months' notice of dismissal or, if they were removed from the classroom immediately, three months' salary instead.[42] When a manager sided with a teacher against the commissioners, however, the commissioners could overrule the manager, as they did in the Mansfield case in Tipperary in 1912.

The majority of school managers were priests, and they distrusted INTO from its start, insisting that "the efficiency of our schools comes before the comforts of our teachers." Between 1899 and 1905, in fact, school managers in Ulster banned the hiring of INTO members, and in Armagh a new teacher had to swear, ". . . I am not a member of the National Teachers' Organization and I furthermore undertake not to become a member of the aforesaid association . . . without first tendering my resignation."[43]

According to INTO's historian, T. J. O'Connell, the "strained relations" between teachers and district inspectors was another "hardy annual [item] on the INTO Congress agenda" in the early years of the twentieth century. INTO members especially resented the 1899 appointment of Dr. W. J. M. Starkie as the new resident commissioner of the National Schools. Starkie, a former professor of Greek at the Queen's University in Galway and a Catholic, possessed a domineering personality "entirely unsuited for [his] position" as national school commissioner, according to INTO members. Teachers especially disliked his willingness to fire teachers who dared to criticize him and the fact that his district inspectors were given wide new powers over classroom instruction and personnel matters. Since incremental pay depended on three successive "satisfactory" inspector reports, many teachers found themselves receiving two "satisfactory" ratings only, followed by an "unsatisfactory" rating that denied them the salary increment in the third year. INTO members claimed that Starkie ignored teacher appeals against unfavorable inspector reports, and "hundreds" of teachers were fired for alleged "inefficiency" in Starkie's first twelve years on the job.[44]

INTO members singled out two inspectors as being particularly unfair to teachers, and one of the two was the same Inspector Welply who had denied Kerry teacher Mary Morris her third "satisfactory" report in 1907 and who had caused Mansfield's dismissal from his Tipperary post in 1912.

In 1913, at closed hearings, the commissioners learned that in the course of one year, over nine hundred teachers had appealed to Starkie against unsatisfactory inspector reports such as Welply's. Starkie had, without consulting the other commissioners, denied the vast majority of these appeals. Moreover, some appeals were even sent back to the inspector who wrote the offending reports, often causing reprisals against individual teachers by the same inspectors in future reports.[45]

The commissioners overruled Starkie's request to allow Welply to testify before them and instead made recommendations designed to prevent abuses of power in the future. Henceforward, all appeals against inspectors' reports were to be given full consideration by all commission members, and the inspector's dreaded "Observation Book" would be renamed the more teacher-friendly "Suggestion Book." Furthermore, annual increments in salary would be automatic in the absence of a bad report. Even with these reforms, however, inspectors retained the right to deny promotions, and teachers continued to dread the inspector's visit. Inspectors were aware of these fears. In May 1910, for example, two inspectors complained that their visit to a school in Queen's County (Laois) "was hampered by the unwillingness of the [teacher] to teach. Where no refusal was made it was clear that the teacher was in such a condition of nervousness that she could not do herself justice. . . ." The inspectors found the same fear at a school in County Kilkenny. Here, "the teacher claimed to be quite unable, and even unwilling, to teach before an inspector." Another inspector named McGuire had even worse luck when he visited a school in Mayo in that same year. "I visited [the school]," he reported, but, "the Headmistress informed me that she . . . did not wish the school to be inspected. . . ."[46]

A teacher's nervousness in the face of an inspector's visit may have been increased by the occasional arbitrary dismissal in spite of reforms. Faced with unfair firings, many individual teachers took their protests to court. In 1897, for instance, a County Kildare school manager ordered thirty-two-year veteran principal teacher Mrs. O'Sullivan to leave her classroom on only four days' notice and without severance pay because of her unrecorded reaction to a complaint about the behavior of her girls' choir. Like Aghaloora's Margaret Smyth before her, O'Sullivan refused to turn in the school key until she received the three months' severance pay due her. Instead, the manager forced the school door open and installed a new teacher in O'Sullivan's place. O'Sullivan took her case to court and won a £200 settlement.[47]

Some school managers tried to interfere in their teachers' lives in even more drastic ways than denying them their salaries. In September 1914, for instance, County Clare teacher Michael O'Shea was fired by his manager, the local parish priest, when O'Shea refused the priest's demand that he marry the school's assistant teacher. Since O'Shea occupied the school's official teacher residence and female assistants were hard to keep, the priest insisted that marriage to O'Shea would provide the assistant with both housing and incentive to remain at her post. O'Shea refused to go quietly, and as in so many of the controversies between managers and teachers, he also refused to give up his key—in this case, to the teacher's residence. He also married someone else, who was not a teacher at all. When the priest finally evicted him, the parents of his students gave O'Shea and his new wife a cottage and withdrew their children from the local school, sending them instead to O'Shea. The priest retaliated with denunciations from the altar, going so far as to deny the sacrament of confirmation to children being tutored by O'Shea and other sacraments to their parents.[48] Although O'Shea's colleague's feelings about her very public rejection have not been recorded, the priest/manager's attempts to dominate his teachers in even their most personal decisions, and the local populations' active resistance to these attempts, indicate that even in 1914, teacher rebellion had not been entirely quelled. Despite their vehement protests and the support they received from local taxpayers, however, teachers like Kildare's Mrs. O'Sullivan, Clare's Michael O'Shea, and Cavan's Margaret Smyth all ended up unemployed.

"Thank God for America!"

Despite their teachers' often restricted lives and low salaries, the seemingly independent, educated, well-groomed *ladies* teaching in Irish schools offered a new possibility for female potential to the girls under their care.[49] In an era when few went beyond four years of primary education, teachers were women who had achieved their status not through birth or marriage, but through diligence at school, a diligence any school girl could imitate. Instead of creating thrifty workers satisfied with their lot in Ireland, therefore, the schools and their teachers unintentionally opened a window of opportunity for young women destined to leave their homeland for American cities.[50] Inspired by memories of their teachers in Ireland, the immigrant generation would see their American offspring achieve the same lady-like

and educated status as the glamorous women in the classrooms they remembered from their Irish childhoods. Geographical and educational
mobility for schoolchildren was the unintended consequence of the window
of opportunity opened by a conservative Irish school system.

Mary Crowe Lennon, who left Ireland for Chicago in 1927, was one
beneficiary of the system. "I was born on September 2, 1907, in . . . Logua-
mullane [County Mayo]," Lennon recalled many years later in her handwritten memoirs.[51] Lennon, the oldest of three sisters, "went to Lehinch
school about a mile away [from our farm]. . . . When I finished in the Lehinch school, I went on to Ballinrobe Convent School for two years. I walked
two miles to get to the train—about a half hour ride—then walked from the
train to the school[,] about two blocks. We spoke Gaelic in our house. . . .
[M]y Dad had a very limited amount of English [language] learning, [but]
Mom had a good English [language] education. . . . My Mom was great
for sending us to school . . . she valued education. . . . [She] was the go-
getter in the family."

"To get a position in Ireland," Lennon continued, "one needed a well-
rounded education as there [weren't] enough jobs for everyone. Many of us
had to travel far to places of opportunity and so at the age of nineteen I
de[c]ided to come to America . . . and get a job. . . . It was extremely hard
leaving my family at Home—and I was very lonesome. . . . [A] girl from
near my home . . . and I stayed close together during the trip . . . we were together like sisters . . . supporting each other." After landing in New York,
Mary took a train to Chicago, where she was met by her aunt.

Lennon's adjustment to life in Chicago accelerated once she found
paid work. "I was on my own to get a job and take care of myself . . . ," she
remembered. "I started to work as a clerk in an A and P grocery store—
fifteen dollars a week. . . . I saved most of it to buy some American clothes
and also [to send money to] my Mom and Dad at Christmas." Her adjustment to American life was also eased when she "started keeping company
[with] Michael Lennon [an immigrant] from Athlone. . . . [H]e seemed to
have the qualifications I was looking for—Irish Catholic, steady work and a
nice lad! (ha!) A year later we became engaged but hadn't any marriage
plans for another year and a half—time to save enough money. . . . [O]n
June 22nd, 1935, we were married. . . ." Eventually, the Lennons had nine
children, four boys and five girls altogether. "The children all went to good
schools and all have . . . well-rounded educations with Dr and Master's
degree[s]," Lennon tells us. Her eldest daughter Kay got a master's degree

at DePaul University, an accomplishment that allowed her to pursue a career in education.

A mother's pride in her children's accomplishments is further reflected in the concluding sentences of Lennon's memoir. "I am extremely happy," she wrote, as "my priority and heartfelt wishes [were] that [my children] would all have the opportunities I didn't. This can be done in America, thank God. [My children] are all doing well. [They have] good jobs, nice homes, and [are] good American citizens which does my heart good. . . . Thank God for America[!]"

CHAPTER 3

"Boston Schools for Boston Girls!"

Campaigning on the slogan "Boston Schools for Boston Girls!" in 1901, Julia Harrington Duff became the first Irish-Catholic woman to win a seat on that city's school committee. Born in Charlestown, Massachusetts, in 1860, the oldest child of seven and the granddaughter of Irish immigrants from County Cork, Julia spent four years at Boston's Girls' High School before graduating from Boston's Normal School in 1878. For the next fourteen years, she taught in the Boston public schools and traveled extensively in Europe and the Holy Land, sending her lively and well-written impressions back to be published in the *Boston Pilot*, the city's widely read Catholic newspaper.[1]

In 1892, Julia left teaching to marry her childhood sweetheart, John Duff, a Massachusetts Institute of Technology and Harvard-educated physician. The son of an Irish immigrant father, Dr. Duff had completed his medical residency in Dublin after spending several years as a mining engineer in Colorado. On the day of their marriage, a headline in the *Boston Herald* announced, "Brilliant Society Wedding in Charlestown: Bride: Julia Harrington; Groom: Dr. John Duff: Both Bride and Groom Hold Leading Positions in Catholic Circles in Boston."[2] While her husband, dressed always in a white hat, walked to his house calls in hilly Charlestown or stitched up the wounded in the local police station, Julia raised their three surviving children, sending them also to the city's schools.[3] The Duffs'children eventually earned advanced college degrees. Like their father, sons John and Paul became physicians. Daughter Mae followed in her mother's footsteps by becoming a teacher, after completing two degrees simultaneously in art and education. Mae eventually became the head of the Boston Public Schools Art Department before entering a convent at the age of forty-four, where she continued to teach art.[4]

Funded by her husband's money, the well-to-do and always elegant Julia canvassed Charlestown in her carriage, winning her school committee seat by showcasing her fourteen years of "practical" experience as a public school teacher and by promising to protect access to city teaching jobs for the largely Irish-American graduates of her alma mater, the Boston Normal School. Duff believed that the Normal School provided the single best opportunity for the professional advancement of women from working-class, largely Irish neighborhoods. While better-off women could obtain their educations at expensive private colleges, Duff knew that city-funded teacher training was essential for the social and educational mobility of growing numbers of Boston's Irish working-class women.[5]

According to a contemporary newspaper report, Duff joined the Boston School Committee because she "had seen good teachers rejected for promotion." Since she knew "more about the schools from a practical standpoint than all the reformers . . . combined," the article's headline announced, Duff had "Sized Up the Boston School Committee Before She Became a Member, and Knows Its Weaknesses." The same article also reported that "It has long been known that the Public School Association [PSA] is nothing more than a shell of a public movement, controlled by a half dozen . . . men with money and no children." In contrast, as a former teacher and the mother of three, Duff was a long-time reformer who had already saved the city's normal school from extinction. "[I]n her career as a schoolgirl, schoolteacher and active woman of society," the article concluded, Duff was not "obeisant . . . because she can talk so well and hit so hard. . . .[6] In another newspaper article, headlined "How Mrs. Duff Compelled Machine to Oppose the P.S.A.: What Men Have Failed to Do a Woman Has Accomplished," which was accompanied by a large pencil portrait of Duff superimposed on a page from a school text, readers learned that Duff single-handedly prevented local Democratic Party bosses from endorsing PSA candidates.[7]

Fearing that he could not control the fiery reformer, Democratic Mayor John "Honey Fitz" Fitzgerald joined Duff's PSA enemies and successfully stopped her bids for reelection. Accused of political graft when one of her brothers was hired by the school department and of political manipulation when another brother won a seat in the Massachusetts State Legislature, Julia's political career was over.[8]

By the time Duff lost her seat on the school committee, she was a veteran of the war between the Yankee Protestants, whose ancestors had created the first public school system in the nation, and the Catholic Irish, who were becoming an ever-larger proportion of the system's student body and teaching force. Recognizing that her opponents' aim of restricting the number of Irish teaching in the schools was an attempt to rescue the Protestant "American" basis of school culture, Duff fought back. Qualified Irish Americans like herself, she insisted, had earned the right to places in the Normal School and jobs in the classroom.

Duff's campaign hit a nerve in Boston's turn-of-the-century school culture wars. Her opponents among the wealthy Protestants of the PSA opposed her with their own slogan, "Keep the Schools Out of Politics!" The PSA's advocates of "good government" insisted that using the city's Normal School as a conduit to teaching jobs for its largely Irish-Catholic graduates was the spoils system run amok and therefore a threat to American democracy. They promoted the hiring of the "best men and women in the country" as city teachers instead. City-funded teacher training, Duff replied, provided working-class, and mostly Irish, Bostonians with access to professional employment otherwise unavailable to them. The Normal School was an agency of democracy, Duff insisted, and not a threat to American values.[9]

In her years in the public eye, Duff also faced scrutiny as a wife and a mother. Contemporaries reported that she was "distinctively and essentially domestic." To allay suspicions among traditionalists, Duff declared that "I am not a new woman." Instead, she "believe[d] in devotion to the home and not the desertion of the home."[10] To further publicize Duff's housewifery, the *Boston Sunday Post* ran a two-page illustrated article announcing that "Dr. and Mrs. Duff Have a Collection of Chinaware and Pitchers That Are Admired By All Who Are Permitted to See Them."[11] The city's most influential newspaper, the *Boston Sunday Globe,* also ran a two-page illustrated article entitled "Home Life of the Real Mrs. Duff: The Aggressive Woman of the Boston School Board Never Neglects Her Family . . . She Enjoys a Honeymoon Trip Semiannually." The article was decorated with a large central portrait of Duff with smaller portraits of her husband and three children on each side. A view of the front of the family's handsome townhouse at Five Dexter Row in Charlestown completed the display.[12] While many of Duff's working-class constituents must have marveled at her ability to combine family life with a career in politics, Duff was backed by a devoted husband and "the work of her maids."[13] According to her descendants, despite her small stature and physical fragility, she ran her household with an iron hand.

One of Duff's contemporaries, Mary Elizabeth Blake, was also active in turn-of-the-twentieth-century Boston school politics. The Irish-born Blake graduated from high school in Boston and completed her education at the Convent of the Sacred Heart in Manhattanville, New York, where she studied four foreign languages—Latin, French, German, and Spanish. Returning to Massachusetts from New York, she began her teaching career in Quincy, just south of Boston. Like Julia Duff, Blake married a physician, the Irish-born Dr. John Blake. After her marriage, she moved to Boston, became a writer and a mother, and sent her five children to the city's schools.

Blake's husband John had been a member of the school committee in the 1880s when he led the protest that eventually banished Swinton's *Outline of the World's History* from Boston's classrooms. Insisting that this required text was intensely anti-Catholic, John Blake took his campaign to the city's Irish community. In 1888, the offending book was removed from use in the public schools despite vigorous anti-Catholic demonstrations demanding its retention.[14]

In 1901, campaigning like Julia Duff for a school committee seat, Mary Blake also met stiff opposition from her Protestant opponents, especially women. If the PSA-dominated board needed "for the good of the schools to have ten Romanists on the board," the *Women's Voice* opined in its December 1900 issue, "let them at least not wrong the Independent Women Voters by the nomination of as objectionable a Romanist as Mrs. Blake." Apparently, Blake's husband's textbook activism twenty years before had not been forgotten. The *Women's Journal* of November 10, 1900, however, praised Blake, noting that the Manhattanville graduate was "a woman of unusual scholarship." This support, however, failed to get Blake a seat on the school committee.[15]

Although Blake met defeat at the polls in 1901, Duff did not. She and other Irish Americans demonstrated their new-found influence on school policy in many ways during the next few years. By 1906, in fact, the Irish members on Boston's school committee partially reversed the Protestant-dominated school culture of the nineteenth century when they ordered the distribution of 605 copies of an Irish history textbook, Johnston and Spencer's *Ireland's Story*, for use in all city schools.[16] Yankee domination of school curriculum matters appeared to be eroding.

Boston's school wars had by no means ended, however. Forced out of office after one term, Duff's achievements on behalf of Irish-American aspirants to city teaching jobs was eclipsed by a new wave of "progressive" school reform that was designed to limit the influence of female teachers over school curriculum and administration. These changes would also be as inimical to teacher autonomy and mobility as earlier sectarianism had been.

In 1910, reformers again tried to demolish what they saw as the Irish political machine's stranglehold on the schools by reducing the twenty-four-member board representing individual wards to only five at-large candidates, thereby increasing the power of anti-neighborhood progressives like the Harvard-educated lawyer James Jackson Storrow. As a further safeguard against undue political influence in school matters, including the hiring and firing of teachers, the school committee would henceforth be concerned with overall school policy only. The actual day-to-day running of the schools and the hiring and firing of teachers was to be left in the hands of appointed university-trained educational "experts." Between 1910 and 1920, professional administrators ran the schools along these progressive lines.[17]

A quarter of a century after her defeat at the polls, the now-widowed Duff was interviewed by a reporter from the *Boston Herald*. In an article headlined "Julia Duff Scores Boston's School System," the "stormy petrol of the Boston School Committee . . . Who Ever-Championed the Cause of the Boston Schoolteacher," had the "same old Duff fire in her eye." Deploring the current trend of male administrators marking down the top students' grades on city teachers' examinations in order to prevent them from becoming eligible for school jobs, Duff insisted that the problems with the schools were, "not the fault of our own Boston girls who are teachers, either." Instead, she continued, "Our schools have been overrun with an army of specialists, philanthropists, statisticians, and would-be directors, to the detriment of reading, writing, and arithmetic." In all, the seventy-year-old Duff concluded, "I feel as young as I ever did. Some day I will be on the school board again and you will see things happen!"[18]

Although Duff died in 1932 and never rejoined the Boston School Committee, over thirty years later an April 1953 *Boston Post* editorial titled "Tribute Long Overdue" reminded readers that a half century ago, "before women were enfranchised," Duff had been a member of the city's school committee. Bravely, she, "entered a bitter political fight to improve the Boston school system," even though "she was well aware[,] . . . having been a schoolteacher, . . . that the odds were against her." Nevertheless, "She broke the power of the Public School Association" Concluding that Duff's efforts "ought to be memorialized," the newspaper urged that one of the new public schools then being built in the city be named after "Mrs. Julia Elizabeth Duff . . . [to] recognize her lifetime of service.[19]

A Common Citizenship

The divisions between Irish Catholics and Yankee Protestants in Boston's school politics were at least a half-century old by the time Julia Harrington Duff and Mary Elizabeth Blake campaigned in 1901. In fact, Boston was the first American city to have a public school system when, in 1789, the year of the revolution in France, the Boston Education Act established the city's first tax-supported free schools open to children aged four to sixteen. By 1820, Boston had a citywide primary school system. These schools were designed to teach the "three Rs" to the city's children, but they were also charged with instilling discipline and patriotism in the hearts and minds of Boston's youth. Thus, even in the early nineteenth century, when Boston's population was still largely Protestant and of English-stock, the city fathers stipulated that school lessons be designed to foster the Protestant and republican values held by most of their fellow citizens at the time. This homogeneity in ethnicity and culture remained unchanged, for the most part, even after 1833, the year the Commonwealth of Massachusetts erased the last vestiges of its connections to the Congregational Church established by the Puritans two centuries before. From then on, schools would be the chief vehicles for filling the cultural void left by the separation of church and state, as they would bring children from all social classes together and instill in them a sense of common citizenship.[20]

Since theirs was the first American city to establish a public school system, Bostonians had no blueprint to follow in creating a curriculum designed to inculcate what were seen as the fundamentals of citizenship in the new republic. In addition, in the first decades of the nineteenth century, as the growing city's increasingly diversified industrial economy divorced the workplace from the family home, parents now spent their days in factories rather than in home workshops, where they had once been able to watch over their children. The unsupervised young were more and more familiar on city streets.[21] In the face of rapid urban growth and economic change, public schools formed a cutting edge for the creation of a new urban order, prompting reformer Horace Mann, named the first Secretary of the Massachusetts State Board of Education in 1837, to promote schools rather than prisons as a means of transforming the growing numbers of undisciplined urban poor into useful citizens.[22]

In a term of office that lasted until 1848, Mann modeled Boston's schools on the new factories pioneered in nearby Lowell. His age-graded "common" schools used uniform texts—such as Noah Webster's new school readers that deemphasized the wrathful Puritan God in favor of edifying tales of good citizenship—which pupils read while they learned the three Rs and uniform spelling. In this way, the interchangeability of the factory assembly line was mirrored in the "culture factories," as the new schools were sometimes called, which would efficiently produce a reliable citizen-worker in the new economy.[23] Despite these changes, however, Mann's "common" schools remained Protestant in their cultural assumptions. The product of a God-fearing rural Massachusetts upbringing, Mann believed that the Protestant Bible belonged in the public school curriculum by "common consent," and Catholics and other marginal groups went unacknowledged. Under Mann's leadership, Boston's schools with their Protestant values became the spearheads for school reform throughout the country.

Inundation

In the late 1840s, Boston's model school system faced a new and unprecedented challenge as hundreds of thousands of impoverished, often Gaelic-speaking refugees fleeing the Famine in Ireland descended on the city. Whereas overall immigration into Boston had never before exceeded 4,000 people annually, according to one count the number of Irish settling in the city reached 29,000 in 1849 alone. Suddenly, one-quarter of Boston's population was Irish Catholic, and Catholics were now the city's largest single religious group. A decade later, in 1860, the number of Irish-born equalled the number of indigenous Yankees in Boston.[24] By the end of the nineteenth century, the Irish were the majority of the city's population of over a half million.[25] This inundation was to have a far-reaching impact on the city's common schools.

The flood of Irish into the city led to massive school overcrowding as the public elementary-school enrollment rose from a little over 4,000 in 1830 to over 17,000 in 1846, the first full year of the mass influx of Famine Irish. The mushrooming school system got its first superintendent, Nathan Bishop, in 1851. By 1852, the city employed 190 teachers, and, according to Primary School Board Secretary Alvan [sic] Symonds, more than half of the city's schoolchildren in that year were Irish. Out of the fifty-eight pupils in the Endicott School alone, Symonds reported, forty-five were Irish. In that same year, Massachusetts enacted the first compulsory school attendance law in the United States, in hopes of forcing all children between the ages of eight and fourteen to attend school for at least three months each year. By 1859, over 25,000 children were sitting in public school classrooms, and more and more of these children were Irish.[26]

By the 1870s, Boston's Irish population was growing faster than all other ethnic groups in the city. The city's registrar noted in his annual report of 1874 that the Irish were, "as usual," responsible for the highest marriage and birthrates of any ethnic group in the city. The one marriage for each forty-five Irish-born in the city outstripped the one marriage for each sixty-six native-born in Boston in 1874, and marriages between Irish-born brides and grooms comprised over one-quarter of the total marriages in the city that year.[27] High Irish birth rates matched the high Irish marriage rates. In 1874, for instance, almost one-third of the city's 11,717 births were to Irish-born parents, while only slightly more than a quarter of this total were to American-born parents.[28] By 1890, census-takers estimated that the mostly Irish foreign-born mothers in Boston had twice the number of children under five than their native-born counterparts.[29]

High birth and marriage rates among Boston's Irish were mirrored by equally high death rates, owing to the persistent poverty of the city's Irish neighborhoods. In 1874, for instance, the city registrar reported that almost a quarter of the Irish-born in Boston died in that year, achieving the dubious distinction of having the highest mortality levels among all groups in the city at all ages over fifteen. Lamentable as this statistic was, however, the registrar did note that Boston's Irish mortality was lower than New York City's and Baltimore's. Nevertheless, Boston's Irish had the third highest recorded mortality in the nation, dying in greater numbers than their compatriots in

Buffalo, Louisville, Richmond, Philadelphia, Providence, and San Francisco. Furthermore, Boston's Irish infant mortality rate was second only to New York's in the United States, standing at 23.59 per 1,000 births compared to New York's 27.10 per 1,000 births. Irish babies in Boston were statistically better off than Irish infants in Leeds, Manchester, and London, however, where death rates per 1000 Irish in the population reached 30.9, 27.3, and 23.9, respectively, in that same year.[30]

Despite their poverty and appalling rates of premature death, Boston's Irish neighborhoods continued to grow because, as census official Carroll D. Wright noted in 1885, "great bodies of immigrants coming in . . . conspired to increase our population beyond the normal rate."[31] As the number of Irish Bostonians rose, the number of students in the city's public school classrooms grew apace. In 1880, when well over 50,000 children aged five to fifteen were enrolled in the city's schools, Boston employed 989 primary and grammar school teachers who taught classes of over fifty students apiece. In that year, each of an additional eighty-three high school teachers taught twenty-five out of the 2,090 students enrolled in the city's high schools, and 107 evening elementary school teachers taught classes of almost forty each.[32] By 1900, 60 percent of the students in Boston's public schools were the children of the foreign-born, and this percentage was even higher in the lower grades, where two-thirds of the city's pupils in grades one to four had a foreign-born father. According to one contemporary authority, no city school system in Massachusetts, including Boston, could accommodate its growing school-age population in the late nineteenth and early twentieth centuries, and classes of over sixty were not uncommon in those years.[33]

Poverty and the large class sizes prevented most Boston children from remaining in school beyond the first few years. A 1904 study noted that only 6,927 out of the 10,721 pupils entering the first grade in 1892 eventually finished the three primary grades. Only 3,457 of that number had completed the eight elementary grades by 1900. Drop-out rates among the city's high school students were equally dramatic. According to the same 1904 study, only 559 out of the 2,306 who entered Boston's high schools in 1892 ever graduated.[34]

Despite these dropout numbers, truancy in Boston fell from one-quarter to only ten percent of the enrolled students between 1870 and the mid-1890s, and Boston and other Massachusetts cities continued to be educational leaders into the early twentieth century. By the mid-1890s, in fact, the 125-day average length of the Massachusetts school year was the longest in the United States, and an 1894 Massachusetts law was the first in the nation to require each Commonwealth town to build its own high school. Tax expenditures on public schools also increased in the late nineteenth and early twentieth centuries, and Boston schools were part of this trend. By the 1910–1911 school year, fully one-quarter of Massachusetts state taxes went to fund public education.[35]

In addition to its educational innovations and generous school funding, Massachusetts was also atypical because it was more heavily industrialized than most other states in the late nineteenth and early twentieth centuries. Its industrialization fostered a high level of urbanization, and the growth in the number of available skilled and unskilled jobs that resulted from these changes attracted an above-average number of the foreign-born. In turn, Massachusetts cities had to create school systems able to cope with the rapidly intensifying urban problems of disease and poverty, as well as large numbers of non-English-speaking students. While classes in American history and civics had been required subjects in the Boston schools since 1857, these subjects took on an even greater importance in the school curriculum as more and more immigrant children crowded into the city's classrooms.[36] Boston school authorities, in fact, relied on the growing number of Irish-American teachers in the city's public schools to "Americanize" this even more alien population. Sara O'Brien, for example, wrote two texts in wide use in the city's classrooms, which provided literacy lessons for the foreign-born that emphasized proper etiquette, personal hygiene techniques, the workings of American democracy, and methods of obtaining naturalization and citizenship papers. The Irish-American O'Brien's thoroughly "Americanized" texts also included warnings against the urban political machine and extolled the values of rural America to the urban foreigners reading her texts.[37]

In the 1880s, as immigrants swelled the school population, girls' industrial education classes in homemaking and needlework were also added to the curriculum, reflecting the spirit of the times in much the same way as O'Brien's texts. Needle crafts had long been seen as vital to school girls on both sides of the Atlantic, as many educators believed that sewing skills instilled moral qualities of patience, aesthetics, and industriousness in young women. Since Boston school reformers held that the city's increasingly multicultural schoolgirls lacked both the moral and the domestic skills required to support healthy family life, training schoolgirls in the domestic arts was all the more urgent. As a result, Boston's first public school sewing class appeared in 1879, followed by cooking and laundering classes a few years later. These lessons were also designed to provide immigrant girls with salable skills, since almost all of them would need to earn money during the course of their adult lives, even after marriage.[38]

Culture Clash

Although officials had originally envisioned the schools as "culture factories" for inculcating discipline and American Protestant values into the city's growing number of school-age children, the schools' success in attracting the children of immigrants posed an unforeseen threat; and fear grew that the alien Catholic Irish would overwhelm the system and destroy it. This fear—perhaps coupled with the "pungent odor . . . suggestive of cholera . . . [and] the fumes of New England rum" that supposedly emanated from Irish children—prompted large numbers of the better-off native-born to remove their children from the public schools in favor of more exclusive and expensive private education elsewhere.[39]

The common schools were indeed an arena for a culture clash between the Anglo-Protestant "common" values of Boston's original settlers and the Irish Catholic attitudes of the city's new immigrants. Even before the influx of Famine refugees, Boston's Catholics and Protestants had had bloody conflicts, most famously in August 1834, when an Ursuline Convent in the city's Charlestown neighborhood was burned to the ground by Protestant workers. The attack so outraged Horace Mann that he began his campaign for the creation of the common schools to combat such sectarianism. Mann's campaign received further impetus in 1837 when an anti-Irish riot broke out in the center of Boston. His common schools, Mann insisted, would create a common sense of values that would transcend sectarian divisions.[40]

Despite Mann's good intentions, anti-Irish and anti-Catholic prejudice remained strong in Boston, and nativist extremists like Samuel F. B. Morse, inventor of the Morse Code, declared that Boston's Irish were the worst of all Catholics, since they were especially prone to slavishly following the will of Rome. The Irish would have to abandon their religion entirely, Morse insisted, if they ever were to become free citizens of the American republic. Morse was not alone in his beliefs, and in 1850, even the more moderate voices on the Boston School Committee expressed similar anxiety when they noted that there was only one "American" in a class of fifty girls. The forty-nine other students were, they claimed, unassimilable Irish Catholics. In the mid-1850s, when Know-Nothings like Morse won control of both the state and Boston city governments, new laws made the reading of the King James version of the Bible mandatory in Boston's public schools.[41] When they were forced to read the Protestant Bible in the classroom, however, Irish pupils staged walk-outs and sit-down strikes patterned on those of real factory workers. Irish parents and clergy were also suspicious of the 1852 compulsory attendance law, especially since its enactors saw the schools as the single most important public institution for inculcating Protestant "American" values in an alien Catholic poor. Increasingly, the Irish saw the schools as a poorly disguised effort on the part of Protestants to convert their children. As a result, by the end of the 1850s more and more Irish sent their children to the new Catholic schools appearing in the city.[42]

Nevertheless, the city's parochial school system never accommodated more than a minority of Boston's Catholic Irish. Instead, most Irish parents continued to send their children to the well-established public schools and to fight sectarianism in school curriculum from within. Boston's Catholic leaders supported this trend. Bishop Benjamin Fenwick, who led the Boston diocese from 1825 to 1866, oversaw the transformation of Boston from a city with only one Catholic church to a large and growing city with over twelve Catholic parishes for a population that was now half Irish Catholic. As a graduate of the Boston schools himself, Fenwick supported the city's public schools. The Catholic rank-and-file, he believed, should quietly co-opt the public schools rather than withdraw from them. After all, he reasoned, Boston possessed an excellent school system that predated the arrival of the Famine Irish, and Catholics should use this system to enter mainstream American life. Furthermore, Fenwick pointed out, Boston's public schools received almost twice as much city tax revenue as the schools in any other American city, and, since the Irish were taxpayers, they were already paying for the city's schools. Boston's public schools were therefore already in place, better-funded, and provided a superior education in comparison with any school under the auspices of a single parish church. Rather than building makeshift schools for the Catholic poor in the city's burgeoning number of parishes, Fenwick instead built secondary schools for the Catholic elite and impressive church buildings designed to awe Protestant passers-by.[43]

Fenwick's successor, Archbishop John Williams, led the diocese between 1866 and 1907. Williams, like Fenwick, was the son of Irish immigrants and a former pupil in the Boston schools; and like his predecessor, Williams also promoted public, not parochial, education for the city's Catholics. In fact, despite the Church decree of 1884 requiring that every Catholic parish provide a school and that Catholic parents send their children to these schools, Williams told his priests not to reprimand parishioners who sent their children to the public schools.[44]

Williams's preference for public education struck a chord among the city's Catholics. Although the number of Boston parishes with a school rose from ten to sixteen in the decade after 1880, less than two-thirds of the city's twenty-seven parishes had schools in 1890. Furthermore, the percentage of the city's school-age Catholics enrolled in parish schools barely increased in that same decade, rising only from slightly more than ten percent to slightly less than thirteen percent of their total number between 1880 and 1890.[45] As one Boston priest noted in 1895, "Parents think their children will have greater success in life, and obtain positions more easily if they have gone to public school."[46] The numbers bear him out.

In much the same way as their counterparts in Ireland, Boston's Yankee reformers and Roman Catholic prelates alike viewed public education in the same positive light, although for different reasons. Despite this apparent harmony, however, serious rifts between the growing Catholic public school population and the Protestant school authorities poisoned relations between Catholics and Protestants in Boston's schools in the second half of the nineteenth century. As early as 1843, for instance, Bishop Fenwick protested what he believed to be anti-Catholic bias in public school texts, particularly in the *Elements of History,* a book in wide use in Boston's schools. Perhaps the single most notorious case of sectarian conflict in the city's schools occurred in 1859, however, when an Irish-Catholic Eliot School pupil named Thomas Wall was beaten by his teacher and suspended from classes for refusing to recite what he saw as a Protestant version of the Ten Commandments. Local priests rallied around the boy and, although the teacher was acquitted in court for merely doing his job and upholding the law, the school committee changed its policy on classroom recitations the following year. Henceforward, no child would be compelled to recite anything that offended his religious principles. This victory, however, did not change the school curriculum, which remained Protestant in content. Readings of the

Protestant version of the Bible, the Ten Commandments, and the Lord's Prayer remained in place even if Catholic conscientious objectors were no longer forced to join in.[47]

Another Catholic challenge to the Protestant-inspired common-school curriculum occurred in 1888 when Boston high school teacher Charles B. Travis defined the Catholic belief in indulgences as "permission to commit sin . . . sometimes bought with money." Using a defense similar to the one that acquitted the teacher in the Wall case almost thirty years before, Travis claimed that he was merely quoting from an approved school text and therefore was fully within the law. This time, however, with men such as future school-board candidate Mary Blake's husband John sitting on it, the Boston School Committee was almost half Irish in composition; the city's first Irish-Catholic mayor, Hugh O'Brien, was serving the last of his four one-year terms; and Boston's Irish had become much more militant about their rights than they had been during Bishop Fenwick's era of appeasement. The newly militant committee banned the text from the classroom, censured the teacher, and reassigned him to classes in ancient history, where it was thought that his treatment of the subject matter would do the least harm to impressionable young minds.[48]

These victories notwithstanding, the growing influence of Boston's Irish in the city's schools was again eclipsed by a Protestant backlash. In 1888, after three decades of steady advance into positions of political power in the city, Hugh O'Brien, the city's first Irish-Catholic mayor, was driven from office when a coalition of Yankee elites and Protestant Evangelicals reclaimed City Hall. By 1890, in fact, only two Catholics remained on the twenty-four member school committee, and the committee promptly adopted two anti-Catholic texts on medieval and reformation history for schoolroom use. One member of the newly revamped committee, Samuel Capen, later founded the Immigration Restriction League, which sought to end the open immigration policies that had already allowed the Irish and so many other "undesirables" into the country.[49]

The schools, even more than other city agencies, attracted the most attention from Protestant reformers. While they had learned to tolerate the rapid growth of the numbers of Irish Catholics in the city's fire and police forces, Protestants could not countenance an Irish takeover of the schools, which they viewed as the last bastions of the traditions of their Puritan forebears. The most committed among them formed the Committee of One Hundred, a distinctly anti-Catholic group organized to defend Protestantism and "Good Government" against the inroads of Catholic values and Irish political control in the city's schools. The committee's program for using the schools to reinforce the Protestant version of good citizenship was supported in leading educational journals of the day. In 1888, for instance, the editors of the *Journal of Education* reminded their readers that the public schools were "our sacred inheritance of independence." In the journal's 1889 issue, the editors added that, "In earlier times, all that was expected of the school was the teaching of the three Rs. The home disciplined, the church looked sharply after morals, and the people, being homogeneous, had no problems to solve through the school."[50] Like the Committee of One Hundred, the *Journal's* editors feared that the social changes wrought by the influx of Irish and other aliens into the country had fundamentally altered the former social harmony of American life.

Academic papers buttressed the *Journal's* point of view. In "The Contents of Children's Minds," an 1880 study of Boston children entering the first grade, author G. Stanley Hall noted that Irish children were ignorant of even such basics as beehives, sheep, pine trees, and the triangle. Amazingly, Hall claimed that these descendents of Famine refugees were unaware of what a spade or even a potato was! As a result of studies like Hall's, educational reformers in Boston joined the national trend promoting early childhood education as a means of altering the deprived environments of the urban poor and of enhancing their educational potential through cultural remediation. Consequently, in 1887, Boston approved the creation of public kindergartens, and by 1894, there were fifty-four of them housed in the city's schools. By 1905, the city possessed ninety-eight kindergartens with 188 trained teachers and over 5,000 pupils.[51]

In an effort to stem the rising power of the Irish in the schools, in 1875 Boston's leaders reduced the school committee to twenty-four members elected in citywide campaigns less vulnerable to political manipulation in the city's Irish wards. Four years later, in 1879, in the hopes that Protestant women would counteract Irish male voting power, Boston's female citizens won the right to vote in school committee elections; thus, by the 1880s, Protestant women held five seats on the school committee. Until Julia Harrington Duff's election in 1901, in fact, the female minority on the now more compact Boston School Committee fulfilled sectarian hopes, as each woman member was a conservative Protestant who had campaigned on an anti-Catholic platform.[52] Agreeing that American values were Protestant and the schools needed to teach this "common" culture to the children of immigrant aliens, these women promoted patriotic school exhibits and ceremonies. They also welcomed, from the very Protestant Sons of the American Revolution, a donation of reproductions of Gilbert Stuart's portrait of George Washington for display in every city classroom.[53] To these women, Protestantism and patriotism were identical.

In the 1890s, liberal Protestant organizations like the Citizens Public School Union reemerged in Boston school politics, helping Catholics regain seats on the school committee and promoting the adoption of more balanced school history texts.[54] School expenditures continued to increase in these years, reflecting the dramatic near-doubling of the number of pupils in Boston's classrooms from 50,543 to 90,086, between 1880 and 1907.[55] Between 1890 and 1900, the city built fifty new schools to house the mushrooming school population.[56]

Raising the Bar

In spite of the hostility of certain Protestant groups toward them in the last decades of the nineteenth century, the desire of Irish Catholics to remain in city schools was reinforced by the backing of the city's Church hierarchy and Catholic school committee members. Boston's Irish were eager to partake in the increasingly sophisticated range of educational opportunities made available to them in the city's growing number of classrooms. Moreover, the number of Irish Americans teaching in these classrooms was also growing.

Although the venerable Boston schools may have been somewhat slower to hire large numbers of Irish-American teachers than newer cities farther west, the number of Irish graduates of the city's public high schools and normal school and the number of Irish Americans teaching in the city's classrooms more than doubled in the quarter of a century after 1880. Even in 1880, when Protestants controlled school policy, and four years before the election of the city's first Irish-Catholic mayor, teachers with Irish last names were fully seventeen percent of the 415 teachers in the city's primary schools (grades one to three) and ten percent of the 574 teachers in the city's grammar schools (grades four through eight).[57]

An examination of the diplomas granted by the Boston Normal School and Girls' High School in 1880 also indicates that the number of Irish Americans in the city's teaching force would continue growing. In that year, almost one-fifth of the total number of Boston Normal School graduates were young women with Irish last names; and one-quarter of the female fourth-year graduates of the Girls' High School, a major supplier of Normal School entrants, had Irish last names. An additional one-fifth of the third-year class at the high school were also Irish Americans.[58] Since only obviously Irish last names are included in this total, these percentages are probably an undercount.

In 1900, at least one-half of the students enrolled in the Normal School were Catholics, mostly Irish, and Irish Americans were the largest single ethnic group among Boston's teachers in that year. By 1908, Irish Americans comprised one-quarter of the city's teaching force, according to one reliable estimate. In those same years, the percentage of Catholics enrolled in the Normal School rose to between one-third and one-half of the student body; and in Boston, these Catholics were mostly Irish.[59]

School officials had long noted the importance of teaching as an avenue of female social mobility. "The Normal School is doing good work in affording to the children of the citizens of Boston an opportunity to prepare themselves in a profession," the school committee reported in 1886, "whereby they may participate in the benefits of an institution which their fathers have contributed to build up and sustain."[60] The school committee also noted that teachers already in the school system's employ were no less enthusiastic than trainees about the opportunities offered by the Normal School for professional enhancement. Noting that the now mostly female teachers in the Boston schools were willing to give up their weekends for career betterment, the committee reported that "The practice was begun [in the winter of 1879–1880] . . . of giving courses of lectures to teachers. . . . The plan worked admirably. [Their] presence was voluntary, but hundreds of our teachers attended these exercises. They were held on Saturdays, thereby not interfering with the schools."[61]

Formal teacher education had begun in Boston in 1852, when a year-long normal school course was made part of the new Girls' High School curriculum to train female assistants for the city's still mostly male teaching force. A year later, in 1853, as more and more young women displaced men teachers, more rigorous training requirements were instituted, and the normal school course was increased from two to three years. In 1854, added luster was given to teacher training when the high school was renamed the Girls' High School and Normal School. In 1872, the normal school separated from the Girls' High School, and normal school classes coalesced into an extra one-year postgraduate course. In 1888, the training program was increased to one-and-a-half years, and in 1892, the training program was again lengthened to two years. In 1904, the first male students were admitted to the normal school.[62]

The intensification of Boston's teacher training in the late nineteenth and early twentieth centuries mirrored the nationwide push in those years to produce better qualified public school teachers. Boston's new, more-stringent training requirements were also designed to raise the bar for entrance into city teaching jobs, and not only for the purpose of improving the quality of education in the schools. The new requirements also reflected the desire of Protestant-dominated school committees to stem the tide of Irish Americans into public school teaching jobs. As a result, as the number of Irish-American normal school students rose, the length and rigor of their training was increased. In 1904, entrance examinations for normal school applicants were introduced as a further means of culling the faint-hearted.[63]

Raising the bar for graduation did not prevent large numbers of Irish Americans from graduating from the Boston Normal School, however, and other ways of curtailing the number of Irish eligible for a Boston teaching job were devised. James Jackson Storrow, for instance, began a campaign to eliminate what he saw as political corruption in the appointment of the city's teachers. In 1906, after the ouster of "Boston Schools for Boston Girls!" champion Julia Duff, the Storrow-led school committee mandated a merit system for teacher appointments designed to excise what they believed to be the evident nepotism between Boston's largely Irish politicians and the growing number of Irish-American normal school graduates receiving teaching appointments.

In 1913, in order to further restrict political pull in teacher appointments, the committee again tightened teacher-training requirements by extending the normal school curriculum to three years. In 1922, normal school students could earn a bachelor's degree after four years of study. Two years later, in 1924, Boston Normal School became Boston Teachers College, able now to grant a master's degree as well as a bachelor's degree to its qualified students.[64]

By the early twentieth century, then, working-class Irish-American women could no longer expect to enter the paid teaching force within a year or two after completing high school. Since the vast majority of Boston's public school pupils left school before the eighth grade to enter the waged workforce, spending up to sixteen unpaid years in school in order to qualify for a city teaching job represented a significant financial sacrifice on the parts of aspiring teachers and their families. Moreover, since new normal school graduates were hired first as permanent substitutes, earning only $500 a year, novice teachers continued to face restrictions on their ability to earn livings. Only after a novice teacher completed a two-year trial period did her salary reach $690 a year.[65]

Despite the increasing obstacles of rising training requirements and extremely low pay, especially in the early years of a teacher's career, thousands of Boston's Irish were drawn to teaching, including some men. By 1919, there were 3,500 teachers in Boston's schools, 3,000 of whom were women.[66] Large numbers of these women were Irish Americans. In spite of the PSA, Julia Duff's campaign to keep Boston's schools open to Boston's girls had apparently worked.

Even though rising numbers of applicants from Boston's Irish-American neighborhoods eagerly sought city teaching jobs, working conditions in the public schools were far from ideal. In addition to enduring criticism from unsympathetic school committees about their inadequate training and deficient cultural backgrounds, teachers faced classrooms filled with fifty or more students, many of whom were underfed, unwashed, disease-prone, and unable to speak the English language.[67] In fact, health and sanitation issues in the schools took on a new gravity beginning in the 1880s with the problem of tuberculosis, a highly infectious disease which spread rapidly in the damp, dirty tenements that housed Boston's immigrants, threatening teachers and students alike in the crowded classrooms. "The need for practical instruction in school hygiene," the school committee warned in 1880, "is as great as ever. The laws of health are daily violated in our schools through ignorance rather than wilful neglect."[68]

In 1885, the Irish-American Dr. John Moran was hired as the hygiene instructor in the city's schools. Although Moran was purged by the school committee three years later, a number of anti-tuberculosis measures were launched during his watch, including a move to replace communal chalk and chalkboards with more sanitary individual paper and pencils. Along with vaccinations and quarantines, these measures helped combat the spread of deadly infection. In addition, Moran inaugurated a school lunch program and installed seat backs for student desks to promote better spine support for youthful bones.[69]

Besides working in unhealthy and underventilated classrooms, teachers also faced ever stricter supervision designed to force them into utter conformity with the values of Protestant school committee members. By the early twentieth century, these values had merged with those of Progressive reformers who also viewed the large numbers of Catholic-Irish teachers with unease. The first wave of tightening teacher oversight came in the form of new "Rules and Regulations" to correct the supposedly poor hygiene and work habits of a teaching force with largely working-class origins. Whereas teachers had once come from the city's genteel Protestant lower-middle classes and had possessed the same manners and mores as their supervisors on the school committee, the new "breed" of teachers from the rough and tumble of Irish neighborhoods were viewed with suspicion and distaste by their employers.

Able to meet the ever more difficult entrance qualifications for a classroom job, Boston's teachers organized themselves into a militant union designed to protect their jobs and provide them with pensions and adequate pay. Some even challenged the gender bias that allowed male teachers to earn larger salaries than their female counterparts. The growing militancy of teachers was met with school committee intransigence, however.

In 1880, for instance, the school committee rejected a life-tenure plan for teachers, "set on foot" in 1879, on the grounds that the committee preferred the system already in place that elected teachers on an annual basis according to the results of classroom observations of their teaching talent. Teachers who objected to this yearly scrutiny were suspect, according to the committee, as "no competent and acceptable teacher need fear the ordeal of stated elections." Teachers seeking job security risked being labeled as inferior. In that same year, the school committee also refused to oversee a teacher pension fund based on public money. Instead, the school committee men argued, pensions were a private matter for teachers, and the teachers themselves should create and administer the fund themselves. They were not entitled to public money after they left the classroom.[70]

Job security in the form of tenure, pensions, and better pay that teachers had secured by the early years of the twentieth century would meet a new challenge with the advent of Progressive-era "reforms" designed to replace teacher autonomy and mobility with a more rigid workforce stratification. When Julia Duff lost her seat on Boston's school committee, her campaign to keep Boston schools open to the city's largely Irish normal school graduates like herself was under attack.

By the second decade of the twentieth century, Boston's teachers were denied access to school supervisory jobs, as appointed university-trained male "experts" took over the administrative jobs once open to female teachers rising up from the ranks. Adding to the largely Irish teaching force's difficulties was the renewed polarization between the city's old guard Protestants and its Irish-American majority, a polarization personified by the victorious mayoral election of John "Honey Fitz" Fitzgerald in 1910 and, especially, James Michael Curley in 1914, whose successful campaigns emphasized the gap between working-class Irish Catholics and Protestant elites.[71]

By the time Julia Duff died in 1932, ethnic politics in Boston were once again as entrenched in the city's consciousness as they had been before Bishop Fenwick forged a truce between the city's Protestants and Catholics a century before. Despite the growing ethnic animosity in the city, however, by 1910, one-third of Boston's Irish held white-collar jobs.[72] Boston's Irish teachers were prominent among those who had made the leap from blue- to white-collar status.

(above)
Irish immigrants aboard
the S.S. Vedic in Boston
Harbor, 1921. Courtesy
of Brother Michael
Grace, S.J., Loyola
University Chicago
Archives, Catholic
Church Extension
Society Photo
Collection.

(left)
Julia Harrington Duff,
Charlestown,
Massachusetts. Courtesy
of Dr. John Duff, M.D.

Julia Harrington Duff and her husband, Dr. John Duff.
Courtesy of Dr. John Duff, M.D.

Kate Kennedy,
San Francisco, c. 1860s.
Courtesy of the
San Francisco
History Center.

Amelia Dunne Hookway,
Chicago, c. 1880.
Courtesy of
Mrs. Edward Hilts.

*Catherine Dunne
Bancroft,
Chicago teacher, c. 1890s.
Courtesy of
Mary Foerner.*

*Angela Bancroft Hillan,
Chicago teacher,
c. 1900s. Courtesy of
Mary Foerner.*

Frances Bancroft,
Chicago teacher,
c. 1900s.
Courtesy of Mary Foerner.

Chicago Normal School graduates (Frances Bancroft 2d from left, front row),
c. 1890s. Courtesy of Mary Foerner.

Armour School Faculty, Chicago, 1910s
(Frances Bancroft standing, 3d from right). Courtesy of Mary Foerner.

Oakland School Faculty, Chicago, 1910s
(Angela Bancroft Hillan standing, far left). Courtesy of Mary Foerner.

Margaret Hillan and Frank Foerner, Chicago, 1928.
Courtesy of Mary Foerner.

*Margaret Haley,
New York, 1910.
Courtesy of the
Chicago Historical
Society. ICHi-21781
(photo by Marceau).*

*Mary Ellen (Ella)
Martin Moakley,
Gloucester, Massachusetts,
c. 1900.
Author's collection.*

Mary Ann Donovan Nolan, Lynn, Massachusetts, 1895.
Author's collection.

National School, Skibbereen, County Cork, Ireland. Author's collection.

*Sisters of Mercy Convent School, Skibbereen, County Cork, Ireland.
Author's collection.*

William Francis Nolan, graduate, Salem Teachers College, Salem, Massachusetts, 1935. Author's collection.

Janet Moakley Nolan, graduate, Salem Teachers College, Salem, Massachusetts, 1935. Author's collection.

William Francis Nolan, naval officer and Master of Physical Education, Long Beach, California, 1945. Author's collection.

Janet Ann Nolan, teacher, Taconic High School, Pittsfield, Massachusetts, 1973. Author's collection.

San Francisco

Pioneers in the Classroom

In 1872, after four years in a national school classroom, sixteen-year-old Catherine Harrington left Ireland for America. In 1884, after twelve years in the East working as a maid, she arrived in San Francisco, where she continued working before she married Irish-born James Curry in 1889. Catherine gave birth to two children: Viola, born in 1892, and John, born in 1894. Both children graduated from high school, and John's teachers urged his mother to send him to college. Patrick O'Donnell, the son of an illiterate father, also spent four years in an Irish national school before arriving in San Francisco at the age of twenty in 1876. All seven of his children graduated from high school, and three of his daughters graduated from San Francisco's Normal School and began teaching in the city's public schools in the late teens. Mary, the eldest of O'Donnell's teacher-daughers, later married the Currys' son, John; but she continued to teach, retiring only in the 1950s. Their daughter, Catherine Ann Curry, became a member of the Sisters of the Presentation, a Ph.D., an archivist, and a teacher in San Francisco.[1]

Patrick O'Donnell taught his daughters the value of education. He called the family's dining room, where the girls did their homework, the "library"; and he hung on the wall a map of Ireland emblazoned with Thomas Moore's poem, "The Harp That Once in Tara's Halls," in bold letters across the bottom. Although Mary thought it "pretentious" for her father to call the dining room a "library," Patrick felt very differently. Although his own father couldn't read, he could, thanks to his Irish education. His American daughters, he insisted, would surpass him and go to high school.[2]

The O'Donnell girls' upbringing illustrates an already familiar pattern among Irish Americans of their daughters joining the teaching ranks in cities such as Boston and San Francisco. In fact, by the end of the first decade of the twentieth century, Irish-American women comprised almost one-half of all the teachers in San Francisco's public primary and grammar schools, making them the largest single ethnic group among the city's teachers at that time.[3]

The high percentage of Irish-American women teaching in the city's public schools at the turn of the last century demonstrates an important point of the Irish experience in San Francisco that has been too-long overlooked: by the turn of the twentieth century, large numbers of Irish-American women had entered the lower middle class by becoming teachers. Since San Francisco's boys, like their counterparts throughout Irish America, could more easily than girls find well-paid skilled work without years of advanced study, the daughters of Irish San Francisco stayed in school longer and entered white-collar work at least a generation before their brothers.[4] These women also entered professional work in numbers unrivalled by any other second-generation immigrant women in San Francisco at the time.[5] Ironically, in an era when social mobility was measured almost exclusively in male terms, women were often the leaders in Irish San Francisco's advance.

The remarkable success of the daughters of Irish San Francisco was tied to their educational achievements, achievements realized at a time when educating women was restricted for the most part to an upper-class few among native-born Americans. In an age when most Americans spent less than eight years in school altogether, San Francisco's women teachers had spent a minimum of thirteen years in school, including four years of high school followed by one or more years of normal school training.

As in the rest of Irish America, the beginnings of women's educational mobility in San Francisco can be found in Ireland's national schools, which had become training grounds for emigration, particularly for girls, by the late nineteenth century.[6] San Franciscan Hannah Casey Cotter, for instance, dreamed of becoming a teacher while still a child in Ireland. According to her granddaughter, Caren Cotter Ellis, Hannah loved her Irish school days in County Cork, and she told her descendants how she had often played teacher after school by reading to a stone circle of "pupils" arranged around her. After immigrating to San Francisco in 1913 at the age of thirty-three, Hannah worked as a housemaid before marrying County Kerry native Sylvester Cotter, a city fireman. Their daughter-in-law, Ellis's mother Clare McGrath Cotter, realized Hannah's childhood dream by becoming a teacher in San Francisco.[7] Women like the O'Donnells and Cotters led their families and their communities into the ranks of America's educated middle class.

Pioneers

The city of San Francisco grew up in a hurry after gold was discovered in the mountains to its east in 1848. By 1849, it had a population of 10,000. By 1850, the year California entered the Union, San Francisco was already an important commercial center and had a public school.[8] San Francisco could boast of having the first free public school on the Pacific coast by 1851.[9] The following year, Catholics, mostly Irish, were one-third of the city's total population of 37,000.[10] As early as 1860, 6,100 of the city's 14,000 school-age children were enrolled in the public schools; and an additional 2,100 attended private schools, almost two thirds of which were run by pioneering Irish-born nuns. Catholic school enrollment peaked in 1863, then dropped as the state withdrew funding from denominational education.[11] As a result, San Francisco's largely working-class Irish Catholics, much like Boston's, went to public, not parochial, schools for the most part.

In 1865, elite "cosmopolitan" schools joined the public system, attracting well-to-do students with their foreign language curriculum.[12] With the advent of the transcontinental telegraph in 1861 and the transcontinental railroad in 1869, San Francisco's isolation ended, and the city's population doubled between 1870 and 1890, rising from almost 150,000 to nearly 300,000. By 1880, almost 45,000 attended the city's public schools. On the eve of the earthquake in 1906, approximately 58,000 pupils sat in the city's public classrooms. Rapid recovery from the devastating earthquake allowed the population to reach 456,000 by 1915.[13] In order to accommodate the growing demand for classroom space, San Franciscans embarked on a rapid building campaign. By 1891, the city supported seventy-four schools: forty-nine primary, sixteen grammar, four high schools, and five evening schools. By 1909, the city's schools numbered ninety-five.[14] As the Irish proportion of those living in the city rose along with overall population in those years, the Irish presence in San Francisco's schools became ever more pronounced.[15] The number of Irish Americans teaching in San Francisco expanded along with the public school system. By 1886, 245 of the 752 teachers in San Francisco, or about a third of the total, had Irish last names. In 1910, 390 of the city's 804 primary school teachers had Irish last names, an astonishing 49 percent of the total.[16]

San Francisco hired its first Irish-American teachers when it was still a Gold Rush boomtown reachable only by trek across an isthmus or a continent, or by sea around Cape Horn. Three sisters—Alice, Kate, and Lizzie Kennedy—are representative of the Irish presence in San Francisco's earliest decades. The product of an Irish education begun at a local school two miles from her childhood home in County Meath, Kate had completed her education at a convent in Navan, where she studied four languages besides English. She home-taught her younger sisters, basing their lessons on her convent-bred language skills. The Kennedys emigrated to New York during the Famine of the late 1840s. Alice was the first of the family to reach San Francisco, arriving in the city in the early 1850s. Alice was also the first of the sisters to take a teaching job in the Gold Rush boomtown's fledgling public schools. When the nativist Know-Nothings briefly won control of the city's government in the mid-1850s, however, Alice lost her teaching post, supposedly because of her Irish accent. Despite this setback, Kate and Lizzie joined her in San Francisco in 1856. In 1858, Kate and Lizzie passed the San Francisco teacher examination with "top grades" and received their primary school teaching certifications. The Kennedy sisters were especially proud of this accomplishment. Despite their Irish birth, they had bested their American-born rivals on the examination, a vindication of sorts for Alice's rude treatment by nativists a few years before.[17]

Although Kate claimed to have abandoned her Catholicism in Ireland when a local priest blamed the Famine on Providence rather than on what Kate insisted was British misgovernment, her Irish convent education served her well when her teaching career began in one of the twelve classrooms of San Francisco's Greenwich Primary School in 1858. By 1862, she had risen to the rank of principal teacher at the school; and in 1867, on the strength of her foreign language abilities, she was appointed principal of San Francisco's North Cosmopolitan Grammar School, which offered instruction in French and German. At the time of her appointment, Kennedy was the only woman holding such a high rank in the city's teaching hierarchy; but, at a salary of $180 a month, she earned considerably less than the $202.50 a month paid her male counterparts.[18] This injustice spurred Kennedy to launch the first of her many campaigns on behalf of women teachers. Insisting that women ought to be paid the same as men for the same job, she succeeded in getting the California State Legislature to pass an equal-pay-for-equal-work law in 1874, one of the first such laws in the world.[19] Kennedy also won tenure and pensions for San Francisco teachers, safeguards that would allow them, for the first time, to make teaching a lifetime career.[20] Although many of Kennedy's hard-fought gains on behalf of San Francisco's female teachers were later rescinded, her efforts set precedents that eventually prevailed throughout the United States.

After Kennedy's death in 1890 at age sixty-three, Superintendent of Schools John Anderson noted that although she had fought many uphill battles in her long teaching career, she "possessed . . . admirable qualities of head and heart. . . . It is sad," he continued, "to record here there were those who would not accord her the esteem and honor which were justly her due." Nevertheless, he concluded, "She lived to triumph over those who sought to wrong her. . . . Hers was the courage of honest conviction."[21]

Kennedy's work was again recognized in 1908 when the Kate Kennedy School Women's Club was founded in memory of her determination to better the working lives of San Francisco's teachers. Margaret Mahoney, a physician and a city teacher, served as the club's first president. The daughter of Irish immigrants herself, Mahoney later became the president of the San Francisco Teachers' Federation.[22] Dedicating themselves "to further teachers' rights professionally, to secure equal salary for equal work, [and] to gain recognition for promotion based on credentials regardless of sex," the Kate Kennedy clubwomen carried on Kennedy's campaign to improve the pay and working conditions of San Francisco's teachers.[23]

Lizzie Kennedy's teaching career mirrored her sister Kate's. By 1885, she was the principal of San Francisco's South Cosmopolitan Grammar School and held a "Life Certificate" permanently guaranteeing her position in the city's schools. Lizzie's daughter, Elizabeth Burke, followed her mother and aunts into the ranks of San Francisco teachers. By 1892, she held a Grammar Grade Certificate to teach in the city's schools. In 1910, she was teaching the seventh grade in the Croker Grammar School, earning a salary of $1,224 a year.[24] The Kennedys received posthumous recognition for their lifelong commitment to public education in San Francisco when two new schools were named in their honor. Today, San Francisco's Kate Kennedy School and the Burke/Delmar School, named for Lizzie, are community landmarks reminding San Franciscans of these Irish-American teacher pioneers.[25]

As the careers of the Kennedy and O'Donnell sisters suggest, teaching was often a family affair among San Francisco's Irish, and the city's teacher directories document this pattern. In 1891, for instance, eighteen of the twenty-eight pairs of sisters with Irish last names teaching in the city's schools lived at the same address.[26] Teacher directories also provide insight into the volatility of teaching careers in the city. Despite their hard-fought campaigns to secure "Life Certificates" guaranteeing them permanent employment in San Francisco's schools, city teachers did not often remain at any one school for their entire careers, and the rapidity of their transfers between schools suggests chronic insecurity in terms of individual careers. Sisters Emma and Alice Stincen of 816 Chestnut Street, for example, first appear in the 1891 directory when Emma held a principal teacher position at the Whittier Primary School on Harrison Street and her sister Alice was the principal of the same twelve-classroom North Cosmopolitan Grammar School on Filbert Street where Kate Kennedy had once been principal. By 1909, the Stincens had moved to a house on a corner lot at 976 Chestnut Street, and Alice was now the principal of the Pacific Heights Grammar School. Emma joined her sister at the Pacific Heights School, teaching the third and fourth grades under Alice's supervision. A year later in 1910, however, the sisters left the Pacific Heights School and their mutual workplace, with Emma returning to the Whittier School and Alice moving to the Grant School. Both continued to share the same home.[27] Like the Kennedy and O'Donnell sisters before them, the Stincens moved among the city's schools and, apparently, up and down the career ladder.

Alice Rose Power's career, on the other hand, demonstrates that permanent upward mobility was possible for some Irish-American women teaching in San Francisco. Encouraged by her Irish-born parents, Power began her career as a teacher in San Francisco's Edison Grammar School and was soon made principal of the Washington Irving School. After her election in 1919, she sat on the San Francisco Board of Education until 1932; and between 1934 and 1939, she served on the California State Board of Education. In addition to her teaching and administrative duties, Power wrote several classroom texts, including the *Power Graded Speller, Jingles: A Reader for Beginners,* and *Poems for Memorizing.* When she retired in June 1943, the Council of San Francisco School Women issued the "Alice Rose Power Commendation" with the hand-lettered inscription: "You will always be re-

membered for your devoted career of civic and professional activities. . . .
We attest to your leadership, loyalty to your pupils and teachers, and your fidelity to educational ideals."[28]

The impact of education on the mobility of San Francisco's Irish-American women is also revealed in the life of Urania Cloney Moran. The daughter of Irish immigrants, Moran was born in 1873 in rural Illinois. She graduated from St. Vincent's Academy for Girls in LaSalle in 1891. At nineteen, Urania enrolled in a teachers' college in Fort Jefferson, Iowa, where she wrote "True friends are like/ Diamonds pre[c]ious but rare/ False ones like leaves/ Found everywhere" in the flyleaf of her copy of the *Twelve Lectures on the History of Pedagogy.* Perhaps because she found few true friends in Iowa, after graduating in 1894, Urania migrated further west to teach the children of cavalry men stationed at Fort Crook, Nebraska. Eventually, she rejoined her family when they moved to Kansas, where she found another teaching job. By 1901, at the age of twenty-eight, she abandoned the Great Plains forever and began teaching in San Francisco. Although her career in the city was cut short by her marriage to County Leitrim–native Michael Moran, Urania remains a pioneer of Irish-American female mobility. She was the first in her family to attend college, the first to leave home alone, and the first to travel unescorted by train over the Rockies to San Francisco.[29] Her grandniece recalls that Urania's daughter, Urania Moran Garner, was "so proud of her mother's teaching skills that she, too, became a teacher after graduating from Berkeley in 1928." Mrs. Garner taught for thirty-seven years before retiring in 1966.[30] The teaching careers of San Franciscans Patricia Fleming Walsh, the daughter of County Galway–educated Mary Huvane Fleming, and thirty-year veteran San Francisco teacher Judith Comisky McGovern, whose grandmother also attended an Irish national school before immigrating to San Francisco, illustrate the female educational dynamic among the city's Irish as well.[31]

Although most Irish-American teachers worked in San Francisco's public schools, women belonging to Irish religious orders were also pioneers in the city's educational history. Mother Theresa Comerford, for example, joined the Presentation Order in her native Ireland before emigrating to San Francisco in 1854, just six years after the discovery of gold and fully two years before Kate Kennedy arrived. Shortly after her arrival, Comerford and her Presentation Sisters started the Powell Street School, the only tuition-free Catholic school in the city. In 1869, Comerford opened a second school at the corner of Taylor and Ellis Streets. Another Gold Rush pioneer and cofounder of San Francisco's Sisters of Mercy, Mother Mary Baptist Russell, left her native Ireland for the city in 1854.[32] Today, women religious remain integral to the success of education in San Francisco, as the career of Catherine Ann Curry, a member of the Presentation Order and the daughter of San Francisco teacher Mary O'Donnell Curry, attests. Curry's unpublished doctoral dissertation remains the most definitive history of the city's schools, a history shaped in part by her own family, as we have seen. Her work as a scholar, teacher, and archivist has also spurred new generations to reach high educational goals.

Margaret O'Sullivan, later known as Sister M. Columba, was another pioneer in San Francisco's educational history. Born in 1893 near Listowel, County Kerry, O'Sullivan was the fifth of the seven children of Timothy and Mary O'Sullivan. According to her memoirs, "In the year 1909, an important letter arrived in the farming area of Fingue, a suburb of Listowel. It was addressed to [my father], and was sent by Mother Camillus, superior [and foundress] of St. Gertrude's Academy, in Rio Vista [on the Sacramento River]. It said: 'Having learn[ed] from your two sisters, Sisters Benedict and Martha, that you have five daughters, I am wondering and hoping that two of them would be blessed with vocations to the religious life, and would like to come to California.'"[33]

"My father and mother took several days to talk over this matter before mentioning it to us . . . ," Sister Columba continued. "We [already] knew quite a bit about the academy from our aunts' letters [and] glances seemed to rest on Mary and me, as Mary had finished at Presentation School that year, and I . . . had two more years to go. I was all for it, . . . but [Mary] didn't seem too enthusiastic . . . and Mary [withdrew] before it was too late [but] Elizabeth stated that she would love to become a sister. . . ."[34]

In 1911, at age eighteen, O'Sullivan left Ireland with her sister Elizabeth and traveled to Burlingame, California, near San Francisco. "It was arranged that Mother Camillus [would] take care of the trip, . . . have a person meet us in Sacramento, get us to the river boat where we would be met again and taken to St. Gertrude's," Sister Columba remembered. "Thank God, we got the Postulants' caps five days after arrival, on the Eve of All Saints, 1909."[35] The O'Sullivans were now Sisters of Mercy.

In 1917, at the age of twenty-four, Sister Columba took her final vows. After teaching in Rio Vista and Sausalito for many years, she spent the remaining two decades of her career at San Francisco's Holy Name School. Her community remembers her love of Ireland as a "holy passion," and that

her classroom gifts had been so great that "she could teach a radiator frac-
tions."[36] In these ways, she exemplified the devotion to education found in
so many women in Irish America.

"The Horace Mann of California"

Like their counterparts in Boston, the San Francisco Irish also faced discrimination in terms of their ethnicity and religion. Anti-Irish and anti-
Catholic rhetoric had circumscribed teacher autonomy and mobility since at
least the 1850s, when Alice Kennedy reportedly lost her teaching job because of her Irish accent. After the election of an Irish Catholic mayor,
Frank McCoppin, in 1867 and the advent of "Blind Boss" Christopher Buckley's political machine in the 1880s, Protestants of all classes, fearing further
political losses, allied against the growing Irish and Catholic presence in the
city's schools.[37] As a result, throughout the late nineteenth and into the
twentieth century, San Francisco's Irish teachers faced serious challenges to
their upward mobility, despite their growing qualifications.

The clash between Protestant and Catholic cultures in San Francisco's
public education was apparent in California Superintendent of Public Instruction and future San Francisco school superintendent John Swett's
insistence in 1865 that the schools were embarked on a "great mission . . .
to train the children of the common people for the occupations of the common life."[38] This "common life" was to be based on the Anglo-Protestant
traditions inherited from the Founding Fathers and championed by common
school pioneer Horace Mann of Massachusetts. Acclaimed as the "Horace
Mann of California," New England–native Swett saw Mann's common
school ideal as a continuation of the Pilgrim and Puritan traditions, the
very bedrocks of American civilization.[39] Swett insisted that San Francisco
school personnel be fully versed in this heritage also. Lessons were to be
based on a specified group of school texts, and primary schools were to
teach the "rudiments of an English education," while grammar schools
were to teach "the common branches of an English education."[40] While
these dictates surely referred to an English *language* rather than an English
cultural education, the distinction between the two would probably not
have seemed significant to most school authorities.

To facilitate this immersion in Anglo-American culture, Swett created
a book list for teachers that included Arnold Guyot's *Earth and Man,* a

geography with a distinctive point of view. According to Guyot, there was a great contrast even among superior European races between the "free and intelligent . . . Protestant of the north, and the . . . superstitious . . . Catholic . . . of the south." To Guyot, the United States was the culmination of European civilization and the "true offspring of the Reformation."[41] The Protestant point of view was reiterated in an 1888 American history textbook in wide use in the schools, which informed its readers that "Luther and his followers protested against the sinfulness and impurity of the Church of Rome."[42]

Perhaps because of the steady increase in the number of Irish among San Francisco's public school teachers and pupils, however, sectarianism in the classroom became more muted over time. Although the Board of Education in 1851 required teachers to open each school day with a reading from Scripture, by 1864 Protestant Bible reading was no longer common in the schools. In 1870, a now more-inclusive Superintendent Swett could report that, although "Occasionally we hear of sectarian difficulties in our public schools, common sense, concession, [and] compromise will bring us to . . . understanding and harmonious action. . . ." By 1874, even the recitation of the Lord's Prayer was outlawed as sectarian.[43]

Anti-sectarianism, of course, could cut two ways, and measures designed to curtail overtly Protestant values in the classroom could also be used against those of Catholics. In 1891, for instance, the Board of Education's "Course of Study" pamphlet warned the increasingly Catholic teaching force to "avoid all occasions [of] alluding to sectarian subjects," threatening immediate dismissal if they used any "sectarian or denominational" publications in the classroom.[44]

By the late nineteenth century, in fact, San Francisco's Protestants and Catholics alike supported the inclusion of "American" values in the school curriculum. In the same Board of Education pamphlet that warned against sectarianism in the schools, teachers were instructed to "impress on the minds of their pupils the principles of morality, truth, justice and patriotism; . . . teach them to avoid idleness, profanity and falsehood; . . . instruct them in the principles of free government, and . . . train them up to a true comprehension of the rights, duties and dignity of American citizenship."[45] In 1898, the Department of Public Instruction further required "every classroom be supplied with a national flag and the same should be saluted every morning." On Mondays, the salute was to be accompanied by the pledge of "allegiance to my flag and to the Republic for which it stands—one people, one language, one flag."[46]

Despite the encouraging reduction of overt sectarianism in the schools in the course of the late nineteenth century, San Francisco's Irish-American teachers faced other obstacles in those years. In his *Annual Report* of 1890, for instance, Superintendent John Anderson indirectly expressed his concern over the Irish presence in the city's schools by remarking that the teaching corps was increasingly composed of unqualified political appointees rather than fully trained educators. Complaining that he "is seldom, if ever, consulted . . . in the selection of teachers," Anderson insisted that choosing personnel for the city's classrooms was "the most sacred duty imposed on the Board [of Education]." Nevertheless, this was the duty "more than any other[,] the members of the Board are least capable of performing." Instead, teaching jobs had become political spoils. "Nominally there is an election of teachers," Anderson noted, but, "practically there is no election . . . the Board . . . appoints some friend or favorite to the Substitute class, and the party thus named . . . is sure to be elected. . . . We have never known a rejection."[47] Since the Irish at this point held powerful positions in city and school government and their numbers among the city's teachers were steadily rising, Anderson's targets are clear.[48]

Eight years later, in 1898, Superintendent Reginald Webster took up Anderson's cry. In his *Annual Report* of that year, Webster wrote that "the method employed in electing teachers . . . is antagonistic to scholarship . . . It is eminently political and the application of 'personal patronage.'" By this time, the Board of Education had Irish-American members, including a Miss P. M. Nolan, and Webster implied that teacher appointments were going to friends of sitting members rather than to fully qualified applicants. After all, he continued, "There are more persons who want to teach than there are schools to be taught," but, "[a]s long as the Board of Education is elected at large, there is little hope of an improvement in the method of the appointment of teachers."[49] By implication, as long as San Francisco's large Irish population elected its own to the school board, Irish-American teachers would be even more numerous in the city's classrooms, regardless of their qualifications. In his *Annual Report* of the following year, Webster continued his campaign against appointing teachers on a political basis by quoting Cecil W. Mark on the lack of standards in selecting teachers. "For many years," Mark wrote, "Boards of Education have been governed entirely in their selection of teachers . . . not by the fitness of, but by personal friendship for, the teacher appointed, or by the request of some personal political friend."[50] In 1900, when a new city charter ended school board elections in favor of mayoral appointments, critics like Webster and Mark may have been crestfallen that Irish-American James Duval Phelan won the mayoralty, and the numbers of Irish-American teachers continued to rise.[51]

Stemming the Tide

Even more subtle approaches aimed at stemming the tide of supposedly unqualified Irish political appointees into teaching appeared as school authorities tightened teacher training requirements and classroom supervision. Educational standards for teachers rose, and by the late nineteenth century, a four-year academic high school diploma was a prerequisite for a city teaching post. Undaunted, San Francisco's Irish girls flocked to the city's high schools. In 1886, almost 15 percent of the 910 Girls' High School graduates had Irish last names. By 1909, girls enrolled in the, by then, five high schools in San Francisco outnumbered boys by almost two to one, 1,825 girls to 971 boys, and many of these girls were Irish Americans.[52]

Although formal teacher training beyond high school was not mandatory in San Francisco until after the turn of the twentieth century, the city's Irish also took advantage of the educational opportunities offered by San Francisco's Normal School.[53] First opened in 1857, the Normal School graduated thirty-one new teachers by 1877. In 1880, seventy graduated, more than doubling the normal school class of only three years before. The proportion of Irish Americans among the graduates grew apace. In 1888, over one quarter, or twenty-seven of the ninety-nine graduates, had Irish last names; by 1898, almost one-third of the graduating class (thirty-seven out of 127), had Irish last names.[54]

Unable to stop the influx of Irish San Franciscans into high school and normal school classrooms, school authorities were forced to try other means of restricting their entrance into teaching. After 1880, teachers with high school diplomas but no normal school training, still the vast majority of the teaching force, had to sit for a new "Examination for Teachers," which in 1885 included questions on "Algebra (through quadratics), Physiology, Music, Drawing, Book-Keeping, Elementary Physics, Science of Living

Things, and Herbert Spencer's Essays on Education." Normal school graduates were exempted from the teachers' examination, presumably because
they had already demonstrated their competence and cultural conformity by
mastering a difficult curriculum of algebra, arithmetic, grammar, geography, word analysis, American history, the "elements of natural philosophy
and botany," as well as zoology, astronomy, elocution, and practice teaching, all taught with a "special reference to the methods of teaching."[55]

Perhaps because of the success of Irish Americans in gaining seats in the
Normal School, however, a proposal to limit the number of normal school
students to one hundred was suggested by watchdogs on the school board
in 1890. In addition, a stiffened normal school curriculum was introduced
in 1892 as another hindrance to fainthearted applicants. Among its course
requirements were "Methods of Teaching" along with lessons in science,
entomology, arithmetic, grammar and composition, freehand drawing, psychology, "light gymnastics," and a four-month stint of practice teaching
in a city school. By 1897, normal school entrants had to provide proof of
graduation from a four-year academic high school, a feat so rare among the
students in the city's schools that, as late as 1914, school authorities estimated that less than one child in a hundred graduated from high school.[56]
Irish-American women were, however, able to meet these challenges, as
their growing numbers in the teaching force at the turn of the last century
attest.

Perhaps even more than ethnicity, gender posed problems for the
women teaching in San Francisco's schools; and by the late nineteenth century, female teachers faced growing restrictions on their professional autonomy as male "experts" wrested control of school curriculum and administration from them. Women who had formerly been able to rise up from the
teaching ranks into positions of authority in the school system now faced
career roadblocks, much as Kate Kennedy had at the end of her own career
a generation before. The formal reduction of female supervisory authority
began in 1880, when the word of the principal, usually a former teacher promoted from the ranks herself, as to the competence of her teachers was no
longer sufficient by itself. From that point on, a principal had to report "any
and all incompetent teachers" to the school board. Furthermore, "a single
neglect . . . to make such a report shall subject such principal to suspen-
sion." The deputy superintendent, almost always a man, must "observe
carefully the methods of teaching and discipline pursued by teachers"; and,
twice a month, he was to present a written report to the school board on the

"efficiency of the teachers . . . visited by him." After all, Superintendent Anderson noted in 1888, "teachers are made for the schools, and not the schools for the teachers."[57]

As the ethnic composition of the city's teaching force changed in the late nineteenth and early twentieth centuries, the heightened supervision of teachers and their still mostly female principals also manifested itself in ever more precise rules and regulations governing teacher behavior. In 1880, the school board issued new "Duties for Teachers." Henceforward, teachers must "punctually keep the hours for opening and dismissing school" and must "be in their classrooms fifteen minutes before 9 o'clock. . . ." Principals must report any teacher "late three or more times in one month," and such transgressions were punishable by dismissal.[58] At the end of the school day, teachers were "expected to correct papers in their homes . . . ," focusing on "good penmanship." After all, the report concluded in a bit of a non sequitur, "A man might be an excellent accountant, but none will want him as a book-keeper, unless his writing was good."[59]

Despite the new regulations, school officials still fretted over teacher deportment. In his *Annual Report* for 1888, Superintendent John Anderson lamented that "[f]ew of our teachers devote themselves to . . . any well-devised plan for self-improvement . . . , [that] day has passed. . . ." Nevertheless, he insisted that his suspect teachers take "every opportunity to teach civility and courtesy. . . . In dress and manner, [they] must *be* what they want their students to *become*." After all, "No teachers can expect to make their pupils more civil or more courteous than they [are themselves]." In the same report, Deputy Superintendent Babcock added his voice to Anderson's. "Every teacher should be a lady or a gentleman in taste, dress, carriage and character," he wrote, "and every Principal should be a model for the . . . teacher. . . . [But] it may not be too much to say that the average . . . teacher is not in habits or manners what . . . youth . . . should copy."[60] Principals, therefore, needed to "give due attention to [a teacher's] personal neatness and cleanliness, and any who fail in this respect must be sent home to be properly prepared for school." Since a teacher lost a fifth of a day's pay for each hour she was absent from the classroom, being sent home to wash her hair was not only embarrassing but expensive.[61]

Official suspicion against the women teaching in San Francisco continued after the turn of the twentieth century. In 1902, teachers became part of the civil service system, and the school board no longer chose San Francisco's teaching staff.[62] In 1917, the Department of the Interior's Bureau of

Education added its authority to the curtailment of teacher mobility in a series of recommendations for improving the city's schools. Noting that only seventeen of San Francisco's 1,104 elementary school teachers were male in that year, the report's "Summary and Recommendations" urged that "the proportion of men principals should be increased, and the present unwise policy of appointing all principals from the San Francisco corps of teachers should be abandoned."[63] Since the overwhelming majority of the city's teachers were women, the report's implications were clear: schools should henceforward be run by university-trained men, not locally trained women. School officials took this advice; and by the late 1920s, access to principalships and other administrative posts in the school system had been effectively closed to the, by then, largely Irish-American female teaching force. These women would now remain in the classroom under the supervision of male administrators.

The curtailing of upward career mobility for women teachers did not go unchallenged, however. As early as 1888, Superintendent Anderson had noted that if "the charges of incompetency be produced against any teacher, however undeserving, . . . immediately the cry of persecution is raised . . . with the allegation that the removal is attempted [because of] some political or religious bias."[64] This "cry" took on a new life in the 1920s when, in a pamphlet widely distributed among city voters, San Francisco union leaders denounced the school department's policy against teacher promotions. Claiming that twenty-one recently hired San Francisco school principals "have been imported from other states, . . . over the heads of local college graduates," the pamphlet also revealed that all but three of these new hires were men. Furthermore, in a list of 163 additional "imported principals and teachers," fully 112 were men. Only three of the fifty-one women named on the list were Irish. "Graduates of San Francisco and California colleges have been barred from the public school department and numerous teachers [have been] imported to take the places they could fill," the pamphlet concluded.[65] The pamphlet's message was clear: the city's public schools had been taken over by male outsiders and female teachers were being denied their rightful place in the city's educational hierarchy.

Despite these attempts to limit their access to teaching jobs and to curtail upward teacher mobility into principalships, the daughters of Irish San Francisco overcame many of the challenges imposed by the gatekeepers. Ironically, these challenges not only failed to stem the influx of Irish Americans into the city's classrooms, they also served as goads to even greater educational achievement among the very women they were designed to displace.

In an era when women were not yet full citizens of the republic, the talents of San Francisco's Irish-American women teachers enabled their families and untold numbers of their students to make the leap into America's middle class. Except for the extraordinary success of individuals like Alice Rose Power, however, the days of upward career mobility for the women teaching in San Francisco's schools were on the wane by the second decade of the twentieth century. Henceforward, ever fewer "principal" teachers rose from the ranks of the classroom teacher. University-trained male "experts" now supervised the schools and their teachers. As the largest single ethnic group among San Francisco's teachers throughout the late nineteenth and early twentieth centuries, however, Irish Americans fought for better working conditions, salaries, and pensions for the mostly female teaching staff in the city's public schools. Despite the challenges leveled at them, the daughters of San Francisco's Irish were the pioneers of public education in the city.

CHAPTER 5

Chicago

Paradigm Shift

The sisters Mary Theresa Meehan McGowan and Norah (Nonie) Meehan McNeela spent their childhoods in a Kilasser, County Mayo, classroom. After six years in school, McGowan left the classroom at the age of nine to care for her brothers and sisters when her mother died giving birth to Nonie in 1915. McGowan and her younger brothers and sisters went to live with a neighbor whose children had left for America, leaving her alone in her cottage. "When pension day arrived," McGowan's daughter, Chicago public school teacher Mary Ann McGowan Clancy writes, "the little lady would send my mother and her sisters to town to buy a delicious fresh loaf of bread.[1] By the time the children had walked all the way into town . . . , they were 'famished with hunger.' They would start eating 'the heart out of the bread.' Upon their arrival home, there was often nothing remaining but a circle of crust."[2]

The Kilasser school had two rooms and two teachers, a husband and a wife. The wife taught the "infants" classes that McGowan attended, and the husband taught the upper classes. According to Clancy, her mother "had happy memories of her early years in school and often related stories of her teacher being kind to her."[3] Despite her mother's happy memories of her Irish schooldays, Clancy acknowledges that even the youngest girls were frightened in the classroom. "If you knew the answer, you were afraid to say it," her mother told her, for fear of being hit if you were wrong. Although McGowan said she was never a victim of physical abuse, she never forgot how "her teacher would call her husband into her classroom to administer punishment to other students when she felt it was warranted." Boys in the upper grades were the primary targets for corporal punishment, however; and, according to Clancy, her father John, who also attended the Kilasser school, "had horror stories to tell when he recounted his days at the national school."

McGowan's childhood was marked by hunger and poverty, unlike the local girls who had "stylish beautiful items of clothing or fancy shoes. They would have money for fancy treats. They were the fortunate ones who had *[Y]anks in their families* [emphasis in the original]. An older brother or sister, or aunt or uncle, would send parcels from America. . . . Mom always wished she had a relative in America who could send a package to their house." Since none of McGowan's close relatives yet lived in the United States, McGowan, "decided she would have to take the responsibility on herself to be the paradigm shifter. . . . There was no future in Ireland for her. There were only a few jobs in town and [my mother] had to work for little more than her keep while 'serving her time,'" Clancy writes.

Not quite fifteen years old when she left Ireland for America in 1921, Mary McGowan had never before been beyond the borders of her hometown. Two elderly aunts in St. Louis paid her passage and arranged a job for her as a live-in maid in a wealthy home in that city. The trip to America began with a train trip to Dublin, which was "frightening" to the farm girl from Mayo. She took a hotel room and had "the rude awakening to discover there was no lock on the door . . . the anxiety over the unlocked door . . . combined with the city noises such as milk cans clanking on the horse-drawn carts beneath her windows," kept her from sleeping on her last night in Ireland.

The morning after her arrival in St. Louis, McGowan went immediately to work. She was "overwhelmed by the mansion" where she was to live and work, she later told her daughter. "[I] had left a home with a thatched roof, a fireplace that served as a stove and furnace, kerosene lamps and no indoor plumbing. . . . Talk about culture shock!" While McGowan marveled at the material luxuries of her new home, she quickly learned that many of the difficulties she had faced in her childhood in Ireland had not completely disappeared in America. "Class distinctions were evident among the [servants]," she told her daughter years later. "The cook and the woman's personal maid earned the most money, and enjoyed the most prestige. . . . Newcomers like [me] . . . received the least compensation." Furthermore, the cook, an Irish woman from Kerry, "was very stingy with the food," and McGowan once again didn't have enough to eat. Although grateful to her aunts, McGowan wanted to leave St. Louis for Chicago, where her friends were and where job prospects would be brighter. When the money she owed her aunts was repaid, she "was able to send money home to help the rest of the family, and save enough to steal off to Chicago."

The paradigm had indeed shifted, especially after McGowan found a job as a maid in the palatial home of the Donahue family on the Chicago lakefront. Her Chicago earnings paid the passage of her sister Annie, who joined her as a maid in the Donahue household. Mrs. Donahue, the scion of a family fortune, insisted that McGowan borrow her new shoes for the [Irish community's] dances on weekends, to "break them in." From that time forward, McGowan "was always a wise judge of quality shoes and wearing apparel." Life with the Donahues also taught McGowan about the finer points of architecture. "Mom would refer to our front hall at home as a 'vestibule,'" Clancy writes, "a word I am sure she never heard of in Kilasser." Later, when McGowan's brother Patrick and sister Nonie came to America, they too went to work at the Donahues'. According to Clancy, the siblings "considered the Donahues' home their home. The entire third floor of the house was theirs."

Even after leaving her position at the time of her marriage to former Kilasser classmate John McGowan in 1937, and after the births of their daughter Mary Ann in 1939 and son John in 1943, McGowan continued to practice the household arts she had learned in Irish schools and in the Donahue household. According to her daughter, "Mom was adept at making hors d'oeuvres. . . . Years later she continued to utilize these skills when she catered food for society parties" at local hotels. McGowan also earned needed dollars by taking in a lodger and cleaning the upstairs rented apartment for its tenants. She also took in ironing, another skill introduced to her at the Kilasser school. "The men's shirts were starched, sprinkled with water, and placed in the refrigerator before ironing," Clancy recalls. "They always looked professionally done when Mom finished with them."

When the local parish kindergarten in Chicago was too full to admit her daughter Mary Ann, McGowan tutored her at home, again demonstrating the legacy of her national school days. "Although my parents never went past the fourth grade in school . . . ," Clancy explains, "[a] day did not pass that they did not read a newspaper. Their comprehension and retention w[ere] remarkable. . . . [and] it was imperative to do homework before anything else. I remember tracing letters on a piece of paper and learning my [alphabet]," just as her mother had been taught in Ireland. "I also learned to do my sums. I remember later, when I was a big first grader, I assertively wrote my name the way my mother had taught me. . . . When I brought home a report card . . . I would come home and say, 'Well, I made it!' Mom never had a doubt. She expected us to 'make it.'"

"I hadn't intended to teach in the Chicago Public Schools," Clancy, herself a mother of six, contends. But after completing her college degree in 1973, this daughter of an Irish national school–educated mother took a job teaching on Chicago's South Side. Later, McGowan proudly saw Clancy earn a master's degree in education. Today Clancy has completed a doctorate in education, as well, and is the coordinator of the Citywide Gifted Program for sixth, seventh, and eighth graders in Chicago's public schools. McGowan insisted that her daughter "Get a good education. No one can ever take that away from you. . . . Go to school. That is where you belong, so you don't have to work like your father and I did." McGowan's dreams for her daughter have been realized.

Born just before their mother's death in 1916, McGowan's youngest sister Norah Meehan McNeela, known as Nonie, also attended the Kilasser national school. Arriving in America in 1937 to work with her sisters and brother at the Donahue's Chicago house, Nonie left service in 1940 when she married Michael McNeela. In 1970, one of their three children—their only daughter, Annmarie McNeela Ricker—joined her cousin Mary Ann Clancy in the ranks of women teaching in the Chicago public schools.

Ricker credits her mother's influence for her career choice. Like her cousins, Ricker insists that "I would have never been able to accomplish any of my life goals without the specific support of my mother. [She] encouraged me to be whatever I wanted to be in life. After my father died [in 1966], my mother returned to the workforce and literally washed floors so that I could receive the education she deemed necessary." Nonie also helped her daughter continue her teaching career after Ricker's three children were born. "My mother came to my house . . . everyday to watch my three toddlers so that I could go teach," she remembers. Today, Ricker teaches at Chicago's Pierce School of International Studies and holds a doctorate.

Nonie remains her "strongest support in all areas of my life. . . . My mother always iterated that it was important for girls to be educated in the advent of a husband's demise. 'Always be able to support yourself. . . . Be a . . . teacher . . . provide for family and self-support,'" Nonie told her daughter.[4]

Daughters of St. Patrick's

The educational mobility of Irishwomen, personified by the Meehan sisters and other daughters of Irish Chicago, can also be seen more than a generation before in the career of Chicago teacher and school principal Amelia Dunne Hookway, the eldest sister of Finley Peter Dunne, the creator of the literary character Mr. Dooley. As the founder and director of a nationally known children's theater in the city's Howland School, her efforts were so exceptional that Mark Twain, a devotee of children's theater himself, congratulated her in a 1908 letter. "Dear Mrs. Hookway," the world-famous author wrote, "[Your work] supports & reaffirms what I have so often & so strenuously said in public: that a children's theater is easily the most valuable adjunct to any educational institution . . . [I]ts lessons are not taught wearily by book & by dreary [homily], but by visible and enthusing *action*. . . ."[5]

Born across the street from Saint Patrick's Church, the city's first Catholic parish, in 1858, Hookway was the first child of Irish immigrant parents who had met and married in Chicago. Her Irish-born mother, Ellen Finley Dunne, encouraged her daughter's intellectual curiosity by filling the Dunne home with the works of Dickens and Thackeray and the children's magazines *Youth's Companion* and *St. Nicholas*. Amelia and her younger brother Peter Finley, as he was then known, spent many hours reading together in their mother's library.[6]

Amelia was the first of her seven surviving siblings to attend Saint Patrick parish grade school. Successful female graduates of the parish school like Amelia and her sisters then entered the four-year Saint Patrick's Girls' High School, situated in a tree-filled garden around the corner from the church. In an era when most Americans attended only a few years of primary school, the Girls' High School prepared the daughters of local Irish Catholics on the rise, like the Dunnes, for teaching careers. Offering a rigorous curriculum in English, Latin, mathematics, science, and social studies, St. Patrick's equipped its graduates to become self-supporting teachers who could also make significant contributions to their family's economic well-being.

Although St. Patrick's, like the public schools, offered secondary education for boys also, young men in the parish were less willing than their sisters to put off entering the labor market since males could find skilled work more easily than females without the benefits of an advanced formal education. In 1880, however, when Amelia was elected an assistant teacher at the Scammon School—the elementary school where her brother Peter was enrolled—she struck up a friendship with the Scammon School's principal, Ella Flagg Young, who later became Chicago's first woman school superintendent. With Young's support, Amelia convinced her father to send the precocious Peter to high school, a career path none of her other brothers had taken.

Peter enrolled only at the insistence of Amelia, and he proved to be an unmotivated student at Chicago's West Division High School.[7] Without Amelia's influence, however, he might never have attended, instead becoming a carpenter like his brothers, leaving "Mr. Dooley" unborn.[8] Peter's lackluster performance in high school might be attributable to something more than his own indifference, however, as Chicago's high schools in the 1880s offered a demanding curriculum focused on the classics and foreign languages. Called the "crown jewel of our public school system" by then superintendent George Howland, the city's high schools were a "citizen's college," taking great pride in their "thorough and intelligent instruction."[9] Although ambitious girls like the Dunnes needed no inducement to tempt them to enroll in high school classes, the imbalance in the educational aspirations of young men and women in the parish had become so noticeable by 1881 that the Christian Brothers began offering a three-year commercial course aimed at preparing young men for jobs in the front offices of city businesses. The public schools soon copied the Brothers' curriculum in hopes of luring young men into their own high schools.[10]

Altogether, three of the Dunne sisters—Amelia, Kate, and Mary—became teachers in the Chicago public schools, a pattern that became increasingly common among the city's Irish in the 1890s. Equally significant, the Dunnes' upward mobility was directly linked to the careers of the daughters. Not long after Kate joined Amelia on the Scammon School faculty in 1882, for instance, the entire family moved out of the deteriorating neighborhood around St. Patrick's to a new home on Laflin Street. They continued to move to better and better neighborhoods in the wake of Amelia's steady rise from assistant teacher at the Scammon School to head assistant at the Central Park School on Walnut Street and Kedzie Avenues.[11]

After her mother's premature death from tuberculosis in 1884, Amelia had become a mother substitute for her younger siblings, particularly Peter and Charlotte. When their father died in 1889, several of the adult Dunne children continued to live together and pool their resources. No doubt, Amelia, Kate, and Mary's salaries as schoolteachers, along with Peter's newspaper earnings, helped pay the rent on their new Warren Boulevard address. Multiple paychecks also made it possible to send their youngest sister Charlotte to the prestigious Mount Saint Joseph Academy in Dubuque, Iowa.[12]

As a rising star in the city's school system, Amelia was her family's chief breadwinner, especially after she was named principal of the George Howland School on the city's west side in 1895, with an annual salary of $1,700. In 1901, she married William Hookway and moved out of the family home into an apartment over her new husband's pharmacy on the corner of Harrison Street and Independence Boulevard. A landmark on Chicago's west side for many years, the Hookway Drugstore building became a favorite gathering place for younger generations of Dunnes.

Hookway retained her school principalship until her death from meningitis at the age of fifty-six in November 1914. After her death, she was lauded not only as the sister of the internationally famous newspaper columnist now known as Finley Peter Dunne, but also in her own right when the Chicago Catholic newspaper, *The New World,* remembered her as "One of the city's best-known Catholic educators, . . . a recognized literary authority . . . , [and the author of] several plays."[13] The *Chicago Daily Tribune* also noted her talents at the time of her death, acknowledging that "some of her Irish dialect is said to be as clever as that which brought fame to her brother's 'Mr. Dooley.'"[14] Her brother also testified to her impact on his career: he remembered her urging him to "keep it up" when he first began writing; and he maintained that his sister was "responsible for the continuation of the Dooley series," when he once thought of abandoning it.[15] In her published eulogy, Ella Flagg Young, school superintendent and Hookway's friend and mentor, wrote that "Mrs. Hookway achieved marvelous results in arousing a sense of personal dignity and responsibility in [her pupils] through literature and drama."[16]

Despite her key role in shaping not only her brother's but her family's destiny, Hookway was eclipsed by her younger brother's fame. Even on the day before her death, a newspaper headline proclaimed, "Finley Peter Dunne at Bedside of Sister Mrs. Amelia Hookway . . . [Who] Is Dying." Only on second thought did the article let its readers know that it was Amelia who "encouraged [her] brother to write 'Mr. Dooley' stories."[17] Her long career as a teacher and a principal was recognized in 1928, however, with the opening of the Amelia Dunne Hookway School at Eighty-First and LaSalle Streets on Chicago's south side.

Along with the Dunnes, St. Patrick's parish nurtured many other Irish-American families whose mobility was spearheaded by daughters who taught school. One family had, in fact, six generations of teaching daughters. The dynasty's founding mother, Irish-born Mary Leonard, left Liverpool, England, in 1847, at the age of nineteen, for Rahway, New Jersey. By 1850, the city census listed her as a teacher. After her marriage to another Irish immigrant, Nicholas Dunne, Mary and her husband left New Jersey for Chicago, settling in the city just before the Civil War. Two of the Dunne's five children—Catherine, born in 1854, and Mary, born in 1859—became teachers in the city's schools. Catherine Dunne married James Bancroft of Philadelphia, son of Irish immigrants, at St. Patrick's church in the summer of 1873, and continued her work in the city's classrooms for the next thirty years. The Bancrofts, in turn, had three children: Mary Angela, born in 1877; Frances, born in 1881; and Edward, who died prematurely at the age of nineteen in 1898. Mary Angela and Frances followed their mother into public school teaching. In 1898, Mary Angela married Irish-born John Hillan. Their daughter, Margaret Mary Hillan, born in 1906, graduated from the Chicago Normal School, earned certificates at the Chicago Teachers' College, and taught at the city's Barnard primary school until retiring in 1971. Margaret Mary and her husband Frank Foerner's daughters, Pauline and Mary, in turn, became Chicago schoolteachers themselves. Today, Pauline's daughter, Amy Miniat, teaches in the Chicago suburb of Lake Forest.[18]

A Fighting Irishwoman

Teacher and labor-union activist Margaret Haley, a contemporary of the Dunnes and Bancrofts on Chicago's west side, was born in 1861 in Joliet,

Illinois, thirty miles southwest of downtown Chicago. The second of eight children of Irish immigrants, Maggie, as she was known to her family and friends, spent her childhood on farms and in small towns in Illinois as her labor-activist father Michael tried his luck—often bad—at various small business ventures supplemented by farming. When her brother Tom drowned at the age of twelve, Maggie became the eldest in a family of six surviving siblings.[19]

Haley's political consciousness had been born when she was a child listening to her father's outrage at the injustice accorded workers in Ireland and the United States. She heard her father, a one-time whiskey "jigger-carrier" for the Irish workers building the Illinois and Michigan Canal south of Chicago and later the elected Democratic treasurer of the Illinois State Federation of Labor, talk to his friends. "I heard as much about [Irish nationalist leader Charles Stewart] Parnell in my girlhood . . . as James Joyce ever did . . . in Dublin," Haley wrote; but she learned about American politics as well. Henry George's *Progress and Poverty* also influenced Haley's thinking about government responsibility to citizens, and she connected George's theory of the single tax on land to the relationship of taxation to "fundamental human justice."[20]

"My father's and my mother's people," she wrote, "left Ireland in order that they might have . . . independence of mind." In fact, Haley saw her Irish heritage as the founding principle of her reform impulse. "The fighting Irish," thrilled her, she later wrote, along with their Irish nationalist heroes, the "Tones, and the Emmetts [*sic*], and the Parnells." Haley also wrote that her mother Ellen emphasized the importance of intellectual development to her when she was a child, "as only the Irish, who have been denied a full measure of education, could value it." Paraphrasing Young Irelander Charles Gavan Duffy, Haley's mother told her to "[e]ducate in order that your children may be free."[21] Like Amelia Dunne Hookway, Haley was also destined to make her mark in the Chicago schools.

"I was catapulted into teaching," Haley recalled, when, in 1877 at the age of sixteen, she needed to find paid work to supplement the family income after her father lost his business. Having just graduated from a convent school in downstate Illinois herself, Haley began her teaching career in a nearby one-room school. "From the first day I went into the school," she wrote, "I loved the work." Nevertheless, she was not content to remain in so small a school for long. "[M]y one thought," she acknowledged, "was to find another teaching job."

In 1880, at the age of nineteen, her fight for what she believed were teachers' fundamental rights began when she left her teaching post in Joliet because the superintendent would not raise her $35-a-month teaching salary by $5. By 1882, after spending the next two years taking teacher-training courses and moving up the career ladder to ever larger school districts, she had her raise and her first teaching job in Chicago's Cook County. "Chicago in the Eighties was still a frontier town," she wrote, but, "even then, Chicago was the lodestar for ambitious girls of the Middle West."[22] Two years later, she was hired to teach the sixth grade at the Hendrick's School in the Stockyards District, the home of many of Chicago's most recent immigrants. When the district was incorporated into the city limits in 1889, Haley became a Chicago public school teacher at last.[23]

Conditions at the Hendricks School planted seeds of rebellion in Haley. While her students were "eager to learn . . . the school itself was almost hopeless" because of an incompetent principal. Although she later remembered herself as being "a tremendous conformist in those days . . . [with never] a thought of any kind of revolution," she began to protest against school mismanagement. Haley had found her battleground.[24]

After almost a quarter of a century in the classroom, Haley left teaching in 1901 to become the paid business secretary and vice president of the newly formed Chicago Teachers' Federation (CTF), the first teachers' union in the United States and, in 1902, the first teachers' organization to affiliate with the American Federation of Labor (AFL). Together with former Chicago teacher and CTF president Catherine Goggin, herself the daughter of Irish-born parents, Haley spent the rest of her life fighting for teachers' and women's rights.[25]

The CTF provided Haley with a platform for her crusade against the entrenched powers she believed were undermining public education. "I had no choice to make. It had been made for me," she wrote. "Only through the freedom of their teachers could the children remain free."[26] As a CTF leader, Haley campaigned for equal pay for equal work, pensions, and tenure for Chicago's largely Irish-American female teaching force. While powerful opposition among the businessmen on the city's school committee eventually dismantled many of Haley's initiatives, she declared that as a descendant of the "fighting Irish," she had "never . . . feared anything or anyone, least of all established authority."[27] After all, she wrote, "My father's and my mother's people had left Ireland in order that they might have . . . independence of mind," and, as a "child of generations of men and women who battled for something beyond material gain, [I had the duty to participate] in the gigantic struggle for justice" promised by America's public schools.[28]

Haley's Irish heritage was one of the founding principles of her reform impulse. Her Catholic education further fueled her political development. In the mid-1890s, for instance, when she attended a Wisconsin summer school for teachers, run by largely Irish-American Dominican nuns, she "came into the knowledge . . . for the first time . . . of the fundamental issue in the unending war for academic freedom: the right of a teacher to call his soul his own."[29] Her taste for rebellion against unjust authority, born in her parents' home, would soon find a public stage.

Haley entered the public battleground beyond the classroom for the first time when she challenged the leadership of the Women's Catholic Order of Foresters, a mutual aid society with a largely Irish membership, founded in Chicago in 1891. The issue that forced Haley to fight was the fact that the "authoritarian" leaders of the Order allowed older women past the upper age-limit to join the organization, thus violating the Foresters' own rules and threatening to bankrupt the insurance cooperative before younger members like Haley grew old enough to draw a return from their investment. When the Chief High Ranger of the Foresters undemocratically proclaimed that she would remain the organization's chief executive for life, Haley saw the move as "wrong, unAmerican, autocratic," and said so when she stood up from the floor at the Order's convention to challenge the leadership's position. Met with "terrible passions . . . faces twisted with hatred . . . they would have [torn] me limb from limb," Haley was expelled from the Order. Undaunted by this open hostility, Haley successfully fought her expulsion in court and was reinstated by Judge Edward F. Dunne, later the Chicago mayor who defended teachers in many of Haley's future battles with entrenched power in the city.[30] Her forty years of battle had now officially begun. By the time of her death in 1939, however, Haley had lived long enough to see the end of a golden age of teacher organization and mobility that her efforts had brought about.

Backlash

By the turn of the twentieth century, Chicago had the largest Catholic school system in the country. Created in the 1840s as a haven for the Irish and later Catholic immigrant groups seeking freedom from the Protestant values they believed were widespread in the public schools, Chicago's "separate but equal" Catholic schools seemed poised to undermine the city's public school system by the end of the nineteenth century. Even though such an obviously Protestant practice as reading the King James version of the Bible in the public schools was outlawed in 1910, the city's Catholic schools were by then so well-established that few of Chicago's Irish families with enough income to afford the modest fees for a Catholic education sent their children to the public schools. When they were growing up, for instance, neither Amelia Dunne Hookway nor Margaret Haley attended a public school.

In the thirty years between 1890 and 1920, however, the number of Chicago public elementary school students also rose, doubling from 130,000 to 260,000. At the same time, the number of public elementary school teachers almost tripled, rising from 2,600 to 7,400.[31] Although Irish Catholics had been the primary founders of the city's English-language Catholic school system and remained the single largest ethnic groups in parochial school classrooms in those same years, the rising numbers of city teaching jobs attracted more and more Catholic school graduates to public school teaching. By 1908, in fact, Catholic school–educated Irish-American women were the largest ethnic group among graduates of the city's public normal school. By 1910, at least one-third of Chicago's public school teachers were Catholics, and most of these Catholics were Irish. By 1920, according to one count, they were an astonishing 70 percent of all the city's teachers.[32]

The entrance of so many Irish-American women into public school teaching was noticed by contemporary critics, especially in Chicago where most Irish-American teachers, like Hookway and Haley, had been educated in Catholic, not public, schools. In contrast to Boston and San Francisco, parochial education had attracted the majority of Chicago's Catholics since the mid-nineteenth century, making that city's Protestant establishment especially hostile to the influx of so many Catholic school–educated teachers into the "common schools." As early as 1891, the *Chicago Tribune*, in an article headlined ". . . Romanism's Power . . . and the Public Schools . . . ," quoted a member of the Women's Christian Temperance Union as saying: "The situation [in the public schools] is becoming alarming. . . . Our school teachers are 70 percent Catholic. . . ." Another member urged: "We must protect the schools of this country against the Romish church. . . . We must take sides and the public–school system is to be the pivot." The clubwomen's fears were justified; so much so, in fact, that by the 1920s, almost all of the city's teaching force who were Irish Catholic had graduated from local Catholic girls' high schools.[33]

As the number of Irish-American women among the ranks of Chicago's public elementary school teachers grew larger and larger, the school board ruled in 1903 that only graduates of the city-run normal school could be employed in city classrooms. Graduates of all other teacher preparatory classes—most notably graduates of Chicago's Catholic high schools and colleges—would henceforth be required to gain between two and four years' teaching experience outside the city limits before becoming eligible to apply for a city position. Chicago's diocesan archbishop, George Cardinal Mundelein, immediately declared that the ruling was an indirect attack on the graduates of Catholic colleges. As Catholic public opinion rallied around Mundelein and as swelling public school enrollments made the hiring of more teachers imperative, the school board was forced to withdraw its ruling in 1904.[34]

Attempts to limit the numbers of Irish Americans teaching in Chicago's schools did not end in 1904, however. Two years later, education officials decreed that examinations for entrance to the Cook County Normal School were now required of all candidates for admission who had not graduated from "approved" public high schools. Once again, Chicago's Catholic community saw this ruling as openly discriminatory against graduates of their schools. In 1915, the year after the death of her protégé Amelia Dunne Hookway, Superintendent Young proposed yet another quota system that would allocate a certain percentage of Chicago's teaching jobs to graduates of the Normal School only, thereby limiting by default the number of teaching jobs open to graduates of the city's Catholic school teacher-preparation courses.[35] Despite these measures, more and more graduates of the city's Catholic high schools entered the city's normal school in the first decades of the twentieth century. The influx of the Catholic Irish into Chicago teaching jobs had not been stopped.

From its inception in 1897, the Chicago Teachers' Federation had striven to combat the backlash directed against the largely Irish-Catholic female teaching force in Chicago's schools, and their efforts were to inspire similar efforts among teachers in other parts of the country. The CTF was a remarkable and in many ways unique professional organization for educators. Unlike the powerful and long-established National Education Association (NEA), the CTF deliberately excluded all administrators—usually male—from membership. Instead, the CTF promoted the economic interests of the rank-and-file elementary public school teacher, the mostly female proletariat of the educational world. Furthermore, the CTF concentrated on improving the material well-being of its members, rather than imitating the NEA's emphasis on annual meetings, including lectures from the podium that reinforced the educational hierarchy.

The CTF also deviated from the pattern established by literary discussion societies, the only other organizations besides the NEA open to classroom teachers at the time. These genteel reading circles promoted modest intellectual, not economic, improvement. Members of the CTF, however, eschewed the polite passivity imposed on them by both the literary societies and the NEA; discussion of the classics or appreciation of curricular schemes designed by their superiors had no place on the CTF's agenda. Instead, the women of the CTF actively and sometimes impolitely pursued their economic interests as paid professionals entrusted with the education of Chicago's youth.

According to the CTF's constitution, the organization's primary goal was "to raise the standard of the teaching profession by securing for teachers the conditions essential to the best professional service."[36] Fundamental to this mission was the fight to protect the recently enacted teachers' pension fund from alterations that would favor the mostly male administrators and (better-paid) mostly male high school teachers, at the expense of the mostly female elementary teachers for whom the fund had originally been designed. The CTF saw the preservation of the pension fund as fundamental to teacher economic security, since pensions allowed the largely female elementary teachers to make teaching a lifelong career. Furthermore, since the long-awaited teachers' pension plan had only gone into effect in 1895, its elimination so soon after its inauguration would be a severe setback to all other potential reforms designed to uplift the elementary teacher's economic and professional status. As a result, Margaret Haley and her staunch ally Catherine Goggin declared "No Surrender" on the pension-fund debate.

Also at issue in the CTF's early deliberations was the securing of tenure and the raising of salaries for teachers. In pursuit of these goals, Haley moved the CTF's fight for financial equity for Chicago's teachers beyond the city limits to the state legislature in Springfield. As a lobbyist, Haley attended every legislative session between 1898 and 1935.[37] Throughout these "forty fighting years" as she called them, her main consideration remained securing adequate and reliable funding for the schools and their teachers.[38]

In this quest, Haley went up against the most powerful financial and political institutions in Chicago.

Haley's first major battle on behalf of the CTF began in 1899 when the Board of Education reneged on a promised salary increase for the city's elementary teachers on the grounds that sufficient funding for the increase was not available. Rejecting this explanation, Haley campaigned to restructure the city's tax base so that high profit corporations would lose their tax-exempt status and begin paying their rightful share of property taxes, the public schools' revenue source. The issue was simple to Haley. "If the great corporations paid their legal taxes," she insisted, "there would be plenty of money to operate the schools."[39] Haley and the CTF took these corporate giants to court and won. As a result, in 1907, a citywide reassessment collected a windfall of current and back taxes from corporate scofflaws, providing the schools and their teachers with a stronger financial foundation than they had ever had before.

The efforts of Haley and the CTF to improve the economic well-being of Chicago public school teachers can also be seen in the CTF's affiliation with the Chicago Federation of Labor (CFL) in 1902. This controversial alliance of the mostly lower-middle-class female CTF with the mostly working-class male CFL embodied Haley's position that teachers must recognize that they were not too genteel or too "professional" to fight for their rights as workers by joining a labor union. She also realized the value to presuffrage women teachers of an alliance with vote-wielding union men.

The pragmatic and idealistic union of the CTF with the CFL was without precedent at the time.[40] Never before had female white-collar workers joined male blue-collar workers in defense of their mutual rights as employees. As Haley saw it, the "school, alone, was powerless against organized wealth. . . . [I]f we [want] to preserve not only our own self-respect but [also] the basic independence of the public schools, we must make a powerful political alliance . . . with the social group which [has] the same elemental interest as our own—the welfare . . . of public school children. That organization [is] the Chicago Federation of Labor."[41]

By joining the CTF to the CFL, Haley and CFL leader John Fitzpatrick publicly acknowledged the strong labor commitment to public education. No longer could public schools be seen as ploys of the privileged to impose social controls on the poor. From 1902 on, at least in Chicago, public education was wholeheartedly supported by organized labor. The schools were the means of working-class betterment, not oppression; but, according to Haley, American society itself could not be democratic unless the teachers in its public schools were free themselves. "To me," she wrote, "Chicago is the proving ground of American democracy."[42]

Haley had come of age in the late nineteenth century, imbued with the heady reform impulses of the era that have come to be called Progressive. Her progressivism was an inherited instinct stemming from her view of herself as one of the "Fighting Irish . . . child of generations of men and women who battled for something beyond immediate gain, beyond material welfare," who had a part to play "in the gigantic struggle for justice [which must be waged until] the last war for man's freedom has been won."[43] Her deep belief in the role of the public school in protecting and furthering the cause of American democracy was based on its ability to educate all social and economic classes and both sexes together in the same classrooms. This ability made the schools the unique key to democratic self-government and social justice.

Unlike the "administrative progressives" who wanted to bureaucratize the schools and replace teacher decision-making in curriculum and other school matters with that of mostly male university-trained educational "experts," Haley's progressive impulses were in the direction of decentralizing school decision-making and returning the power to decide educational issues to the teachers.[44] Haley supported the teacher council movement advocated by Superintendent Young, the first woman to head the Chicago school system and also the first woman elected president of the NEA, the CTF's rival organization.[45] While the businessmen who sat on the school board sought to reorganize school decision-making along the lines of a corporation, from the top down, Young's teachers' councils were designed to tap into the growing professionalism among grade school teachers by giving them a say in the selection of textbooks and in other curricular matters. As Haley saw it, "Two ideals are struggling for supremacy in American life today: one the industrial ideal . . . which subordinates the worker to the product . . . ; the other, the ideal of democracy, the ideal of the educators, which places humanity [first]. . . ."[46] The teachers' councils, Haley insisted, were the only things standing between "[t]he tendency toward centralization in education [that] was sweeping the country, and would probably have engulfed us hopelessly if it had not been for [teacher determination] that we would see its dangers."[47] Her support of Young's decentralizing counter-force demonstrated Haley's desire to widen the franchise to include elementary school teachers, women who had been denied a role in public decision-making.

This belief in democratization led Haley to her feminism, which had been nurtured by her parents in her youth. "I don't know Susan B. Anthony . . . ," her father once said after hearing a lecturer disparage the famous feminist, "but she's a woman who is working for a cause, a just cause, and I will not allow my children . . . to listen to any half-baked nincompoop who sneers at her."[48] Haley's relatively high level of education—she was a high school graduate with lifelong post-graduate teacher training—and her early entrance into the world of paid work outside the home further fueled her belief in the importance of women's economic and social autonomy, key planks in any feminist's platform. To Haley, women's work was as important as men's, and women workers should be accorded the same respect and pay as their male counterparts.

Haley was a major player in the women's suffrage movement, which she equated with her struggle for teachers' rights. To her, women needed the vote because women teachers could not teach their students how to exercise their democratic rights unless the teachers themselves were enfranchised. While campaigning for women's suffrage in 1911, Haley explained that, "when I'd seen the hate of men unleashed against every woman who took the stump to demand the vote, I . . . realize[d] that woman suffrage was not an end in itself but a means to a more important end, the governmental establishment of fundamental justice to all men, women, and children of the nation."[49] In 1913, her work on behalf of democracy for all was instrumental in making Illinois the first state east of the Mississippi River to grant the vote to women.[50]

Haley's feminism was not confined to suffrage alone, however, as can be seen in her recognition of the misogyny of male school reformers such as William Rainey Harper, Chicago school board member and president of the University of Chicago. Harper, she claimed, "scorned women," and his anti-teacher proposals advanced the cause of women's suffrage "further [in one] day [than] in fifty years in Illinois. . . . Voting women today owe more than they know to William Rainey Harper."[51]

Haley also realized that "there was . . . no concerted movement [in the early years of the century] toward women's active participation in political life. We were stumbling along in the dark."[52] Haley did not trust prominent women progressives like the aristocratic Jane Addams, whom she called "gentle Jane" in contrast to Haley's "fighting Irish." She was, however, a great admirer of the "New Woman" of her day, unlike her Boston contemporary Julia Duff. Haley recognized that, "it was my lot . . . to come into maturity just when women were struggling for political, economic, and social independence." If women were "to win rudimentary justice," she realized in classic feminist fashion, they "had to battle with brain, with wit, and sometimes even with force."[53]

Haley began writing her posthumously published autobiography *Battleground* early in the new century, finishing it only shortly before she died in 1939. Although she expressed her feminist convictions in the manuscript, however, she downplayed her feminism in more public venues during her lifetime, perhaps fearing that her convictions on women's issues were too liberal for even the CTF's membership. In the final draft, however, written shortly before her death, she expressed her disillusion with feminism's retreat after women won the right to vote in 1920.[54]

Despite her reticence on the subject in public, Haley saw close connections between women's rights and what she saw as anti-Irish discrimination in the Chicago schools. Her ethnic and feminist consciousness was aroused, she claimed, when her colleague Catherine Goggin was nominated for the CTF presidency in 1899. The Irish-American Goggin's candidacy prompted a flood of anonymous letters attacking her "race and religion"; and to Haley, Goggin's victorious campaign against the non-Irish Mrs. Bratton, whose supporters "brought in as much dirty politics as any precinct brawl," was a clear-cut defeat for anti-Catholic and anti-Irish discrimination.[55] Haley was not, however, a blind supporter of all things Irish. Instead, she divided Irish America into two political camps, each originating in "the same cause—the oppression of their race in Ireland. . . . Persecution had crushed one group of Irish into submission to an established authority and a correlative intention of getting from it, by fair means or foul, whatever might be grasped [while i]t had roused the other group to continuing struggle against any and all injustice."[56] There was no doubt as to which camp Haley favored.

In fact, Haley opposed politicians she believed belonged to that first group of persecuted Irish who bowed to authority while grabbing whatever spoils their betters sent their way. Once, when she was warned by the Democratic Party boss of the Illinois State Legislature, Roger C. Sullivan, to stop her activities against the [State] Board of Education on the grounds that "we were all Irish Catholics and ought to stand together," Haley rejected his demand. "I'd be damned," she insisted, "if I'd stand with any

Catholic, Irish or Dutch or anything else, who'd defend procedure like that of the State Board." She opposed Sullivan, she said, "not only because it's always been my creed [to do so], but because it's the creed of so many others of my faith and race."[57]

Many non-Irish also opposed Haley and the CTF's initiatives, of course, including the school board's antifeminist Harper Commission chairman, University of Chicago president William Rainey Harper. Charged by Mayor Carter H. Harrison in 1898 to draw up a plan for school reform, Harper's Commission urged school reorganization along the lines advocated by the administrative progressives—that educational "experts," university-based men like Harper himself, should manage the schools. Teachers were to be hired "hands," allowed only to carry out the dictates of their superiors on a day-to-day basis in the city's classrooms.

Harper, Haley wrote, was "the head of the Rockefeller-endowed institution on the Midway" and an "educational 'mossback'" who had already denied pay raises to his University of Chicago faculty by claiming that "he could get all the teachers he wanted for $600 a year and that he couldn't see why public school teachers should even get that much."[58] Furthermore, Harper supported the leasing of school land to large corporations for ninety-nine years without tax reevaluation. Thus, even before the publication of the Commission's Report in 1898, Harper stood foursquare against two fundamental issues of Haley's "forty fighting years" in the teaching profession: raising teacher salaries and creating a firm financial foundation for the public schools by ending the tax privileges of the largest corporations in the city, whose directors sat on the school board.

Despite the opposition of Haley and the CTF, the influence of the Harper Commission Report was felt on all levels of Chicago's educational world. In 1903, the fledgling teachers' councils, designed to rekindle teacher initiatives in curriculum and school discipline, were abolished.[59] Although these councils were later reinstated by Superintendent Young, the overall thrust of school reform in the first three decades of the twentieth century was away from the CTF's democracy and towards Harper's administrative efficiency.

Teachers' ties to organized labor also came under direct attack when, in 1915, the school board passed the infamous Loeb Rule, named after school board president Jacob Loeb. At issue was the vastly enhanced power of the CFL-backed CTF in its contract negotiations with the Board of Education. In order to end the affiliation between teachers and organized labor, Loeb's

Rule forbade teachers from joining labor unions or any "teachers' organizations which have officers, business agents, or other representatives who are not members of the teaching force. . . ."[60] Since the CTF was formally affiliated with the CFL, and since CTF business agent and Vice-President Haley and President Goggin had left the classroom in 1901, the intent of the Loeb Rule was impossible to mistake. Henceforward, teachers who wished to keep their membership in the CTF lost their jobs. Thirty-eight of the teachers dismissed by the board in June 1916 were, in fact, CTF members. According to Haley, this "attempt to annihilate the Chicago Teachers' Federation . . . menaced the integrity and well-being of every teacher in the Chicago public schools." Worse, the rule "put in jeopardy the continued development of democracy in the United States."[61]

The CTF fought back and regained many of their economic and professional advances. Teacher councils were reinstituted in 1913, allowing teachers to meet alone again, without the presence of administrators, to discuss academic issues. In 1917, the Loeb Rule was successfully challenged in the courts, and the teachers who had lost their jobs in 1916 for being CTF members were reinstated. All eligible teachers in the city's schools were given permanent tenure to prevent arbitrary dismissal from happening in the future. In 1915, cooperation between organized labor and public school teachers was further advanced with the merger of the American Federation of Teachers (AFT) and Haley's CTF as Local Number One.

The renewed cooperation between organized labor and public school teachers was short-lived, however. "[T]he entrance of the United States into the World War accomplished what Jacob Loeb [and others] had not been able to do," Haley wrote; "it alienated the great body of teachers in the Chicago public schools from the American Federation of Labor."[62] Haley herself joined in the general disenchantment. At issue was labor's rush to join the pro-war forces in 1917. Haley believed labor had been duped into supporting the war effort by British propaganda, deeply offending her Irish nationalism as well as her labor pacifism. "Chicago public school teachers lost confidence," she asserted, "in the integrity of those Labor leaders who had either blindly followed [AFL president] Samuel Gompers[,] by birth an English Jew . . . [,] or who had been willing to trade their moral opposition to war for the sake of material benefits which certain of their groups would secure from the waging of such a war."[63] As a result of the AFL defection from principle, Haley and the CTF withdrew from the AFT, and therefore from its parent organization, the AFL.

Other separations followed, made all the more poignant by the deaths of such staunch colleagues and friends as Catherine Goggin in 1916 and Ella Flagg Young in 1918. By the 1920s, much of the fledgling professionalism of Chicago teachers had eroded, and teachers faced payless paydays brought about by the very financial crises that Haley's reforms had sought to prevent. Teachers debated among themselves how to best confront these twin menaces to their hard-won advances. Many, citing the professionalism of their work, insisted that teachers should confine their reform campaigns to outside the classroom, but remain on the job at any cost. After all, they argued, teaching was a profession, and therefore carried duties along with rights. Even if many of the profession's rights were being contested, the social responsibilities of teachers were unassailable. It was this responsibility to their students and their city's future, after all, that was the basis for their claim to professional status in the first place. Others argued for more direct action to preserve teachers' professional and economic gains. Since the only truly effective weapon teachers had against their school-board employers, advocates of this stance pointed out, was refusing to go to work until their demands were met, public demonstrations and using their ultimate weapon, the strike, were perfectly legitimate collective actions.

By the 1920s, Chicago teachers in all camps also saw the virtual elimination of the possibility for the most talented among them to rise to the position of "principal teacher" in a school, managing large faculties, staffs, and students. Henceforward, normal school–trained women teachers were permanently confined to their classroom duties, while university-trained, mostly male "experts" were hired as school principals and administrators to oversee them. Teacher input into curriculum in the form of teacher councils was also silenced, and a bar preventing married women from continuing to teach was enacted.[64] For the next generation, Chicago's women teachers could no longer follow in the footsteps of such exemplars of their craft as school principal and wife Amelia Dunne Hookway. Several decades would have to pass before Chicago's women teachers could once again expect to marry while pursuing a lifetime career in the schools.

"The Patrick Henry of the Classroom"

"I never wanted to fight . . . on hectic battle-fronts of an unending war" to gain teachers', women's, and human rights, Margaret Haley insisted in her autobiography. Despite being called "the Patrick Henry of the class-room teacher movement" by poet Carl Sandburg, Haley claimed she "never sought a battle for its own sake . . . ," but, "like all crusaders, I have stormed where kings and courtiers feared to tread . . . [railing] at mayors, at governors, at legislators, at presidents of great universities. . . . [I]f I could have won the same results in any other way," she concluded, "I should never have fought at all. . . ."[65]

Despite her professed reluctance to enter the fray, Haley acknowledged that "It was my lot to come to maturity just when women were struggling for political, economic, and social independence. . . ." Women crusaders, Haley reminded her readers, "were never fighting for [themselves] alone." Instead they "were flung on the frontier of the war for human rights."[66] As a result of her battles, Haley saw women teachers in Chicago gain signifi-cant workplace rights and her beloved CTF become the template for teacher organization throughout the country.

At the time of her death from heart disease on the eve of the second World War, Haley saw her life's work on behalf of Chicago's teachers as, at best, unfinished, or at worst, undone. Nevertheless, her legacy was extolled by her surviving contemporaries. Some remembered her as "a little woman with . . . rich eyes that understand much and saw a lot . . . eyes that were anxious to twinkle with an inherited Irish gaiety but eyes that were mostly looking for the answers to challenging questions." Others, like Irish-American labor leader and fellow-Chicagoan Agnes Nester, believed Haley to be "one of the most brilliant, able, and resourceful leaders of her time." She would eventually be, Carl Sandburg wrote, "a rare memory of the labor world and of politics."[67]

By the end of the nineteenth century, then, many of Chicago's public school teachers were the daughters of women like Ellen Dunne and Ellen Haley, women who had been born and schooled in Ireland. This remarkable female geographical and educational mobility continued into the twentieth century when Mary McGowan and Nonie McNeela likewise inspired their daughters' career achievements in the Chicago schools. Despite the advance of the daughters of Irish America, however, the women working in Chi-cago's classrooms continued to have an uphill fight for professional status well into the twentieth century.

CHAPTER 6

The End of a Golden Age

Believing that Chicago was "more Irish than Cork . . . [and] a magnet for the political boss and demagogue," University of Chicago education professor George S. Counts wrote in his landmark 1928 exposé, *School and Society in Chicago,* that "For more than a generation, the Chicago public schools [have been] the victim of political manipulation" and that the history of public education in the city was a "sordid story of political interference and the general subordination of the fortunes of public education to the passions and selfish interests of organized minorities." The millions spent annually on the schools, he contended, gave the "public schools the same allure to contractors and political bosses as gold was to the conquistadores." Although the Methodist Professor Counts distrusted Irish Catholics, he championed teacher rights and recognized that political interference in the schools could be found everywhere in the United States and not just in Chicago.[1]

According to Counts, the Chicago schools were an enormous public resource, accommodating 406,000 students in 1920, up from a student body of only 410 in 1841. By 1926, over half of the 36,218 people on the city's payroll were employed by the Board of Education. In that year, Chicago's 301 elementary schools, twenty-five secondary schools, and one normal school employed 12,000 teachers. The city's elementary teachers were, however, "distinguished from secondary teachers in training, pay, and social class," Counts noted; and they were also "divided by race, culture, religion, and political affiliation." Since teachers were divided, their supervisors could conquer them, beginning with the Loeb Law of 1915, which broke the CTF's affiliation with organized labor, and the Otis Law of 1917, which allowed mayors to appoint school committee members.[2]

Counts believed that the appointed school boards were unrepresentative of the city at large. Partisan politics, he warned, had been given license to govern school policy, as school boards no longer answered to citizen votes. Furthermore, the superintendent was now "at the mercy of the school board." Noting that in a city with a large immigrant and working-class population, only one of the 120 different school board members between 1903 and 1926 was working-class. Although they composed the majority of Chicago's voters, Democrats and Catholics were also minorities on the school board, and Jews even more so. No African-Americans and only nineteen women had ever been members. Therefore, Counts told his readers, the Chicago Board of Education was composed largely of "American-born, Protestant, upper class, white men with college educations."[3]

Perhaps because the majority of the city's teaching force was in the elementary schools, and therefore largely from working-class Irish Catholic and Democratic Party backgrounds, there was "almost continual strife and suspicion" between the board of education, the superintendent, and the teachers. Perhaps most of all, organized teachers in the CTF were the greatest source of trouble for the unrepresentative school boards in these years. In fact, Counts reported, in the aftermath of the school board's successful attempt in 1915 to sever the CTF's ties with organized labor through enforcement of the Loeb Law, relations between the board and teachers "hardened into antipathy, even though teachers had been successful themselves in winning permanent tenure."[4]

Counts also looked into the history of the teachers' councils, those short-lived attempts to secure teacher influence over curriculum and other school matters. Inspired by Chicago School Superintendent Ella Flagg Young's dissertation, *Isolation in the Schools,* which insisted that teachers should have responsibility over what they taught, the councils would be venues for classroom teachers to formulate curriculum and educational policy without administrative supervision. Between 1913 and 1915, in direct opposition to the trend against teacher professionalization, Young revived the teachers'councils which had briefly met in the 1890s.[5]

Young's teachers' councils did not last long, however. The trend toward teacher de-skilling was too powerful to resist. By 1924, Chicago's new school superintendent William McAndrew, a former Chicago teacher and New York City school superintendent, restored all educational initiatives to supervisory personnel, standardized the elementary school curriculum with a renewed emphasis on the 3Rs, and made student testing the basis for judging a teacher's, as well as a pupil's, abilities. As fast as teacher autonomy waned, supervisory staff grew under McAndrew's administration. By 1926, there were five assistant superintendents, fourteen district supervisors, and fifteen supervisors and directors of special subjects overseeing the work of Chicago's 317 elementary and secondary school principals.[6] As a result of the proliferation of largely male university graduates as supervisory personnel, the classroom teacher was alienated more than ever before from the means of production in the schools: the setting of curriculum and evaluation standards.

By the mid-1920s, 5,000 elementary teachers had joined the CTF, which stood foursquare against the top-down approach inherent in McAndrew's superintendency. The CTF had already waged several successful battles for teachers, beginning with Margaret Haley's campaign for teacher pensions during the first decade after its founding in 1897. Despite this victory, the CTF still faced powerful adversaries among entrenched powers in school politics. According to Counts, in fact, "some see in the Federation the veiled hand of the Pope. Miss Haley herself is a Catholic, and the majority of the members are probably of this faith; yet many of the most important offices [in the school administration] have been held by Protestants [only]."[7] Gender, religion, and ethnicity remained at the core of Chicago's school wars.

Minds to Hands

By the time Margaret Haley entered her battleground, teachers in many of the largest cities in the United States were seeking professional status for their work. Teaching had an ambiguous status at the time, and the debate over whether it was a profession, an art, or merely a craft, was ongoing. Earlier in the century, when the teaching force had been mostly male, many observers simply considered teaching a stop-gap employment for men who had failed at other lines of work. In antebellum America, as in pre-Famine Ireland, male teachers were often stereotyped as well-educated gentlemen fallen on bad times, usually because of some personal failing—often drunkenness. By mid-century, as the numbers of women entering teaching began to rise, the once mostly male pursuit of teaching rapidly and overwhelmingly became a female employment, especially in the lower grades. Now seen primarily as a refuge for the undertrained and otherwise unemployable female, teaching lost even more of its already tarnished status.

The feminization of teaching led to two further developments. First, the vision of the young, unmarried woman in the classroom merged with the growing sentimentalization of women as "angels" destined for lives in the private sphere of the family and the home. Female teachers could be tolerated under the new ideological strictures for women only as long as teaching was seen as a "natural" extension of motherhood, women's only "true" destiny. In 1865, San Francisco school superintendent John Swett summed up the prevailing attitudes towards teachers' proper roles. Teachers did not need intellectual training, Swett argued. Instead, "their great heart, womanly tact, love and kindness" were enough to guarantee their success in the classroom.[8] Teaching was, therefore, a natural female calling, but not a profession. However, although teaching was providing women with an extension of their domestic role, it was also providing them with a new opportunity for economic independence and social mobility that was at odds with this domesticity.

Concurrently with the mass influx of women into teaching, school systems in cities like Boston, San Francisco, and Chicago underwent structural change. As the populations of these cities expanded and became increasingly heterogeneous, urban governments followed Boston's lead and took control over a loose network of private schoolrooms and academies, forging a system of rapidly expanding public education funded by taxpayers and administered by paid superintendents and other public employees.

By the late nineteenth century, as the feminization and bureaucratization of urban public schools reached fruition, a further transformation of the work of teaching took place as more and more Irish Americans entered teaching. A perceived conflict between Irish Americans teaching in the classroom and "American" values led school boards to set new limits on the autonomy of teachers, with the hope that "de-skilling" them would reduce their already shaky hold on professional status. In the face of this influx of a new breed of teacher, boards adopted new rules and regulations designed to increase their authority over teachers; at the same time, they instituted more rigorous training requirements for getting a teaching post in the first place. Nevertheless, while the new credential prerequisites advanced the quality of teacher preparation, they did not keep Irish-American women from entering the classroom. Instead, as we have seen, the daughters of working-class Irish families in Boston, San Francisco, and Chicago flocked to the four-year academic programs offered by new city high schools. School boards upped the ante by requiring post–high school training in city-run normal schools, but Irish Americans again met the challenge. By the early twentieth century, in fact, Irish-American women were the largest single ethnic group graduating from high schools in Boston, San Francisco, and Chicago; and they were increasingly large percentages among normal school graduates in those cities.

As school boards tightened their controls, a growing desire for professional autonomy, along with campaigns for higher pay, tenure, and pensions that would allow women to make teaching a lifetime career, spread throughout the ranks of urban teachers. Irish-American women were prominent in these drives for teacher professionalization. Union leaders such as Margaret Haley in Chicago and Kate Kennedy in San Francisco—along with principals and school administrators like Alice Rose Power of San Francisco, Amelia Dunne Hookway of Chicago, and Julia Harrington Duff of Boston— led campaigns to secure professional status for teachers and reverse the de-skilling process.

Despite the ability of Irish-American women to meet the higher entrance requirements for a teaching job and their leadership in teacher unions and school governance, by the second decade of the twentieth century, earlier gains made in teachers' job security and professional autonomy had eroded. As school bureaucracies were "rationalized" under the aegis of "progressive" reform, tenure and pension rights were revoked. The first equal-pay-for-equal-work law anywhere, won by San Francisco school principal Kate Kennedy in 1874, was unsuccessfully challenged the very next year by school authorities. The law was eventually rescinded in the 1890s. Despite San Francisco's pioneering role in securing equal pay for equal work, salary equity there was reinstated only after the Second World War.[9] Marriage bars preventing wives from getting (or keeping) a teaching job were also put in place in the twentieth century. While Chicago school principal Amelia Dunne remained at her job even after her marriage to William Hookway in 1901, by the late 1920s, a new generation of teachers in Boston, San Francisco, and Chicago, as well as in Ireland, had to retire permanently from the class-room when they married.

The rise of the talented to the position of "principal teacher" overseeing large faculties, staffs, and students in a school was also curtailed in the early decades of the twentieth century. Henceforward, normal school–trained women, primarily Irish-American, in Boston, San Francisco, and Chicago were confined to dead-end teaching jobs, while university-trained male "experts" were hired as administrators to oversee them at much higher pay. In 1917, the United States Department of the Interior's summary of its study of San Francisco's schools went so far as to recommend that, in the interest of introducing more "rigid standards of thinking, . . . the proportion of men principals should be increased, and the present unwise policy of appointing all principals from the [largely female] San Francisco corps of teachers should be abolished."[10] Teacher input into curriculum was also silenced. In Chicago, the teacher councils' inaugurated in the 1890s were abolished despite Superintendent Ella Flagg Young's attempts to revive them. Teachers' councils elsewhere, following the Chicago model, also fell silent under the onslaught of greater administrative control from educational progressives.[11] The luster of teachers' minds seemed to fade as they were reduced to the status of hired hands.

By 1920, not only had teachers' fledgling professionalism waned, their paychecks began disappearing as city governments faced fiscal crises exacerbated by the tax loopholes for the very rich that Margaret Haley had opposed. Teachers in Boston, San Francisco, and especially Chicago endured "payless paydays" during the next two decades, as bankrupt municipalities scrambled to pay the more menacing police and firemen instead.[12]

Teachers debated among themselves how to best confront these reversals of their hard-won fortunes. Many, citing the professionalism of their work, insisted that teachers should campaign for reforms outside the classroom but remain on the job at any cost. After all, they argued, even if many of the rights of the profession were being contested, the social responsibilities of teachers were unassailable and unavoidable. In fact, it was this very responsibility that was the basis for their claim to professional status in the first place. Others argued for more direct action to preserve teachers' professional and economic rights. Since the only really effective weapon teachers had against their diminishing professional status was refusing to work in the classroom until their demands were met, this group argued for public demonstrations, insisting that the ultimate weapon, the strike, was a perfectly legitimate collective action for otherwise powerless teaching professionals.

The debate in the early twentieth century over whether or not teachers were professionals and whether or not professionalism precluded striking compelled Margaret Haley to confront her adversaries in the National Education Association. Haley had already temporarily liberated the NEA from the control of male university presidents and school administrators when, in 1901, she became the first woman ever to speak from the floor of an NEA annual meeting. Her motivation, she later wrote, came from a belief in "the right of my sex to equal representation in an organization where [women] bore the heavier burden of responsibility and obligation."[13] Since women teachers composed 90 percent of the NEA's membership, Haley's action gave them a voice in that organization for the first time.

In 1904, Haley became the first woman to make a formal address at an NEA annual meeting. Her speech, "Why Teachers Should Organize," was a call to arms against the entrenched powers controlling public education. Haley's landmark NEA address made clear her distaste for the rule of "experts" at the expense of democracy in the schools. "If the American people cannot be made to realize and meet their responsibility to the public school," she began, "no self-appointed custodians of the public intelligence and conscience can do it for them." Attributing the sorry state of American public education to abysmal teaching conditions rather than to teachers, Haley continued with a list of correctives that included better teacher pay, tenure, improvements in the classroom physical environment, and increased public respect for teachers. Drawing on the work of educational theorists of the day, such as fellow-Chicagoan John Dewey, Haley stressed the importance of teachers in uplifting the moral as well as the intellectual level of society as a whole. She concluded her speech with a ringing declaration in support of labor unions—not only for industrial workers, but also for teachers. "It will be well indeed if the teachers have the courage of their convictions," she declared, "and face all that labor unions have faced with the same courage and perserverance."[14]

As the number of Irish Americans in teaching increased and as school systems in big cities expanded, educational leaders carefully examined the issues surrounding teacher professionalism in terms of their training and impact on pupils. As early as the 1880s, for instance, when the career of Margaret Haley was just beginning, Chicago Superintendent of Schools George Howland read a series of papers before his assembled teachers that he later gathered into a book, *Moral Training in the Public Schools*.[15] A teacher's moral character was the best way to demonstrate the value of morality to children, he began. "We can conceive of no more sacred duty . . . than that of choosing the teachers of our public schools," he continued, and although schoolteachers had been ridiculed "throughout the ages," teachers, "above all others, mold the character of the young—the future of all society." Therefore, he concluded, "This school-keeping of ours is not a make-shift . . . means for tiding over an unforeseen bar in our business career, a ready resort from the tedium of housekeeping . . . but a high calling. . . ."[16]

Howland also championed his teachers. "There can be no more dangerous heresy for our schools than the sentiment which would depreciate the scholarly attainments and character of our teachers . . . ," he insisted; and, even with inadequate pay, "there are good teachers enough—lovers of the work—to fill our positions." Therefore, "In the character and conduct of the teacher is the strength and hope of the school, and . . . our calling [will] become a profession when we do professional work, and our profession [will] be a noble one when we do its duties nobly." Howland also reminded his listeners that, "The teacher of teachers, the school principal, is as important as the individual teacher in training the intellect and developing the moral character of students. . . ." While he believed that normal schools were vital to a teacher's education, "on-the-job experience, under the guidance of the school principal, [is] still the best training for teachers."[17] Rising up through the ranks from beginner to principal was therefore an appropriate and expected reward for the dedicated teacher in the classroom.

In 1911, less than a quarter of a century after the publication of Howland's thoughts on the teaching profession, a less sympathetic observer, Lotus Delta Coffman of the Columbia University Teachers College, published his influential *The Social Composition of the Teaching Profession*. Since the teacher was the mediator between the pupil and the outside world, Coffman bemoaned the declining social status and manners of teachers, a decline he believed resulted from the changeover in teaching personnel. As well-born young women left the inadequately paid "calling" of Howland's day for more lucrative jobs in retail sales and offices, working-class ethnic women took their places in the classroom. Teachers remained crucial to the success of the schools, nevertheless; and knowing the teacher's background, motives, and values was of the utmost importance.[18]

In a thinly-veiled Darwinian attack on the proliferation of Irish-American teachers, Coffman warned that "the differences in race . . . , social class, . . . economic station, . . . intellectual maturity, [and] . . . academic and professional training" between the native-born, Anglo-Protestant teaching force of old and the new ethnic teachers were major problems in contemporary education. Ominously, "the classes with the least income are contributing the largest percentages of teachers . . . ," he wrote, because the "native stock" are the least "fecund" of all the groups from which the new teachers originate. "The kind of people we get in teaching," Coffman advised his readers, "necessarily affects the kind of teaching we get."[19] Getting a teaching job, Coffman continued, "is comparatively easy, . . . a high standard of fitness is not universally required. . . ." Nevertheless, despite the lamentable deterioration of the teaching stock, he concluded that "professionalization is still the ideal." Nevertheless, he warned, "the lower [teaching] positions are supplied with the young, the immature, the poorly equipped," creating a teaching force "recruited from large families [and therefore] the transmission of our best culture is turned over to a group of [the] least favored and cultured because of its economic station. . . . In other words, the intellectual possessions of the race are by rather unconscious selection left to a class of people who by social and economic station, as well as by training, are not eminently fitted for their transmission."[20] Since Irish Americans had larger households than native-born Americans in 1911, and since Irish-American women were the single largest non-Protestant ethnic group in elementary teaching by that year, Coffman's targets are clear.[21]

Two decades later, in 1929, Mary Ledger Moffett's *The Social Background and Activities of Teachers College Students* offered a response to Coffman's complaints about the changing composition of American teachers. In this study of 1,080 teacher college students from throughout the United States, Moffett noted that, in the years between 1911 (the year Coffman published his book) and the 1920s, the number of teaching jobs and the number of trained teachers both rose. In fact, those years had seen a dramatic improvement in teacher preparation, as more rigorous normal school and teacher college courses of study replaced high school training classes and summer review courses. As teacher training standards rose, the percentage of American-born daughters of foreign-born parents who became teachers had also risen. Teacher colleges, Moffett concluded, can "provide [teacher trainees with] . . . training . . . in the necessary cultural background and experience and social abilities . . . [needed] to prepare them for meeting the demands as progressive educators," even if these trainees came from culturally deprived backgrounds.[22] Extrapolating from Moffett's study, it seems that the republic's hope for its educational system was not doomed by the influx of Irish Americans into the teaching force.

Despite Moffett's findings, complaints like Coffman's about new teachers from the prolific ethnic working class reached receptive ears among the members of urban school boards. In the 1890s, there was a resurgence of anti-Catholic feeling among many San Franciscans; and in Boston and Chicago attempts were made to restrict the number of Catholics, largely Irish, among newly hired teachers by setting quotas on the entrance of Catholics into city normal schools. As late as 1910, Chicago's schools still retained vestiges of their Protestant origins by requiring the reading of the King James version of the Bible in the classroom.[23]

Rulings such as these reflect the anxiety felt by mostly Protestant upper–middle class school board members and education professors over the flood of non-Protestant, often Irish-Catholic, working-class women into teaching. In addition, as the debate over the proper curriculum for "Americanizing" the masses of foreign children inundating urban classrooms intensified everywhere in the country in the late nineteenth and early twentieth centuries, school boards worried even more about the religious, cultural, and political loyalties of teachers. Since teachers were on the forefront of the Americanization process, they had to demonstrate their full compliance with the values of their school committee employers. But, school committee members worried, could non-Protestant daughters of the foreign-born working-class be trusted to indoctrinate their students with proper "American" values?

To meet this end, quotas designed to stem the tide of Irish Americans into Chicago's teaching force were attempted. Despite these efforts, more and more graduates of the city's Catholic high schools entered the Normal School from the turn of the twentieth century on, rendering quotas on Catholics entering teaching increasingly irrelevant. Another way to control the potentially subversive impact of the new teaching force was to reduce its already shaky status as a profession and thereby increase the amount of direct supervision over the classroom teacher. In fact, just as larger and larger numbers of Irish-American women entered teaching at the turn of the last century, new methods of teacher training increasingly segregated those who worked in the classroom from those who administered the schools, even at the level of the school's "principal teacher." No longer would teachers receive a liberal arts education. Future elementary teachers, mostly female and increasingly Irish-Catholic, would now acquire skills in teaching methods for elementary school subjects only at the "training schools" located in the school districts where they would teach.[24] Education in the liberal arts was reserved for the (mostly Anglo-Protestant) males destined for high-school and college teaching or for school administration. The stereotypical "failed" gentlemen teachers of old had been replaced by college-trained male "experts" in the newly structured educational systems of the urban United States.

While the newly expanded teacher training allowed the daughters of Irish immigrants to enter the teaching force, career mobility for female teachers was a casualty of this new pedagogical differentiation. City teachers were now separated not only by sex and ethnicity but also by education and class from even their immediate supervisors.[25] Retiring school administrators with years of on-the-job experience, such as San Francisco's Kate Kennedy and Chicago's Amelia Dunne Hookway, were replaced by male college graduates. The mostly female elementary school teachers were proletarianized by their newly limited schooling, transformed into "hands" to be managed by better and more liberally educated male minds.

Battleground

Teachers were not passive in the face of their de-skilling, however. While their male supervisors professionalized, the female teaching force unionized.[26] Here too, Irish Americans led the way. The CTF organized the city's elementary teachers into an effective lobby for better wages, working conditions, and professional autonomy. Elementary teachers in other American cities soon followed suit and, as in Chicago, Irish-American women led the ranks of teacher activists. In New York City, for example, Kate Hogan and Grace Stachan founded the Interborough Association of Women Teachers (IAWT) in 1906.[27]

Unlike the CTF, the IAWT was a single-issue union, focused on improving the salaries of its members. Comparing New York unfavorably to the "cities in the great free, progressive West" like Chicago and San Francisco, Strachan noted that in 1910, New York's male teachers earned an average salary of $900 a year while the city's female teachers earned only a yearly average of $600. Furthermore, men earned $105 extra for each additional year of experience compared to women's annual increment of only $40. Calling for equal pay for women teachers, Strachan also demanded an end to the inequality of sex inherent in the newly differentiated teacher training system, which had de-skilled the city's elementary school teaching force.[28] By the mid-1920s, the majority of New York's public elementary school teachers had joined the IAWT, forcing the school board and the state legislature to make concessions in favor of pay equity.[29] Despite the success of organized teachers in New York, between 1910 and 1920, San Francisco's elementary teachers faced severe inroads into the equal-pay-for-equal-work law that Kate Kennedy had spearheaded through the California legislature a quarter of a century before.

Chicago's teachers also faced diminishing returns for their work by the second decade of the twentieth century, but they remained divided on the best way to combat the new school administration dictates; and the apparently intractable contradiction between teachers as workers and as professionals persisted into the twentieth century. There were also ethical dimensions beyond bread-and-butter issues in the debate over teacher professionalism. Underscoring this dilemma was the question of whether or not teachers had responsibilities to their calling and to the wider community that superceded their own employment circumstances. If teaching was a profession with certain altruistic duties, did teachers have the right to strike in order to secure workplace demands? Furthermore, if they were professionals, shouldn't teachers, and teachers alone, be the judges of their professional standards, their fees, and their clients? Peer review, not supervisors or strikes, should be the mechanism for making decisions in the workplace. If, on the other hand, teachers were workers, with salaries and working conditions set by their employers, did they have the right to bargain collectively and even resort to striking if all else failed to resolve disagreements?[30]

The impasse between the two views of the teacher as a professional and as a worker stemmed from the fact that teachers were seeking two different forms of professional recognition, each based on different ethical grounds. One argument rested on a teacher's natural rights. Gaining equal pay and pay increases could be justified because teachers, along with all other individuals, had the "natural" right to a livelihood. As Americans, teachers also possessed the inalienable right of revolution if their natural rights were taken from them. A related argument for teacher professionalism was based on a theory that, even if teachers were ethically required to fulfill their social responsibilities before looking to their individual rights, it was still unfair and unwise for their society to underpay and otherwise poorly treat them, since bad working conditions drove the more talented out of the profession and lowered the overall quality of the school system as a whole. If teachers lost, everyone lost. Society, after all, couldn't "win" unless the schools succeeded.

The second ethical dimension complicating the claim of professional status for teachers stemmed from the nature of the work. If teaching was a calling requiring a devotion to duty above and beyond salary, low pay could be justified, especially if the larger society, and perhaps teachers themselves, saw teaching as a natural extension of a woman's biological destiny as a mother. Teaching, in other words, both conforms to and confirms a woman's "nature." It would be unethical and even unnatural for a teacher to forgo her duty for her private gain. After all, no decent mother would steal bread from her children. In this sense, teaching's professionalism stemmed from a Kantian categorical imperative—woman as mother, an "angel in the house," immune to the vagaries of circumstance.

Opponents of teacher professional advance often pitted these two, seemingly contradictory, versions of teaching ethics against the women employed in city classrooms. By appealing to the "natural" self-sacrifice "inherent" in females, adversaries could and did divide and conquer the teaching force, forestalling collective action based on unity. As a result, by the second decade of the twentieth century, while teachers in the CTF saw their professionalism as already defunct and therefore felt less compunction against striking, NEA members sought to preserve the remnants of their professional status at all costs, even if it required tremendous self-sacrifice in terms of pay and autonomy. Both groups faced an internal contradiction in their definition of professionalism. The would-be strikers were willing to give up professional trappings to regain professional status. The nonstrikers were unwilling to give up professional trappings, even if it meant losing their professional status altogether—not to mention their paychecks.

Each of these ethical points of view also offered a different definition of a profession. The strikers accepted the commercial view of a profession, seeing themselves as individuals with a product to sell, entering into a contract with those who wished to purchase that product. Beyond the fundamental ethical obligation of not defrauding the buyer, the professional "seller" was perfectly justified in withholding her product if her sales conditions were not met, just as a doctor or a lawyer who refused to take a case often did. In many ways, this view can be seen as an unintended but logical extension of the political economy of the marketplace espoused by the founders of the Irish national schools in the 1830s—men with whom Margaret Haley and her CTF membership would not have been comfortable consorting had they realized this connection. The nonstrikers, on the other hand, held a normative view of a profession. Unlike their more commercially minded colleagues, they believed that, as professionals, teachers had an obligation beyond self-interest to provide the benefits of their expertise to society. This altruism, in short, is the essence of having a professional status. A professional's expertise is governed by rules that supercede those of the marketplace.

The dilemma facing teachers over the best ways to gain, maintain, and expand their professional status and to reap the benefits such a status would bestow, in terms of autonomy and marketplace power, can also be understood in terms of two approaches to ethical decision-making: value maximizing and rights-based reflection. A value maximizing approach asked teachers to decide which outcome of their actions provided the greatest good for the greatest number. In order to make this decision, teachers would first have to determine who the "greatest number" were: teachers themselves? Teachers and their pupils? Society at large?

A rights-based approach to determining the professionalism of teaching required that two types of rights be considered: natural rights and conventional rights. Natural rights are fundamental to the human being and are not based on any particular social code of values. Conventional rights, on the other hand, derive from social rules particular to a time and place. Did the women teaching in the classrooms of Chicago, Boston, and San Francisco at the beginning of the twentieth century have rights in terms of their workplace duties and status; and if so, what was the source of these rights: nature or nurture? For example, do all workers, professional or not, have inalienable rights such as those enshrined in the Constitution, which Americanizers required teachers to master and teach in the classroom, even after they voluntarily stepped over the threshold of the workplace?

According to this line of thought, if teachers wanted to challenge the diminution of their professionalism in the early decades of the twentieth century, they *had to* disobey the conventional norms governing their work in order to do so. They had to take one step backward (threatening to or actually striking) in order to go two steps forward (securing professional autonomy and responsibility). The growing incongruity between outdated professional norms and democratic social values based on the inalienable rights of individuals indicated that these standards were certain to meet challenges.

In Chicago, at least, the dilemma facing teachers over whether or not they should strike ended in the late 1920s. Just as the McAndrew administration tightened the supervision over and diminished the career mobility of teachers, an extraordinary fiscal crisis broke the stalemate over whether or not it was legitimate for teachers to strike: payless paydays. Without pay, even the most reluctant teachers began to rethink their professional ethics.

By 1929, on the eve of the stock market crash that ushered in the Great Depression of the 1930s, Chicago's 550,000 pupils and nearly 14,000 teachers constituted the second largest school district in the country after New York. In that year, the average Chicago elementary teacher made $2,505 for a forty-week year, placing her earnings well above the $1,405 annual average for all full-time employees in the United States. Although the female elementary teacher's pay was less than the $2,757 paid to the city's largely male junior-high teachers or the $3,366 paid to the men teaching in high schools in that year, most of the women working in the lower grades earned comfortable livings. Compared to a doctor's annual average earnings of $5,000 or a lawyer's of $4,500 in that year, however, even the city's highest paid male high school teachers were an "aristocracy of labor" (or even "wage slaves," according to Upton Sinclair) rather than full professionals. The doctors and lawyers and businessmen appointed to the school board, therefore, earned far more on average than the teachers they oversaw.[31]

In addition to their low salaries, Chicago's teachers faced several reversals in their quest to achieve professional status in the years leading up to the Depression. In 1924, Superintendent McAndrew made student testing the gauge of teaching effectiveness, and he placed new importance on teacher punctuality. Furthermore, the average elementary class size of over forty-five pupils in Chicago's schools was among the highest in the United States. In addition to these tangible setbacks, teachers also increasingly resented the general lack of respect shown them by their superiors. By the end of the 1920s, then, Chicago's teachers, even the majority who belonged to the more conservative NEA, recognized that the hard-won gains of previous decades were under siege. The more militant minority who belonged to the AFT, the national teachers' union founded in Chicago in 1916, and the mostly Irish-American female elementary teachers in its Local Number One, the CTF, were even more resentful. Ethnicity and sex, however, continued to divide teachers.[32]

The AFT, like the CTF before it, sought to raise teaching's professional status by raising the salaries, job security, and working conditions of teachers. It also professed a no-strike policy. By 1924, a truce existed between the schools' administrators and teachers, enhanced by a new harmony between unions and administrators capped by that year's revoking of the 1915 Loeb Rule outlawing teacher unions. When McAndrew was replaced as superintendent by William Brogan in 1927, relations between teachers and administrators reached a new high. By the end of the 1920s, union membership had declined and the schools enjoyed a relative peace.[33]

That peace was shattered when school funding evaporated on the eve of the Depression. Since Chicago's schools were funded by its property taxes, and since many of the largest businesses in the city were able to avoid paying these taxes, the over-extended and corruption-ridden school budget descended into the red. Although Margaret Haley's attempts to reform the school tax structure began in 1926, large corporations refused to pay any city taxes until the courts settled the issue. As a result, by the end of the decade, Chicago faced a tax deficit of catastrophic dimensions, and school funding dried up. Among the casualties of this disaster were teachers' salaries. Despite some friendly overtures to teachers, in 1931 the new mayor, Anton Cermak, cut the school budget even further in the hope of avoiding an entire fiscal collapse. Cermak's cuts were not across the board, however. School janitors and other school employees with clout in the city's Democratic machine kept their salaries, but teachers' pay was drastically reduced. After Cermak's assassination in 1933, the new mayor, Edward J. Kelly, began another round of education cuts, firing ten percent of the existing teaching force while making other draconian reductions in school finances.[34]

Most important of all, between January 1931 and May 1933, the monthly wages of Chicago's 14,000 teachers were paid on time only three times. Otherwise, their pay arrived weeks and even months late. Furthermore, their pay was in school board–issued "scrip" rather than dollars. The scrip's value was calibrated to future tax-arrears payments and could only be exchanged for less than face value. As a result, teachers could choose between lower scrip salaries or no salaries at all during the worst years of the Depression. Further pay cuts, sometimes disguised as shorter school years and hours, continued to erase teacher economic security in the 1930s. When teachers' salaries began arriving late or not at all, Chicago's teachers' unions (there were now several affiliated with the AFT or the CTF) did little to demand redress for their members. The public, sorely pressed itself by the economic crisis facing the entire city, also did little to help the teachers, whom many working-class citizens saw as privileged white-collar workers, usually female, who could not possibly be in desperate need. Once again, the ambiguous social and economic status of teachers worked against them, their opponents this time coming from the bottom up rather than from the top down. [35]

Despite their desperate need, most teachers—and their unions—refused to strike for their lost wages. But, gradually, as the crisis became ever more desperate, more and more teachers, especially the younger hires, became radicalized. In 1932, these radicals met to discuss the possibility of striking. Despite their newfound militancy, however, like most Americans at the time, Chicago's teachers remained conservative in their critique of the prevailing political and economic system. Few wished to overthrow capitalism. Most wanted to benefit from it instead. Reform, not revolution, was their goal.[36]

Chicago's teachers finally rebelled and took their cause to the streets in the spring of 1933, when they learned that, while *they* would not be paid, school janitors were set to receive $5 pay increases. Decades of professionalism had apparently gotten them nowhere. The first salvo of this open war occurred on April 5 when 50,000 Chicago students went on strike to demand payment for their teachers. The student walk-outs began in schools with high Irish-American populations and sparked riots throughout the city, which police found difficult to quell. Three days later, on April 8, teachers themselves took to the streets and marched on the opening ceremonies of the "Century of Progress" World's Fair in Grant Park on the city's lake front. Teachers also organized boycotts of newspapers, stores, banks, and other city institutions that had shown hostility to their cause. On April 24 (a non-school day), 5,000 teachers again gathered in Grant Park. Dividing themselves into five groups, they marched downtown towards the five banks that had refused to pay property taxes and had therefore helped cause the school fiscal crisis at the root of teachers' current woes. Storming the banks, teachers tossed papers, threw ink, and did other damage. One group broke windows and ransacked their target. Police were sent to break up the attackers, but teachers fought back. When the fighting was over, police as well as teachers were found injured.[37]

The many Irish-American teachers at the forefront of these battles found support in long-time school board member and former teacher Helen

Maley Hefferan. Called a "stormy petrol" in a 1953 newspaper obituary, Hefferan had long been known as the "public school Catholic," since both she and her children were all Chicago schools graduates, an unusual accomplishment in a city where the vast majority of Catholic children were enrolled in the largest parochial school system in the nation. After her graduation from Chicago High School at the age of eighteen in 1883, and from Cook County Normal School two years later, Hefferan's talents were immediately recognized by Chicago Normal School principal and educational innovator Francis Parker, who hired her as a training teacher—a post she held until her marriage to Chicago lawyer William Hefferan in 1892. The mother of three children, Helen Hefferan was also an active Catholic clubwoman who used her considerable political and organizational skills to win a seat on the school board in 1923, a seat she held for the next eighteen years.[38]

Hefferan was a founder of the Public Education Association (PEA), an organization seeking greater professional autonomy for classroom teachers, and she fought against the Loeb Rule which had forced the CTF to cut its ties with organized labor. Although she later fell out with the CTF because of her support of Superintendent McAndrew, Hefferan regained teacher support during the payless paydays controversy when she organized a teacher rally at the Chicago Stadium in July of 1933.[39]

Under pressure from sympathetic school board members like Hefferan, and in fear of negative publicity that would compromise the city's "Century of Progress" festivities, Mayor Kelly and the banks were forced to ask the teachers to end their protests in return for all their back pay. The pay was slow to materialize, however; and throughout the summer of 1933, teachers continued to bring their protest to the streets of Chicago. Only when the federal government loaned Chicago over $22 million in August 1934 did the city's teachers receive all their lost pay.[40]

The school crisis of 1929 to 1934 permanently changed the terms of Chicago teachers' dilemma over whether or not to strike. Henceforward, they knew that their professionalism could not survive payless paydays and that carrying their grievances to the streets had indeed been the only way to gain redress. By 1937, the fractionalized teachers' unions in the city combined to form the 5,441-member-strong Chicago Teachers Union (CTU), Local No. 1 of the AFT. Within a year, membership had risen to 8,500, making the CTU the largest teachers' union in the United States.[41]

CHAPTER 7

"The One Thing They Can't Take Away"

While Chicago's teachers struggled to keep their professional rights and se-
curities in the early decades of the twentieth century, Irish girls like Delia
McNeela Tully saw the classroom as the route to a better life. In fact, when
Delia returned to her childhood school in County Mayo in 1999 at the age
of ninety-eight, the local newspaper reminded its readers that if her school
"continues to produce graduates of the calibre of Mrs. Tully, then its future
is very bright."[1]

In her own handwritten memoirs, Delia recalled her Irish school days.[2]
"Starting the first grade at Our Lady of Mercy School was an exciting
day . . . my hair was in braids, and I wore a knee-high dress and black high-
top shoes. Mother . . . gave me a piece of bread and butter for lunch. . . .
The Sisters of Mercy operated [the] school, and I walked the two miles [to
school] with my brothers and sisters. When Sister rang the bell, we lined up
in single file and without a sound. School started promptly at 9:00 A.M. . . .
[W]e were drilled over and over in the three R's—Reading, Writing, and
Arithmetic. There was no nonsense. The nuns believed in punishment and
did not want us to be spoiled. We would be cracked with a cane for
just about anything. . . . If we looked at her crooked, were two minutes
late, or did not hold the pen correctly . . . , she would crack both palms. . . .

We took great pride in our handwriting, and we would methodically copy the alphabet from our writing book. . . . Time was set aside during the school day for sewing and knitting. At an early age I learned to sew and knit.

"I needed school shoes," Delia continues. "My parents did not have much money, and store-bought shoes were very dear . . . [but] Mother enjoyed buying us shoes and other little things . . . with the egg and butter money. . . . After the rosary [each evening], Mother lit the kerosene lamp. We all sat together at the kitchen table and did homework. . . . Father enjoyed reading and encouraged us to be good readers. By lamplight and the fireplace flames, we took turns reading out loud. . . ."

After graduating from Intermediate School in 1918, Delia was ready to emigrate. "I had often considered leaving Ireland," she writes, "but a certain incident helped my decision. . . . Mother . . . said to take a quick peek at a farmer who wanted to marry me. He was nothing to look at. . . . When I told Mother I was not interested, she said she'd rather see me going to America and make my own match. . . . [M]y mind was made up. If I didn't get out of there, I'd be stuck on a farm with some old geezer for the rest of my life. . . . There were no opportunities and nothing for me in Ireland. . . . The ambitious always left. . . . I was 21 when I left Ireland . . . on May 27, 1922."

Delia quickly found a job in Chicago, and Irish Chicago's social whirl also hastened her adjustment to her new life. In fact, she first saw her Mayo-born husband Michael Tully by going to weekend Irish dances. Tully, she remembers, "was a nice-looking man [with] a good job with the Chicago Fire Department. . . . And besides, he was a good dancer, and I loved to dance! . . .We were married on April 23, 1927. . . . The day I left Ireland was a sad day, but I never regretted my decision." In fact, one of Delia's proudest days in America was when her daughter, Irene Tully Ryan, became the principal of a Chicago school. Despite teachers' uphill fight for professional status, their Irish mothers basked in their achievements.[3]

By the time Delia married, the "golden age" of upward mobility for classroom teachers was over. Payless paydays, school system bankruptcies, and a renewed urgency on the part of school boards to limit or dismantle teacher gains made in earlier years had taken their toll. Unlike Margaret Haley, a new generation of Irish Americans entering teaching after 1930 could not become Patrick Henrys for their own professional liberties and financial rights. As salary levels plummeted and job openings disappeared, getting a teaching job at all became even more difficult.

Reversal of Fortune

In 1899, Sr. Mary Justitia Coffey, the daughter of Irish immigrants to Massachusetts, and her Sisters of Charity of the Blessed Virgin Mary opened St. Mary's High School in Chicago. For the next several decades, Sr. Justitia's largely Irish-American St. Mary's graduates earned a citywide reputation for passing the stringent annual entrance examinations for the city's normal school. Their success was so stunning that the school board threatened to impose a quota on the number of Sr. Justitia's students allowed to take the examination in the first place.[4] Since graduation from the normal school was a prerequisite for getting a teaching job in Chicago, denying entry to Sr. Justitia's graduates would be a severe blow to maintaining the Irish-American majority among the city's teachers.

Undaunted, Sr. Justitia kept St. Mary's tuition affordably low for her largely working-class students and upgraded her teacher-training curriculum to meet the requirements mandated for the public schools. St. Mary's graduates continued to top the lists of qualified teacher aspirants, no matter what new threats to their success school authorities contemplated. Although the school board's quota was never instituted, it is an indication of the desire of many Chicago leaders in the early twentieth century to reverse the influx of Irish Catholic school–trained teachers into the city's classrooms.

In 1930, the Sisters of Charity opened their new women's college on Chicago's far north side. Named after the archdiocesan leader, George Cardinal Mundelein, Mundelein College's first president was none other than Sr. Justitia. Under the direction of Sr. Justitia and her successors, Mundelein College continued to produce graduates destined for teaching jobs in the public schools. Mundelein graduates retained their prominence among the city's teachers throughout the Depression years and beyond.

Yet despite Sr. Justitia's success, by the end of the 1920s, the "golden age" of professional mobility for teachers had waned. The Irish-American normal school–trained female majority in urban classrooms in those years watched hard-won victories in the academic marketplace wither as university-trained administrative "experts" undercut their professional autonomy. Nevertheless, only the advent of the Depression in 1929 halted teachers' four-decades–long professional advance. "Payless paydays" became increasingly common as urban school expenditures plummeted in the aftermath of the stock market crash. Teacher influence over the lessons taught in the classroom also ended in these years with the reintensification of top-down administrative control over curriculum. Tenure and pension rights were curtailed, and a marriage bar preventing wives from remaining in the classroom was put in place on both sides of the Atlantic, so that scarce classroom openings could be reserved for economically displaced men. Leadership roles for women disappeared, too, as experienced female "principal teachers" and curriculum supervisors were replaced by male administrators who had spent little or no time teaching in the classroom. By the 1930s, teachers had been reduced to "hired hands," no longer the financially independent professional "minds" envisioned by their turn-of-the-century predecessors.

Teachers fought back against these reversals by taking their protests to the streets and the courts, and they continued to meet the rising educational standards instituted by restrictive school boards. Ironically, while the possibility of making teaching a lifetime career eroded under the weight of administrative fiat, the qualifications of those entrusted with educating urban youth continued to improve. Nevertheless, the professional status of teachers had been fundamentally sabotaged.

Irish mothers still continued to echo the call of Margaret Haley's mother for freedom through education. Unlike land or even a country, mothers told their offspring, an education could not be taken away by outside forces beyond an individual's control. Chicago teacher Lorraine Xavier Page's mother, Margaret Grady, was one such woman. Page recalls her mother's words: "I may not leave you a lot of money but education is something that can't be taken away from you." Margaret's ambitions, in turn, had been inspired by her aunt Kate, who taught school in Boston between 1890 and 1920. Born in Mullinahone, County Tipperary, Kate followed her brother John to Boston, where she took a teaching job while her brother moved west to Galena, Illinois. John's daughter, Margaret, remembered her Aunt Kate's visits, which required taking a train from Boston to Chicago before boarding a stagecoach for the last leg of the journey to Galena on the Mississippi. Kate was an unconventional woman for her time and place. Although she was an unmarried school teacher, she could afford fashionable hairdos and elaborate dresses. Family lore also remembers the lavish gifts Kate brought to her nieces and nephews living in the river town.[5]

Galway-born Della Mitchell Dowd also repeatedly reminded her daughter, forty-year veteran Chicago teacher Joan Dowd Enright, that education "was the only thing we can leave you that can't be taken away." Della's belief in the value of education was inspired by her Coolpora National School teacher Mrs. Savage, who had drilled her in the basics of reading, writing, and arithmetic before she left for Chicago at age eighteen in 1929. Della's aunt Annie McGreal met her when she arrived in Chicago. Annie had also attended the national school in Coolpora before leaving for America a generation earlier than Della. In 1933, Della married twenty-eight-year-old Galway-native Patrick Joseph Dowd, who had also attended a national school before emigrating to Chicago. By becoming a Chicago teacher, Joan fulfilled her family's educational aspirations.[6]

Patrick Dowd was not the only Irish father to support his offspring's educational advance, even if not all these fathers recalled their own student days with affection. Delia McNeely Tully's husband Michael Tully, for instance, regarded his schooling with a certain ambivalence, according to their daughter, Chicago teacher Irene Tully Ryan. "I started infant class at the Callow School in Foxford, County Mayo, when I was five years old," Tully wrote in his memoirs, "and I remember that day very well. Callow was a national public school that was about a mile away, and I walked there. . . . Before leaving for school, Grandmother gave me a little piece of turf about the size of a brick. Heating the school was very expensive, and so in order to keep expenses down, each child was told to bring a sod of turf from home. The master watched very closely to see if each child had his turf.[7]

"There were 100 children in the school," Tully continued, "with two men teachers for the boys and two women teachers for the girls. . . . We had no individual desks, just long, long tables. . . . Catechism and prayers started the day. . . . For arithmetic each child had his own slate. . . . Mr. Cunningham, the master, rarely smiled, and had a very long pointer hanging from the wall behind, reminding us to behave. . . . In Ireland, the teachers were looked up to and very much respected, and Cunningham, in addition to his salary, was given an acre of land, and his own house. . . ."—riches indeed in the eyes of farm children in turn-of-the-last-century Ireland.[8]

"When [my family] all got together," Tully remembered, "the main topic of conversation was going to America." Because by the early twentieth century there were no job opportunities even for males, "it was an accepted fact that an industrious young person would leave Ireland—the ambitious always left. . . . The day I left Ireland in April, 1915, was a sad day indeed. . . ." After meeting Delia McNeela, however, Tully's life in America began to look up. "By saving carefully, we were able to buy our first home. . . . America . . . enabled me to live a life of comparative luxury from that which my forebears led. And most of all, it offered me, and all like me who were not afraid of an honest day's work, an honest wage, and a chance to hold my head high. . . ."[9]

John Hastings, the father of Chicago teachers Dorothy Hastings Valeo and Betty Hastings O'Connor, also "set the tone and encouraged all of us to love education," Valeo remembers. It was almost a foregone conclusion that we would become teachers." John had spent six years in the local school near his birthplace in County Mayo before settling in Chicago with his widowed mother and five siblings. In 1914, John married County Cork–native Mary Ann Hurley and saw his daughters Dorothy and Betty graduate from the Chicago Teachers College and later earn graduate degrees. The sisters taught for over thirty years apiece in Chicago's public schools. Their brother, John Hastings, Jr., spent far fewer years in school than his sisters, however. Instead, he left the classroom to become a steamfitter, choosing an income over advanced education.[10]

The educational legacy of the immigrant generation became important in the lives of Irish America's sons after the stock market crash in 1929. When the Depression forced businesses to retrench, they stopped hiring the boys who had, until that time, been willing to leave school early to take jobs that would lead them into the respectable working class. Prevented from finding paid work in a shrinking economy and encouraged by their mothers and sometimes their fathers too, more and more sons stayed in school in hope of eventually finding steady jobs in urban classrooms. Despite the low pay, teaching remained an avenue of upward mobility to Irish-American sons as well as daughters in Boston, San Francisco, and Chicago well into the twentieth century.

"Radical New Experiences"

The Depression's impact on the job market and the eventual outbreak of war in 1939, in fact, propelled William Nolan into the lower middle class through teaching in Lynn, Massachusetts, following the route pioneered by his older sister Mary. Although two of his five brothers graduated from high school, Nolan alone among his brothers earned a four-year college degree.

Nolan had been unable to find full-time work after graduating from high school in 1929. His mother altered his fate one afternoon in early September 1930. When he returned home from a Labor Day picnic in time to get ready for his Olympia Theater usher's job that night, Nolan recalls, his mother "was waiting for me. . . . 'How do you like your job?' she asked me. I told her it was O.K., but I did not count on it as a life's career, and then she popped her big question: 'How would you like to go back to English [High School] for a post-graduate year?'" Mirroring Amelia Dunne's interest in her brother Peter Finley's educational advance, Nolan's "sister Mary had suggested it. She thought I should go back, take some college prep courses, and apply for admission to Salem Normal School. . . . I was stunned.[11]

"The Wednesday after Labor Day was the first day of school for the 1930–1931 school year," Nolan recalls. "I felt quite light-hearted walking along the [Lynn] Common on my way to register at English. . . . I chose English instead of Classical High School," Nolan explains, because of, "the economic ambitions and fears of Mary Ann Donovan Nolan, my mother. Lynn Classical was the elite high school in Lynn. Only students who were college-bound elected Classical over the more 'practical' Lynn English. My sister . . . Kathleen graduated from the secretarial course at English in 1926, and immediately was hired. . . . It was this last stroke of early employment that convinced my mother that I should also try the commercial course as an entree into the world of commerce. . . . And so, when I made my course selections at the end of the seventh grade year, I elected bookkeeping rather than Latin. . . . If one chose Latin, he was college-bound." Additionally, Nolan took classes in English and penmanship. "I also elected Spanish, . . . civics[,] and general science." Nevertheless, he insists, "Had I been able to read the signs, I would have dropped my commercial aspirations, talked my way into first-year Latin, and aimed for Classical High School. Any A's I picked up that year were in college credit courses, not English, but in Spanish and civics."

Nolan's education was not confined to the classroom. "On my own," he tells us, "I read Coleridge's *Rime of the Ancient Mariner,* which I found fascinating." Despite his mother's assurances, Nolan remembers that he "was not really 'sold' on my planned . . . accounting course at Lynn English." In fact, "a faint hope that I could get into college some day was straying around my sub-conscious. I recall thinking: 'What a fine thing if I could write a series of academic or scientific degrees after my name, like some of the authors inscribed in the title pages of the books I had read.' Consequently, I signed up for second year Spanish and an extra history course as electives. I was also interested in art, and fancied myself as an amateur cartoonist. A nebulous thought about becoming a commercial artist or even a newspaper cartoonist had formed somewhere in the deep recesses, but there was no commitment to the thought. I wonder about people who at an early age declare: 'I'm going to be a lawyer!' or judge, or actor, or teacher or some other fairly definite goal. I never had that experience. I just drifted."

In February 1931, however, Nolan's fate again changed. Miss Lovejoy, the librarian at English who doubled as a guidance counselor," he writes, "called me in for an interview. We went over my grades and ascertained that I had the requisite credits for admission to Salem [Normal School]. The requirements for Salem were as rigid as those for any higher institution for learning in the Boston area, but the costs of a Salem education were far less than those at Harvard, Tufts, or even Boston University. I believe the tuition charge at this state school was twenty dollars a semester. . . . In July [1931], I received my letter of acceptance. . . ." During that first year, "The state legislature enacted a bill changing the name of Salem Normal School to Salem State Teachers College and extended the junior-high teacher-training course [in which both Nolan and his future wife, Janet Moakley, were enrolled] to a four-year course leading to a bachelor of science degree. . . . I looked forward to some radical new experiences in this ultra-conservative environment."

Nolan's Salem experiences were indeed radically new. Salem was a "predominantly female school," he tells his reader. "There were about four hundred fifty girls and only fifty men enrolled among the student body. . . . As a normal school, it specialized in training teachers for elementary education (a two-year course), junior high education (a three-year course), and commercial high school teaching (a four-year course). It also trained a group in a one-year course in special education. When it became designated as a college, all courses became four-year courses, with the exception of the elementary course, which was extended one year to make it a three-year course. However, elementary education students were allowed to take an extra year of training in order to qualify for a B.S. degree.

"My first introduction to the other students at Salem was in the opening day chapel exercises," Nolan remembers. "For this ceremony, the faculty sat in over-sized chairs arranged in two rows on the auditorium stage.

Behind a podium at front center was Dr. J. Asbury Pitman, a Maine native who was president of the college. . . . The main decor of the auditorium was a ring of Greek statuary arranged around the perimeter of the hall. A board at the front announced the numbers of the hymns to be sung at chapel that day. Hymn books were available in the racks attached to the backs of chairs. . . . Tall, cathedral-like windows lined the two sides of the auditorium, . . . partially obscured by the rambling ivy that covered the exterior of the building. Talk about separation of church and state. That Madeline O'Hair person would have had a field day! "The exercises opened with Dr. Pitman reading a passage from the Bible," Nolan continues, "and then he delivered his homily and called for announcements. . . . I used the time during Dr. Pitman's homily to look the place over, taking in the faculty members and cataloguing the pretty girls."

Nolan's "first class of the day was at the Horace Mann Training School, an adjunct to the college. . . . Before the day was over, I made the acquaintance of . . . [a] girl who had a book . . . I was trying to get. [She] was working industriously at one of the long tables [in the library]. I slithered in beside her and struck up a conversation, hoping to share the book. She was quite pretty, and had a lively, infectious smile. She told me her name was Janet Moakley. . . . I thought she was quite energetic and yet very serious. She seemed to be full of fun, and I still think so nearly fifty years later."

"At Salem," Nolan explains, "all classes were assigned to subjects as a group. If you were in Junior High II, for example, you had the same classmates in every assigned class. My schedule called for courses in biology, education, psychology, history, mathematics, and English Lit. (In the second semester, we took geography and an economics course, as well as a course in composition. We dropped the literature and the history.) It was a strictly structured curriculum, geared to prepare one for teaching any subject taught in a junior high school, with a few [others] thrown in for enrichment. Oh yes, we also had music and art, but the men had no physical education. Strange."

Nolan's introduction to his future career culminated in the spring of 1934, when he made his "first try at classroom teaching. All Salem students went on practice teaching assignments of eight or nine weeks duration during the junior and senior years. In the junior year, we were given assignments at the Horace Mann Training Schools, an adjunct of the college. We reported to either seventh or eighth grade classrooms in groups of four or five, and the teacher-in-charge (supervisor) would place us in one of the three divisions that segregated the higher level pupils from the middle and low echelons. . . . [M]y training mates [and I] reported to Miss Small, the seventh grade supervisor, sometime early in April for our launching into the world of pedagogy.

"Miss Small was intimidating," Nolan recalls. "Her size belied her name, standing about six feet tall and weighing in around one-eighty. I believe she would have given Maxie Baer, the new heavyweight sensation, a good go at it. She was quite dogmatic but she was a good supervisor. She kept us moving. . . . I became a sort of a favorite, much to the exasperation of some of my [female] training associates."

Despite his positive feelings for his first classroom experiences, Nolan did not "remember the names of any of the children in the class, . . . [even though] I was very fond of this class, and I enjoyed this part of my college training. It made me more amenable to the idea of becoming a school teacher. I still thought, however, that I wanted to be a reporter."[12]

During the 1930s, getting a teaching job in Lynn had become highly competitive as the ranks of the unemployed swelled with male graduates of four-year universities unable to find other professional work. In 1935, the year William Nolan graduated from Salem State Teachers College, "the school committee thought it was time to establish some sort of list for the filling of any vacancies that might occur in the secondary level of the Lynn School Department . . . [and] I [was] among the host of Lynn aspirants who signed up for the 1935 examinations. [Aspirants] had to indicate our major interest because we would be placed on that list in accordance with the examination results. We were also allowed a second choice. I thought the matter over and finally decided that I stood the best chance in history and science.

"The examinations were conducted over a period of two days, a Friday and a Saturday, sometime in April. The battery consisted of an educational examination combining ed psych, ed sociology and history of education, a general cultural examination, and the two majors one selected. There would be an interview and personality and experience rating at a later date.

"Everyone was there. There were college graduates who had been out of college since 1930. I saw people who had already passed the bar examinations. There were some well-known football coaches. . . . There were many teachers who already had jobs in the Lynn system . . . interested in transferring from junior high school work into one of the high schools. . . .

I heard estimates ranging from five hundred to over 1000 candidates in attendance."[13]

While Salem's teaching curriculum had prepared him to tackle the educational subjects with confidence, the general cultural examination was "a panic." Nevertheless, Nolan hoped his afternoons among the books in Lynn's Houghton Street Branch Library would pull him through. "Beforehand, I thought that my wild reading background ought to pull me through that one, but bluffing and a smattering of general knowledge, or even a shrewd elimination of improbable choices, was not going to help in cracking this one. . . . In the literary section, the question would mention some odd Scandinavian name or situation, or a Russian one, or Greek, and one was supposed to identify the author or the book title in which the character or event occurred. All very well, just find the Scandinavian, or Russian, or Greek book or author and you had the problem licked. No such thing; for the Scandinavian name, the examination listed *twelve* Scandinavian authors. The same thing for the Russians, the Greeks, the French, the Italians, the Germans, and the British. In art, music, and current events, we got the same treatment. I felt pretty good about the Bible and mythology. I *had* read plenty about those subjects"; however, his Salem days had not prepared him for the more subtle test selections.[14]

"The directions warned one not to guess. . . ," Nolan remembers. "If I were truly honest, I believe I would have passed in a nearly blank booklet. But I did know Tolstoi, Dostoevski, *War and Peace, Anna Karenina,* something about Chekov, Strindberg, Ibsen, Grieg, Maeterlinck, Dante, *The Ring of the Nibelung,* Wagner, the Three "B's" [Bach, Beethoven, and Brahms], and so I took more chances than I probably should have. It was comforting to hear my fellow sufferers moan and groan during the break. . . . I wished I had gone to Harvard." On the other hand, Nolan found the history examinations "much more comforting. I felt I was on familiar ground. But the history classrooms seemed to be the most crowded. I began to wish I had taken some exam in which no one else could possibly have an interest. There really was no such thing; all the classes were crowded. Still, I came out feeling pretty good about my performance. I was a bit apprehensive [however] about all the teachers who were already teaching history taking the examinations alongside me. . . ."[15]

"In science, I had some trepidation. It really was not my field. . . . and most of the other science aspirants had probably majored in physics or chemistry in college. Lawrence McGinn was in this class. He had been a Pinkham scholar at Brown University."[16] While McGinn topped the science list when the teachers' examination results were announced later that year, Nolan came in as number three in science, and number five on the social studies–history list for both junior and senior high school teaching, despite his ivy-league competition. "This was far ahead of my associates," he tells us. "I was proud, but there were no hints of any [teaching] openings."[17]

"Meanwhile, I picked up a job as a night school teacher at Classical High School, teaching Civil Service preparation as part of an adult education program . . . netting $3.50 a night, three nights a week. This munificent stipend, along with what substitute teaching pay I could muster, constituted my earnings for the school year 1935–'36." Lawrence McGinn received the nod for a high school job, pushing Nolan into second place on the science list and into third place on the social studies list. "That list seemed to have all the movement of an ice-age glacier. . . . I was rehired for night school [and] my substitute work had picked up a bit and some weeks I even cleared $25.00 or more."[18]

The glacier finally moved on Nolan's behalf in the fall of 1936, a year after his graduation from Salem. "My mother had received a phone call from the school department and they wanted me for work. . . . [She] told me to put on my best duds and report to [Lynn Schools superintendent Harvey] Gruver at the school administration building. He had a job for me. . . . Another substitute job, I believed, but probably an extended one this time. If one held a substitute assignment for four weeks in succession, he was eligible for full pay. Maybe this was it." But to Nolan's surprise, "It was a regular appointment filling a vacancy created by a leave of absence granted to a Mr. Philip Cashman, who was the science teacher and physical education director at the Cobbet Ungraded School . . . [which] catered to abnormal children, kids with learning or emotional difficulties. Apparently I was now number one on the science list. . . . Mr. Gruver made it look like I had been selected over a couple of other candidates who had received special training in that type of education, but that I had been selected because it was believed I could handle the physical education duties along with the science discipline. 'Those other fellows would not do very well in the gym,' he said.[19]

"I did not care. It was a job, a regular one. . . . I see now that this was an excellent device for getting me off the science list and into a position where the teaching of science was minimal. After all, I had never majored in any science that would make me expert enough to teach a high school discipline. . . . At the time, Lynn had the eighth highest pay scale in Massachusetts, and my annual stipend that first year was a whopping $1700, more than twice that of most starting teachers in the small towns of New England," but no more than Amelia Dunne Hookway earned in Chicago in 1895. Despite the low pay, Nolan was amazed by his combined earnings. "Coupled with my night school pay of $15.00, I took home the magnificent bounty of $57.00 per week, a truly astronomical salary, well beyond my fondest dreams. . . . But it was not easy money," he continues. "That ungraded job was a tough assignment. Emotionally disturbed and sub-par children create constant problems, but I did love the gymnasium work. It was like play to me." Nevertheless, Nolan knew that "the Depression was still with us [and it] was quite evident at our school. The kids had little of the world's prizes. They had little beauty, slight intelligence, and certainly were not from the more affluent classes. They were appealing in their way and tried hard. I am proud to say that I did all I could to help them overcome some of their problems. The ungraded school was sort of a dumping ground for the rest of the system. . . . There were some tough kids at that school, [but the teachers] could maintain discipline with [their] own tough guy act that would raise a blush of envy on the faces of Jimmy Cagney or Edward G. Robinson.

"It was fatiguing to put in a full day and late afternoon [coaching] at Cobbet, and then go out in the evening to teach adult education classes. . . . [A fellow teacher] would drive me home after the junior high basketball practice; I would have dinner, take a nap and then go to my evening school class. . . .[20]" Despite his grueling work schedule, Nolan was proud of his new-found ability to earn a paycheck. "My big interest at the time," he recalls, "was in procuring my first car . . . a spanking new 1937 Plymouth sedan, black of course. . . . I was twenty-five years old and had never left New England. . . . I guess I felt the constraints that precluded the open road for me: money and perfect contentment with the status quo." By July of 1937, however, Nolan's earnings allowed him to tour eastern Canada and enroll at Boston University, "starting in three physical education courses: Philosophy of Physical Ed., Psychology of Physical Ed., and Tests and Measurements in Physical Ed."[21] He received his Masters of Science degree in 1940.

By 1938, the Nolans were all at work and their fortunes had collectively risen. "At summer's end," Nolan writes, "we decided to leave our Linden

Street home. For some time we had been discussing the possibility of leaving [working class] West Lynn—another milestone in the upward mobility process. There were seven [out of the original nine children and two parents] still at home. . . . When we found a house on Sluice Pond [in more affluent East Lynn], we were unanimous in our decision. We got rid of the Linden Street property [where] we had lived . . . since 1924 . . . [but] it was with mixed feelings that we packed up and left for . . . a large white Dutch colonial house with a gambrel roof. . . . It was [in] a woodsy location, abounding in oaks and birches, and it had a large pontoon raft tied to the shore in back, an excellent diving platform and dock for our rowboat." Upward mobility was not without its conflicts, however. "For some time after . . . ," Nolan reveals, "I had dreams about the Linden Street move. Like my feelings, they were a mixed lot of dreams, some of them reflecting a genuine respect for the move, and some reflecting disappointment at finding myself back at the old address. Freud would have made something of this. I would dream there were letters in the mailbox, letters that would never reach me, and it was important that I read them. Other dreams would find me back living in the old house, dejected because I had to return. This latter dream . . . I have had in recent times. . . . We did not break with West Lynn. Our roots were there. . . ."[22]

William Nolan's family had regained its equilibrium by the end of the 1930s, after a decade of widowhood, Depression, and mobility. Despite his family's new-found prosperity, however, Nolan realized that his "perfect contentment with the status quo" would soon end. "I [was] listening to the radio as it lamented about the sell-out of [Czechoslovakia in 1938]," he writes. "It was then I realized that war was inevitable, at least war in Europe. . . . I felt a sudden chill. I was twenty-six years old. . . . I considered this night as the sounding knell that presaged the end of carefree days. I should be more serious about life. Time was racing fast. . . . I catalogued the girls I knew . . . planning on steadying my course. . . . There was only one girl in that pretty line of march who looked like she had real staying power. She would be a lovely wife—pretty, vivacious, intelligent. She would keep her looks for a long time. . . . Also, there would be no cultural conflicts, a minor point as far as I was concerned, but it did make it easier. I wondered where Jan Moakley was. . . . I had seen her only once since graduation in 1935. . . . I thought I should get in touch with her." Nolan called on her and found she was "teaching at the Coolidge School in Watertown. I remained at Cobbet teaching math, social studies, and physical education[, along with] coaching. . . ."[23] After her mother died suddenly of a stroke in early 1941, Janet Moakley and William Nolan married in Cambridge, Massachusetts.

America's entry into the second world war released Nolan from the Lynn schools into the wider world beyond a Lynn classroom or gym. Equipped with a master's degree, Nolan enlisted in a navy officer's training program and remembered the morning he left for basic training: "I found three other fellows waiting for me at the Fargo Building [the Navy's administration center in Boston]. They were disconsolate. . . . We were to take the trip together to Norfolk [Virginia]. We shook hands and left for the South Station. We did not have much to say besides a few banalities. The train was announced. We boarded it, and I settled down at the window seat. . . . I stared glumly out of the dirty car window at a bright and sunny Boston."[24]

Mothers and Sons

The Second World War opened a new chapter in William Nolan's life, ending his Depression-era teaching job and widening his personal, geographical, and career horizons. Despite Nolan's accident of fate, however, mothers in Irish America continued to urge their sons to enter teaching even after the war.

Edward Mueller, for instance, remembers his mother, Julia Coyle, "encourag[ing] me to take the Chicago Normal College entrance exam, and [she] was a constant support during my four years there, including [giving me] car-fare and homemade bread sandwiches." He believes her eight years in the Gortnacor, County Donegal, national school made her a "great believer in education," despite her wariness of the strict Master Cannon, who ruled the boys' classroom next to hers with an iron hand. In 1900, at the age of sixteen, Julia boarded a ship bound for America and worked as a maid in New York City before moving to Chicago where she met and married Edward Mueller in 1907. Both their son Edward and his sister Eleanor Mueller King became proud possessors of college degrees and teaching jobs in Chicago's schools, achievements they believe their mother helped them to make.[25] Retired Chicago teacher John O'Leary, too, credits his own professional success to his Sligo-born mother's belief in the value of education. It was a value Bridget Mulloy O'Leary first encountered in the national school she attended in her native Kerry before she left for the United States.[26]

Dudley Nee, a Chicago teacher since 1956, also stresses the importance of his mother's influence on his career. Born in 1895 near Clonakilty,
County Cork, Maryanne Fleming Nee attended the local national school
there for six years before leaving Queenstown for Pittsburgh in 1912. After
working as a maid in that city, Maryanne married County Galway–native
Dudley Nee in 1922, and the newlyweds moved west to Chicago. Although
Maryanne remembered the harshness meted out by her national school
teachers, she, "did learn how to read, write, and compute," her son tells us.
He recalls that she "read to her six children, and continued to read almost to
the end of her life. . . . She also corresponded faithfully with her family
[back in Ireland] as long as she was able." Maryanne and her husband, who
had attended the national school in Roundstown, County Galway, before he
left for America, also strongly believed that a high school diploma for each
of their children would be a giant advance for the family. By becoming a
Chicago teacher, and later a Chicago school principal, Nee realized his parents' already high educational aspirations.[27]

Mary Lyons O'Brien, mother of former Chicago teacher and city plumbing inspector Thomas O'Brien, was born in 1889 in County Kerry. After
several years in a national school near her birthplace in Knockreagh, she
emigrated to Chicago where she worked as a maid before she met and married fellow Kerry native Dennis O'Brien. Three of their five sons became
Chicago teachers, including Tom, who writes that his mother's educational
legacy lives on in his granddaughter, a Chicago public school teacher.[28]

The careers of Chicago teachers William and Daniel King were also inspired by their Irish mother, Ann Hunt King. Born in County Mayo in 1903,
Ann remembered the talents of the married couple who taught in the
Cloonfarna National School in her native village of Knock. After spending
eight years in school, she left her family of fifteen in 1926 to seek her fortune in Chicago. Ten years later, Ann married Patrick King, and thereafter
fostered the educational achievements of her sons, both of whom earned
master's degrees.[29]

"A Steady Job and Mink Coats!"

The sons of Irish America who entered teaching during and after the Depression decade were following the trail into the educated middle class
forged by their sisters. Chicago teacher Margaret (Peg) Brown Cunning-

ham, for example, remembers her mother, County Tipperary–native Helen Ryan Brown, telling her children that if they "wanted to 'get ahead in this world,' it was important to do our very best in school. . . ." Born in 1888, Helen Ryan spent her girlhood in the Tankerstown National School. "She walked through the fields to get to school which was several miles from home," Cunningham writes. Once there, the "very strict" Master McKeon and his wife passed out the ubiquitous Vere Foster copybooks that Helen never forgot. Helen told her daughter that although her "school days in Ireland were difficult, she was proud to be able to recite poetry and remember all of the words of songs written by [the early nineteenth-century Irish poet] Thomas Moore," which she had memorized in the classroom. Helen emigrated from Cobh [Queenstown] in 1905, working as a "lady in waiting" for a wealthy Chicago family for twelve years until her marriage at age twenty-nine to County Mayo–native Michael Brown. They had three children, all of whom graduated from college.[30]

"[My mother] encouraged me to take the test for admittance to Chicago Teachers College," Cunningham recalls, and her education served her in good stead as she continued teaching even after her marriage in 1944, retiring only in 1987. Her mother told her that teaching was "a noble profession and offered many opportunities. . . . She always admired and respected [my cousins who were teachers]. . . . They had a steady job and mink coats! . . . My mother loved to boast about my working in the Chicago Public Schools." In 1982, Cunningham was elected as one of the ten top teachers in the city's school system. "I have fully enjoyed my career [in] the Chicago Public School System. My mother used to say, 'You should be paying them, never mind they pay you!'"[31]

Legacy

Despite being underpaid and overworked, before the setbacks of the 1920s and 1930s, urban school teachers represented a new direction in the public roles and upward mobility of Irish Americans. Before the expansion of the public schools on both sides of the Atlantic in the late nineteenth century, women had little or no access to jobs that would take them out of the dirt and drudgery of domestic service. Teaching ultimately allowed daughters, and eventually sons, of immigrants to leave the working class and enter the educated lower middle class. While their jobs demanded outward conformity and obedience to their superiors, the teachers staffing urban classrooms fought for recognition of their own intellectual skills and financial futures.

The rapid mobility of Irish Americans—from the immigrants' service to the rich to their own offsprings' service to the poor in city schools—is a telling indication of the importance of teachers' contributions to the Irish adjustment to America. Rather than being footnotes to the history of the Irish in America, teachers are at the center of that experience. The mothers who left Ireland after a few years in the national schools, by themselves and alone, and their children teaching in public school classrooms in Boston, San Francisco, and Chicago at the turn of the twentieth century serve as new models for revisiting the history of Irish America and of women's entrance into the educated professions.

The regression of teachers from being trained "minds" to being mere hired "hands" by the end of the 1920s marks a defeat of epic proportions in the history of American public education and teachers' professional advance. Teaching today remains an occupation with an ambiguous status, just as it was in the nineteenth and twentieth centuries. Although teachers are entrusted with society's future, they occupy an uneasy perch between unionized workers and salaried professionals. They are at once blamed for the ills facing mass public education and, at the same time, they are prevented from becoming free professionals able to shape the parameters of their work. Even though teachers are often held in suspicion and sometimes contempt by the larger society, they are still expected to be selfless servants of their community.

Talented women today have to enter medicine, law, or perhaps academe to enjoy the same social status achieved by their teacher counterparts in the public schools a century ago. Many have done so, and their influx into these "higher" professions has raised some of the same barriers to their continued mobility as those erected to impede the progress of teachers. Despite the ongoing struggle facing professional women in our time, these women are the beneficiaries of the pioneering legacy bequeathed by Irish immigrant servants of the rich who sent their daughters, and eventually their sons, to serve the poor in urban schools.

NOTES

Introduction

1. I am grateful to Professor Robert Scally, Director of New York University's Glucksman Ireland House, for his invitation to speak at the International Conference on Hunger in May 1995, and to Hofstra University Professor Maureen Murphy, who was a boon companion on my first visit to Ellis Island made at that time. I also wish to express my gratitude to the anonymous readers who supported my applications for grants from the British Council, National Endowment for the Humanities, Irish American Cultural Institute, and Loyola University Chicago. The funding given by these agencies greatly facilitated the far–flung research for this book.

2. For the Providence and Boston totals, see Joel Perlmann, *Ethnic Differences: Schooling and Social Structure among the Irish, Italians, Jews, and Blacks in an American City, 1880–1935* (New York: Cambridge University Press, 1988), 55, 56; for the Chicago total, see James W. Sanders, *The Education of an Urban Minority: Catholics in Chicago, 1833–1965* (New York: Oxford University Press, 1977), 131. The San Francisco total is derived from counting the number of women primary and grammar school teachers with Irish last names in 1910 (390 out of a total of 804 teachers, or 49 percent) listed in the "Directory of Teachers," San Francisco Public Schools, *Annual Report of the Board of Education, San Francisco, 1910,* 52–100. I decided whether or not a teacher's last name was Irish by looking it up in Edward McLysaght's classic *The Surnames of Ireland* (Dublin: Irish Academic Press, 1997; 1957). Many of the "English" names surveyed by McLysaght have Irish origins. Despite McLysaght's guidance, however, I chose not to count "English" names if their Irish origins were unclear. In addition, teachers with Irish mothers but non-Irish fathers or husbands could not be counted. As a result, the number of Irish–American women among San Francisco teachers in 1910 offered here may be a significant undercount.

3. See Janet A. Nolan, *Ourselves Alone: Women's Emigration from Ireland, 1885–1920* (Lexington: University Press of Kentucky, 1989). See also Grace Neville,

"Dark Lady of the Archives: Towards an Analysis of Women and Emigration to North America in Irish Folklore," in *Chattel, Servant or Citizen: Women's Status in Church, State, and Society,* ed. Mary O'Dowd and Sabine Wichert (Belfast: The Institute of Irish Studies/Queen's University Belfast Press, 1995), 200–214; Suellen Hoy, "The Journey Out: The Recruitment and Emigration of Irish Religious Women to the United States, 1812–1914," *Journal of Women's History* 6/7 (Winter/Spring 1995): 64–69; David Fitzpatrick, "Women and the Great Famine," in *Gender Perspectives in Nineteenth-Century Ireland: Public and Private Spheres,* ed. Margaret Kelleher and James H. Murphy (Dublin: Irish Academic Press, 1997), 50–69; Maureen Murphy, "The Fionnuala Factor: Irish Sibling Migration at the Turn of the Century," *Gender and Sexuality in Modern Ireland,* ed. Anthony Bradley and Maryann Gialanella Valiulis (Amherst: University of Massachusetts Press, 1997), 85–101; and Deirdre Mageean, "To Be Matched or to Move: Irish Women's Prospects in Munster," and "Making Sense and Providing Structure: Irish-American Women in the Parish Neighborhood," in *Peasant Maids—City Women: From the European Countryside to Urban America,* ed. Christiane Harzig (Ithaca, N.Y.: Cornell University Press, 1997), 57–97. Analyses of Irish women's migratory patterns include Hasia Diner, *Erin's Daughters in America: Irish Immigrant Women in the Nineteenth Century* (Baltimore: Johns Hopkins University Press, 1983); David Fitzpatrick, *Irish Emigration, 1801–1921* (Dublin: Dundalgan Press, 1984), "The Modernisation of the Irish Female," in *Rural Ireland, 1600–1900: Modernisation and Change,* ed. Patrick O'Flanagan, Paul Ferguson, and Kevin Whelan (Cork: Cork University Press, 1987), 162–180, and "'A Share of the Honeycomb': Education, Emigration and Irishwomen," *Continuity and Change* 1 (1986): 217–234; Pauline Jackson, "Women in Nineteenth Century Irish Emigration," *International Migration Review* 18 (Winter 1984): 1004–1021; and Kerby Miller, *Emigrants and Exiles: Ireland and the Irish Exodus to North America* (New York: Oxford University Press, 1985). Fitzpatrick's recent update, "Emigration, 1871–1921," can be found in *A New History of Ireland, vol. 6, Ireland under the Union, 1870–1921,* ed. W. E. Vaughan (Oxford: Oxford University Press, 1996), 606–652.

4. See Joanna Bourke, *Husbandry to Housewifery: Women, Economic Change, and Housework in Ireland, 1890–1914* (Oxford: Clarenden Press, 1993) for a discussion of these government schemes.

5. See Janet Nolan, "The Great Famine and Women's Emigration from Ireland," in *The Hungry Stream: Essays on Famine and Emigration,* ed. E. Margaret Crawford (Belfast: Institute of Irish Studies/Queen's University Belfast Press, 1997), 67–75. For analysis of the transformation of the Irish economy in the course of the nineteenth century, see Cormac Ó Grada, *Ireland: A New Economic History, 1780–1939* (New York: Oxford University Press, 1994). For the impact of economic change on women, see Bourke, *Husbandry to Housewifery.* Fitzpatrick's "Women and the Great Famine," in Kelleher and Murphy, *Gender Perspectives,* 50–69, argues that women's loss of employment was no worse than men's after the Famine.

6. The pattern of young unmarried women leaving rural Ireland in numbers large enough to dominate overall emigration totals continued until at least the 1960s. While the destination of the majority of these emigrants changed from the United States to Great Britain and the Commonwealth after the United States instituted immigration restrictions in the 1920s, record numbers of increasingly well–educated Irish women continued to leave their homeland into the late twentieth century. See Patrick Travers, "Emigration and Gender: The Case of Ireland, 1922–1960," in O'Dowd and Wichert, *Chattel, Servant or Citizen*, 187–199; Margaret McCurtain, "Late in the Field: Catholic Sisters in Twentieth Century Ireland and the New Religious History," *Journal of Women's History* 6/7 (Winter 1995): 49–63. For a discussion of the fate of women after independence see Valiulis, "Power, Gender, and Identity in the Irish Free State," ibid., 117–136, and Mary Daly, "Women in the Irish Free State, 1929–1939: The Interaction between Economics and Ideology," ibid., 99–116.

7. See Charles Fanning, ed., "Introduction," *Exiles of Erin: Nineteenth-Century Irish-American Fiction* (Notre Dame, Ind.: University of Notre Dame Press, 1987), 8. According to the 1900 Census for the United States, while 54 percent of the Irish-born women in the country in that year were in service and less than 2 percent of their number were teachers, over 14 percent of American-born women of Irish descent were already classified as "professionals" in that same year. Many of these "professionals" would have been teachers. See Census for the United States, U.S. Congress, Senate, *Reports of the Immigration Commission: Abstracts*, 804–820, and table 21B, 470–471. For unstated comparisons with Irish educational mobility, see John L. Rury, "Urban Structure and School Participation: Immigrant Women in 1900," *Social Science History* 8 (Summer 1984): 219–241, and Timothy Smith, "Immigrant Social Aspirations and American Education, 1880–1930," *American Quarterly* 21 (Fall 1969): 523–543.

8. The classic example of the "gloom and doom" approach to the history of the Irish in America is Oscar Handlin's *Boston's Immigrants: A Study in Acculturation, 1790–1880* (Cambridge: Harvard University Press, 1941), in which the author demonstrates the agonizingly slow adjustment of Boston's Irish to American life. Lawrence J. McCaffrey's *The Irish Diaspora in America* (Bloomington: Indiana University Press, 1976), which has been reprinted and revised recently, disagrees that the dismal experience of Handlin's Boston Irish is a model for the Irish adjustment to American life in other parts of the United States, particularly Chicago.

9. The study of Irish education produced by Donald H. Akenson a generation ago is a case in point. His *The Irish Education Experiment: The National System of Education in the Nineteenth Century* (London: Routledge and Kegan Paul, 1970) depends on the official papers of male elites to develop a narrative of the formation of national education in Ireland. Little mention is made of the individual teachers and students who peopled the national school classrooms. His most recent study of Irish education, "Pre-University Education, 1870–1921," in *A New History of*

Ireland, 6: 523–538, also relies on parliamentary papers and other official documents.

10. With some exceptions such as Joel Perlmann's work, American educational historiography for the most part concentrates on gender, class, and religious variables rather than ethnicity. For example, despite its focus on Chicago, Marjorie Murphy's excellent *Blackboard Unions: The AFT and the NEA, 1900–1980* (Ithaca, N.Y.: Cornell University Press, 1990) does not assess the role of ethnicity in shaping the city's public school system. Nevertheless, Irish Americans were largely responsible for organizing the Chicago Teachers' Federation, as we shall see; and they were fast becoming the majority of all the city's public school teachers by the turn of the last century, as we have already seen. See also Ellen Skerrett, "The Catholic Dimension," in *The Irish in Chicago*, ed. Lawrence J. McCaffrey, Ellen Skerrett, Michael F. Funchion, and Charles Fanning (Urbana: University of Illinois Press, 1987), 46.

11. Regional differences in the American Irish diaspora received more attention with the publication of Dennis Clark's *Hibernia America: The Irish and Regional Cultures* (Westport, Conn.: Greenwood Press, 1986). Some very recent examples of this trend demonstrating the importance of destination as well as origin in the history of Irish America are Timothy J. Meagher, *Inventing Irish America: Generation, Class, and Ethnic Identity in a New England City, 1880–1928* (Notre Dame, Ind.: University of Notre Dame Press, 2001); Kevin Kenny, *The American Irish: A History* (New York: Longman/Pearson, 2000); Ronald H. Bayor and Timothy J. Meagher, eds., *The New York Irish* (Baltimore: Johns Hopkins University Press, 1996); Ellen Skerrett, ed., *At the Crossroads: Old Saint Patrick's and the Chicago Irish*, with a Foreword by Mayor Richard M. Daley (Chicago: Loyola Press, 1997); and the forthcoming Donald Jordan, ed., *The Bay Area Irish*. Earlier notable contributions to the regional study of Irish America include David Emmons, *The Butte Irish: Class and Ethnicity in an American Mining Town, 1875–1925* (Urbana: University of Illinois Press, 1989); Lawrence J. McCaffrey, *Textures of Irish America* (Syracuse, N.Y.: Syracuse University Press, 1992); and Kevin Kenny, *Making Sense of the Molly Maguires* (New York: Oxford University Press, 1998). David Noel Doyle's essay, "The Remaking of Irish-America, 1845–1880," in *A New History of Ireland*, 6:725–763, likewise emphasizes the need to look at the Irish diaspora within as well as to America. *The Encyclopedia of the Irish in America*, ed. Michael Glazier (Notre Dame, Ind.: University of Notre Dame Press, 1999), also highlights the scholarship done on the regional nature of Irish settlement in the United States.

12. See James J. Connolly, *The Triumph of Ethnic Progressivism: Urban Political Culture in Boston, 1900–1925* (Cambridge: Harvard University Press, 1998), for a provocative new look at the prevailing thesis that the Irish in Boston faced greater isolation and discrimination than the Irish in other American cities, especially those in the west.

Chapter 1. Irish Education: The Best Intentions

1. Thomas Healy, "Queries to be Answered on Application to the Commissioners of Education for Aid Towards the Salary of the Teacher or Teachers of Castlegregory National Schools, County Kerry," 6 May 1844, ED1/38, #122, National Archives Ireland [NAI].

2. J. M. Goldstom, *The Social Context of Education, 1808–1870: A Study of the Working Class School Reader in England and Ireland* (Shannon: Irish University Press, 1972), 72, and "Richard Whately and Political Economy in School Books, 1833–1880," *Irish Historical Studies* 15 (September 1966): 131, 133, 134, 135, 136, 139.

3. Grainne O'Flynn, "Our Age of Innocence," in *Girls Don't Do Honours: Irish Women in Education in the Nineteenth and Twentieth Centuries,* ed. Mary Cullen (Dublin: Women's Education Bureau, 1987), 79, 81; Maria Luddy, *Women and Philanthropy in Nineteenth-Century Ireland* (Cambridge, England: Cambridge University Press, 1995), 216.

4. Patrick Dowling, *The Hedge Schools of Ireland* (Cork: Mercier, 1968), 1, 8, 19, 20, 21, 31, 73, 75, 153; Norman Atkinson, *Irish Education: A History of Educational Institutions* (Dublin: Allan Figgis, 1969), 43, 45, 46, 48.

5. Atkinson, *Irish Education,* 70; Census of Ireland, 1821, in Table 3, "Population, 1821–1971," in *Irish Historical Statistics: Population, 1821–1871,* ed. W. E. Vaughan and A. J. Fitzpatrick (Dublin: Royal Irish Academy, 1978), 3.

6. Thomas Wyse, "Elementary Education in Ireland," *American Journal of Education* 2 (1862): 134; Atkinson, *Irish Education,* 51, 58, 90. See also Aine Hyland and Kenneth Milne, eds., *Irish Educational Documents,* vol. 1, *A Selection of Extracts Relating to the History of Irish Education from the Earliest Times to 1922* (Dublin: Church of Ireland College of Education, 1987), 15.

7. Wyse, "Elementary Education in Ireland," 135.

8. The Kildare Place Society itself had been founded in 1811. Atkinson, *Irish Education,* 65, 69, 94.

9. John Lawson and Harold Silver, *A Social History of Education in England* (London: Methuen, 1973), 249, 271.

10. Atkinson, *Irish Education,* 73, 75, 76, 79.

11. Wyse, "Elementary Education in Ireland," 135, 136.

12. *Guide to Educational Records* (Belfast: Public Record Office of Northern Ireland [PRONI], n.d.), 6.

13. John Dee, "Application to the Commissioners of National Education in Ireland for Payment of Teachers' Salaries and Supply of Books, Castlegregory National School, County Kerry," 1 May 1850, ED1/39, #96, NAI.

14. "Castlegregory National School, County Kerry," ED9/file 7394, NAI.

15. Reverend P. Browne, to the Commissioners of National Education in Ireland, 5 March 1901, ED9/14848, NAI.

16. "National Education (Ireland)," in *Irish Educational Documents* 1:192, 193; Censuses of Ireland, 1821–1971, in Table 3, "Population, 1821–1971," in Vaughan and A. J. Fitzpatrick, *Irish Historical Statistics*, 3; and "Education of the People," United Kingdom, *Census of Ireland for the Year 1911: General Report, with Tables and Appendix* (Athlone, Ireland: Athlone Printing Works Co., 1913), lii, liii, lvi, lvii.

17. *Census of Ireland for the Year 1911: General Report*, lii.

18. Ibid., liii.

19. John Kelly, "School Record of John Kelly, School Attendance Officer" (Belfast, June 1896), PRONI, 18–21.

20. Frederick W. Ryan, *School Attendance in Ireland under the Compulsory Education Act, 1892* (Dublin: E. Ponsonby, 1912), 7, 4, 9; Commissioners of National Education in Ireland, *The Seventy-Seventh Report of the Commissioners of National Education in Ireland, Year 1911* (Dublin: Alexander Thom, 1912), 12, quoted in ibid.

21. P. W. Joyce, *A Handbook of School Management and Methods of Teaching*, 17th ed. (Dublin: Gill and Son, 1897). See also P. W. Joyce, *The Teaching of Manual Work in Schools* (Dublin: Gill, 1892; John Logan, "Sufficient to Their Needs: Literacy and Elementary Schooling in the Nineteenth Century," in *The Origins of Popular Literacy in Ireland: Language Change and Educational Development 1700-1920*, ed. Mary Daly and David Dickson (Dublin: Trinity College Press, 1992), 127, 128, 131; and David Fitzpatrick, "'A Share of the Honeycomb': Education, Emigration and Irishwomen," *Continuity and Change* 1 (1986): 234.

22. Thomas Urry Young, *The Teacher's Manual for Infant Schools and Preparatory Classes* (Dublin: M'Glashan and Gill, 1856), 6, 41, 42, 59.

23. D. Fitzpatrick, "The Futility of History: A Failed Experiment in Irish History," in *Ideology and the Historians*, Historical Studies 17, ed. Ciaran Brady (Dublin: Lilliput Press, 1991), 168, 170–172.

24. Board of Guardians, *Children's History Book* (Dublin: Hely's, n.d.), PRONI.

25. Young, *Teacher's Manual*, 170.

26. Vere Foster, *Vere Foster Copy Book of Mata Blackwood [County Down], November 24th, 1882–March 8th, 1883* (Dublin: Blackie and Son, n.d.), PRONI, 1–5, 8–11, 13, 20.

27. Vere Foster, *Vere Foster's Drawing Books—K.2*, drawn by J. Needham (London and Belfast: Marcus Ward, n.d.), PRONI.

28. Quoted in Lorcan Walsh, "Images of Women in Nineteenth Century Schoolbooks," *Irish Educational Studies* 4 (1984): 74.

29. Commissioners of National Education in Ireland, *Reading Book for the Use of Female Schools, Fifth Level* (Dublin: Alexander Thom and Sons, 1862), 194.

30. P. M. Egan, *The National Readers for Irish National Schools Fifth Book (First Stage)* (Kilkenny, Ireland: P. M. Egan, 1897).

31. Commissioners of National Education in Ireland, *Biographical Sketches of Eminent British Poets Chronologically Arranged from Chaucer to Burns . . . Intended for Teachers and the Higher Classes in Schools* (Dublin: Alexander Thom, 1870), 1, 34, 36.

32. Commissioners of National Education in Ireland, *Epitome of Geographical Knowledge, Ancient and Modern, Compiled for the Use of Teachers and Advanced Classes of the National Schools of Ireland,* new ed., rev. (Dublin: Alexander Thom and Sons, 1857), 346.

33. Commissioners of National Education in Ireland, *Fifty-Seventh Annual Report of the Commissioners of National Education in Ireland for the Year 1890* (Dublin: Alexander Thom, 1891), 28.

34. Commissioners of National Education in Ireland, *Rules and Regulations of the Commissioners of National Education in Ireland, 1903,* Rule 174 (Dublin: Office of National Education, 1903), 57. Emphasis in the original.

35. Commissioners of National Education in Ireland, *Rules and Regulations of the Commissioners of National Education in Ireland, 1914–1915* (Dublin: Alexander Thom, 1914), xvi.

36. Commissioners of National Education in Ireland, *Commissioners of National Education in Ireland Manual of Needlework* (Dublin: Alexander Thom and Co., 1889), v, iv.

37. Ibid. Emphasis added.

38. Commissioners of National Education in Ireland, *Simple Directions in Needlework and Cutting Out; Intended for the Use of National Female Schools of Ireland to Which Are Added Specimens of Work Executed by the Pupils of the Female National Model School* (Dublin: Alexander Thom and Sons, 1853), 5.

39. Commissioners of National Education in Ireland, *Manual of Needlework,* v, iv.

40. Student specimens, Commissioners of National Education in Ireland, *Simple Directions in Needlework,* PRONI.

41. "Student Cookery Notebook," in *Miscellaneous Papers,* ED 9/2008/7/22, NAI.

42. Isabella F. Johnston, "Roll for Cookery and Laundry Work, 1912–1913," *District Inspectors' Reports, Coorlespratten National School, Cavan,* ED9/1178/ nos. 26 and 33, NAI.

43. Ibid.

44. Louise Kenny, "A New Irish School of Housewifery," *Irish Homestead* 11 (March 25, 1905), 241.

45. District Inspector James Brown, "Application for Salary for a Work Mistress, Castlegregory National School, County Kerry," 29 February 1856, ED1/39, #163, NAI.

46. District Inspector Denis F. Driscoll, "Queries—Application for Salary of Assistant Teacher, Castlegregory National School, County Kerry," 16 February 1865, ED1/40, #167, NAI.

47. District Inspector's Notes, "Castlegregory Girls National School, County Kerry," ED2/196, folio 26, NAI.

48. Ibid.; District Inspector's Notes, 17 August 1880; 8 November 1892; 14 November 1892; 19 December 1892, "Castlegregory Girls National School, County Kerry," ED2/197, folio 101, NAI.

49. 2 September 1897, ED2/197, folio 100, NAI; Browne, Castlegregory, County Kerry, to the Secretarys [sic] of National Education, Dublin, 20 August 1912, ED9/file 23624, NAI.

50. Robert Little, "Memorandum for the Secretaries to the National Education Commissioners," 5 August 1913; and Browne, "To the Secretary's Office of National Education, Dublin," 20 August 1912, ED9/file 23624, NAI. See also ED9/file 25831, NAI.

51. Joan Crean O'Leary, St. Charles, Ill., telephone interview by author, 30 January 1998; letter to author, 1 February 1998.

52. Bishop Moriarty to Lord Dufferin, 1868, "Emigrant Letters," T.1767, 66, PRONI.

Chapter 2. Irish Schools: Windows of Opportunity

1. See Aghaloora School, County Cavan, "Margaret Smyth and Mathew Comisky Case," ED9/4516/7732/33/1886-87, NAI.

2. Commissioners of National Education in Ireland, *Rules and Regulations, 1914–1915*, xx, 60.

3. See J. Nolan, "The Great Famine and Women's Emigration from Ireland."

4. See J. Nolan, *Ourselves Alone: Women's Emigration from Ireland, 1885–1920.*

5. Seamus Ó Buachualla, "The Language in the Classroom," *Crane Bag* 5 (1981): 18, 21, 22, 25, 27, 30.

6. J. J. O'Neill, "Loreto Convent, Balbrigan [County Dublin], 11–12 October 1909," in Great Britain, *Intermediate Education Board for Ireland. Reports of Inspectors, 1909–1910,* vol. 3, *Girls' Schools,* 5.

7. Table 142, "Percentage of Irish-Speaking Population, 1891, 1901, 1911," *Census of Ireland for the Year 1911,* 291.

8. R. C. B. Kerin, "Convent of St. Louis, Carrickmacross [County Monaghan], 13 and 18 April 1910," in Great Britain, *Reports of Inspectors, 1909–1910,* vol. 3, 7.

9. C. E. Wright and E. Ensor, "Convent of Mercy High School, Carrick-on-Suir [County Tipperary], 4 February 1910," in ibid., 3, 5.

10. D. Fitzpatrick, "Futility of History," 171; Ó Buachualla, "Language in the Classroom," 21.

11. A. S. MacShambrain, "Ideological Conflict and Historical Interpretation: The Problem of History in Irish Primary Education c. 1900–1930," *Irish Educational Studies* 10 (1991): 231; D. Fitzpatrick, "Futility of History," 173, 174, 175.

12. C. E. Wright, "Brigidine Convent, Abbeyleix, Queen's [County Laois]" in *Reports of Inspectors, 1909–1910* (vol. 3), 3 May 1910, 6, 7, 8.

13. R. C. B. Kerin and T. Rea, "Ladies School, Dundalk [County Louth], 7 and 11 April 1910," in ibid., 5.

14. C. E. Wright and E. Ensor, "Presentation Covent, Bagenalstown [County Carlow], 8 March 1910," in ibid., 5.

15. J. J. O'Neill and T. Rea, "Ladies Collegiate School, Carrickfergus [County Antrim], 9, 10, 31 May 1910," ibid., 5.

16. C. E. Wright and E. Ensor, "Carrick-on-Suir [County Tipperary], 4 February 1910," ibid., 5.

17. Josephine Kamm, *Hope Deferred: Girls' Education in English History* (London: Methuen, 1965), 153; John Lawson and Harold Silver, *A Social History of Education in England* (London: Methuen, 1973), 241, 242.

18. A training school for male teachers was located across Dublin, in Glasnevin. Wyse, "Elementary Education in Ireland," 140, 141, 142.

19. J. Kamm, *Hope Deferred*, 157, 158; T. J. O'Connell, *History of the Irish National Teachers' Organization, 1868–1968* (Dublin: INTO/Dakota, 1968), 393.

20. Formal teacher training in England also affected only a minority of teachers. Although the number of certified teachers in England rose from 12,000 in 1870 to 53,000 in 1895, the great majority of teachers in English schools were uncertified in those years. Lawson and Silver, *Social History of Education*, 332.

21. Kamm, *Hope Deferred*, 161, 162; T. J. O'Connell, *History of the Irish National Teachers' Organization*, 333.

22. Commissioners of National Education in Ireland, *Rules and Regulations, 1914–1915*, 35.

23. Ibid., 96, 103, 104.

24. Ibid., 35, 36, 103, 104, 106, 107.

25. Ibid., 15.

26. Louis S. Daly, "District Inspector's Observation Book, Caherciveen Number 2 National School, Kerry, 1874–1917," 12 February 1907, 13 January 1908 (entry dated 28 July 1908), 26 May 1910, ED9/1186/7/11, NAI.

27. J. V. Doody, Jr., 10 November 1908; D. Lehane, 12 September 1910; ? Kane, 21 December 1911; E. T. Darman, 17 May 1917, ibid.

28. W. Erskine, *A Review of the National School System of Education: Its Evils Exposed and Improvements Suggested* (Belfast: J. W. Boyd, 1895?), 12, 14, 15, 18, 25.

29. Commissioners of National Education in Ireland, *Rules and Regulations of the Commissioners of National Education in Ireland* (Dublin: Alexander Thom, 1869), 12, 13. Emphasis in the original.

30. Commissioners of National Education in Ireland, *Rules and Regulations, 1914–1915*, vi, 22, 23, 6.

31. Ibid., 15, 72.

32. Ibid., 23, 27.

33. Ibid., 14, 16, 28, 29.

34. Ibid., 29, 95.

35. Commissioners of National Education in Ireland, *Rules and Regulations [1869]*, 20.

36. Emphasis added. Ibid., 19, 20.

37. W. H. Welply, "District Inspectors' Observation Book, Caherciveeen Number 2 National School, Kerry, 1874–1917, Teachers," 12 August 1907, ED9/1186/7/11, NAI.

38. T. J. O'Connell, *History of the Irish National Teachers' Organization*, 409–410.

39. Women hired as teachers after October 1, 1933, were required to resign from their teaching jobs when they married. Eoin O'Leary, "The Irish National Teachers' Organization and the Marriage Bar for Women National Teachers, 1933–1958," *Saothar* 12 (1987): 47. While women hired before October 1, 1933, could keep their teaching jobs after marriage, teachers appointed for the first time after June 30, 1911, were required to be absent from school for two continuous months before and after childbirth and to provide a qualified substitute *at their own expense* if the two-month period of forced absence was not within the normal eight-week school vacation period. In this way, national school teachers were required to either pinpoint the timing of their conceptions and due dates or lose their jobs or a substantial portion of their salaries. See Commissioners of National Education in Ireland, *Rules and Regulations, 1914–1915*, 24.

40. *Rules and Regulations, 1914–1915*, 37, 30, 32.

41. T. J. O'Connell, *History of the Irish National Teachers' Organization*, 7, 274.

42. Ibid., 42, 43.

43. Ibid., 56, 58.

44. Ibid., 403–405.

45. Ibid., 407.

46. Wright and Ensor, "Brigidine Convent, Abbeyleix"; "Presentation Convent, Bagenalstown"; and ? Maguire, "Mount Pleasant School, Ballinasloe, Mayo–February 25, 1910," in *Reports of Inspectors, 1909–1910* (vol. 3), 5, 3, 1.

47. T. J. O'Connell, *History of the Irish National Teachers' Organization*, 45, 48.

48. Ibid., 62, 63.

49. See Janet Nolan, "The National Schools and Irish Women's Mobility in the Late Nineteenth and Early Twentieth Centuries," *Irish Studies Review* 18 (Spring 1977): 23–28.

50. See the following articles by Janet Nolan: "Education: Irish-American Teachers in Public Schools, 1880–1920," in *The Encyclopedia of the Irish in America*, ed. Michael Glazier (Notre Dame, Ind.: University of Notre Dame Press, 1999), 236–239; "St. Patrick's Daughter: Amelia Dunne Hookway and Chicago's Public Schools," in *At the Crossroads,* ed. Skerrett, 103–117; "Patrick Henry in the Classroom: Margaret Haley and the Chicago Teachers' Federation," *Eire-Ireland* 30 (Summer 1995): 104–117; and "Pioneers in the Classroom: The Irish in San Francisco's Schools," in *The Bay Area Irish*, ed. Donald Jordan (forthcoming).

51. Mary Crowe Lennon, "Pages of My Life," 30 June 1989 (photocopy in author's possession). I am grateful to Mary Crowe Lennon's daughter, Chicago teacher Kay Lennon, and to Joan Crean O'Leary for bringing this unpublished memoir to my attention.

Chapter 3. *"Boston Schools for Boston Girls!"*

1. John F. Duff Collection, in possession of John F. Duff, M.D., Byfield, Mass.

2. *Boston Herald*, 4 October 1892.

3. Polly Welts Kaufman, *Boston Women and School Politics, 1872–1905* (New York: Garland, 1994), 232. Brian Duff recalled the family lore about John and Julia's personal lives and habits during a conversation with the author in Chicago on 10 April 2003.

4. "Three in One Family Win College Degrees This Month: Dr. and Mrs. John Duff of Charlestown Congratulated on Achievements of Their Children." Newspaper clipping (Boston, June 1916), John F. Duff Collection. Additional family lore contributed by Brian Duff, 10 April 2003.

5. Kaufman, *Boston Women and School Politics*, 232, 233, 251.

6. "Practical Politics: Character Sketches. Mrs. Julia E. Duff" (Boston, 1903). Photocopy, John F. Duff Collection.

7. Newspaper clipping (Boston: n.d.), John F. Duff Collection.

8. Fitzgerald opposed Julia, a fellow Democrat, because her reforms threatened his political machine's power over the schools. Although she had three children under the age of ten to care for at home, Julia was devastated by her ouster and never forgave Fitzgerald and his Democratic loyalists. Conversation with Brian Duff, 10 April 2003.

9. Kaufman, *Boston Women and School Politics*, 251.

10. Newspaper clipping, no title (Boston: n.d.), John F. Duff Collection.

11. *Boston Sunday Post,* 29 November 1903.

12. *Boston Sunday Globe,* 22 November 1903.

13. Newspaper clipping, no title (Boston: n.d.), John F. Duff Collection.

14. Kaufman, *Boston Women and School Politics,* 114.

15. Ibid., 229, 230.

16. Boston School Committee, "Report Submitted by Thornton D. Appollonio," *Communication from the School Committee Relative to Text-Books on Irish History in the Public Schools* (December 21, 1906), Document no. 152, 1–3, Boston Public Library.

17. Sam Barnes, "Progressivism on the Wane: The Entrenchment of the Bureaucracy, 1900–1945," in *From Common School to Magnet School: Selected Essays in the History of Boston's Schools,* ed. James L. Fraser, Henry L. Allen, and Sam Barnes (Boston: Boston Public Library, 1979), 94, 96.

18. *Boston Herald,* 21 September 1930.

19. *Boston Post,* 13 April 1953.

20. Stanley K. Schultz, *The Culture Factory: Boston Public Schools, 1789–1860* (New York: Oxford University Press, 1973), 261, vi, vii; James L. Fraser, "Reform, Immigration, and Bureaucracy, 1820–1870," in Fraser et al., *From Common School to Magnet School,* 29, 30, 31.

21. Carroll D. Wright, "Population of the City of Boston," in City of Boston, "Doc. 104—1886: City of Boston. An Analysis of the Population of the City of Boston, as shown in the State Census of May, 1885," *Documents of the City of Boston, for the Year 1886* 3 (Boston: Rockwell and Churchill, 1887), 3–4.

22. S. K. Schultz, *Culture Factory,* x, 242.

23. Ibid., x, vii; Fraser, "Reform," 31, 36, 29.

24. S. K. Schultz, *Culture Factory,* 235, vi; Fraser, "Reform," 29, 38. Oscar Handlin, in *Boston's Immigrants,* sets these figures at 35,287 Irish-born out of a total Boston population in 1850 of 136,881. By 1855, the number of Irish-born in the city had risen to 46,237 out of 160,400. By 1860, 105,331 out of 519,004 people in Boston and surrounding cities were Irish-born. Tables VI, VII, VIII in Handlin, *Boston's Immigrants,* 243, 244, 245.

25. James W. Sanders, "Boston Catholics and the School Question, 1825–1907," in Fraser et al., *From Common School to Magnet School,* 65.

26. Chart I: "Boston," in ibid., 49; Fraser, "Reform," 42, 40; S. K. Schultz, *Culture Factory,* 283, 284, 296; and Kaufman, *Boston Women and School Politics,* 235.

27. City of Boston, Doc. no. 54: "City of Boston Annual Report, by the City Registrar, of the Births, Marriages, and Deaths in the City of Boston for the Year 1874" (Boston Public Library), 5, 6, 12.

28. "Table I: Births in 1874. Parentage," ibid., 5.

29. Marvin Lazerson, *Origins of the Urban School: Public Education in Massachusetts, 1870–1915* (Cambridge: Harvard University Press, 1971), 8.

30. Ibid., 16, 26.

31. C. D. Wright, "Population . . . Boston," 5.

32. City of Boston, Doc. no. 27, *Annual Report of the School Committee of the City of Boston, 1880* (Boston: Rockwell and Churchill, 1881), 6, 7, 8.

33. Lazerson, *Origins of the Urban School*, 9, 242.

34. Barnes, "Reform and the Struggle for Control, 1870–1900," in Fraser et al., *From Common School to Magnet School*, 85.

35. Lazerson, *Origins of the Urban School*, 16, 2, 12, 13, 242.

36. Ibid., 233.

37. Ibid., 219.

38. Kaufman, *Boston Women and School Politics*, 174, 45, 120.

39. S. K. Schultz, *Culture Factory*, 288, 289.

40. Sanders, "Boston Catholics," 44.

41. Ibid., 46, 48; Fraser, "Reform," 38; S. K. Schultz, *Culture Factory*, 236, 284.

42. S. K. Schultz, *Culture Factory*, 302, 303.

43. Chart I: "Boston," in Sanders, "Boston Catholics," 49, and 58, 62, 53.

44. Ibid., 62; Kaufman, *Boston Women and School Politics*, 140.

45. Parochial school enrollments in Boston rose from 10.3 percent to 12.8 percent of the city's school-age population between 1880 and 1890, according to Kaufman, *Boston Women and School Politics*, 142.

46. Anonymous priest, *Annals*, 1895, Sisters of Notre Dame, St. Augustine Parish (Ipswich, Mass.: Archives of the Sisters of Notre Dame). Quoted in Sanders, "Boston Catholics," 74.

47. Sanders, "Boston Catholics," 66, 67, 68.

48. Ibid., 68.

49. Ibid., 69; Lazerson, *Origins of the Urban School*, 21, 33; Kaufman, *Boston Women and School Politics*, xii, 140.

50. Lazerson, *Origins of the Urban School*, 21, 27; *Journal of Education*, December 20, 1888, quoted in Kaufman, *Boston Women and School Politics*, 156.

51. Lazerson, *Origins of the Urban School*, 42, 46; Barnes, "Reform," 77, 81; Kaufman, *Boston Women and School Politics*, 173.

52. Barnes, "Progressivism," 93; Kaufman, *Boston Women and School Politics*, 165, xi.

53. Kaufman, *Boston Women and School Politics*, 165.

54. Sanders, "Boston Catholics," 69.

55. Lazerson, *Origins of the Catholic School*, 13; Chart I: "Boston," in Sanders, "Boston Catholics," 49.

56. Kaufman, *Boston Women and School Politics*, 167.

57. City of Boston, Doc. no. 27, *Annual Report of the School Committee of the City of Boston, 1880*, 7. In 1880, almost all the Irish-American grammar school teachers were third assistants, the lowest teaching rank, however. Irish-American

women had also moved into non-classroom school jobs by 1880. Although only one of the grammar school janitors in that year was a woman, she had an Irish last name—Ryan—and twelve of the thirty-one female primary school janitors in that year had Irish last names. See City of Boston, *Thirty-Seventh Report of the Superintendent of Public Schools (Boston), 1880* (Boston: Rockwell and Churchill, 1881), 279–285, 298–295.

58. In 1880, eight of the forty-three graduates of the Normal School had Irish last names. An additional nine of the thirty-six-member fourth-year class and eighteen of the ninety-six-member third-year class at the Girls' High School also had Irish last names in that year. "Diplomas of Graduation," in City of Boston, *Thirty-Seventh Report*, 54–57.

59. Sanders, "Boston Catholics," 144; Perlmann, *Ethnic Differences*, 55, 56; Kaufman, *Boston Women and School Politics*, 232.

60. City of Boston, Doc. no. 27, John B. Moran, Henry P. Bowditch, and Abram E. Cutter, "Report," *Annual Report of the School Committee of the City of Boston. 1880*, 9.

61. Ibid., 9, 10.

62. Kaufman, *Boston Women and School Politics*, 74, 75; S. Barnes, "Progressivism," 100.

63. Barnes, "Progressivism," 100.

64. Ibid., 94, 100.

65. Ibid., 101.

66. Ibid., 100.

67. In 1880, the average class size in Boston's primary and grammar schools ranged from a high of fifty-six in the primary grades, where most of the Irish-American teachers worked, to a low of fifty in the grammar school grades. Teachers were allowed an assistant if they had over fifty students in their class, which, of course, many did. See City of Boston, Doc. no. 27 (1880), 7.

68. Ibid., 27.

69. Kaufman, *Boston Women and School Politics*, 170, 182, 183.

70. City of Boston, Doc. no. 27 (1880), 27, 29.

71. Jack Beatty, *The Rascal King: The Life and Times of James Michael Curley (1874–1958): An Epic of Urban Politics and Irish America* (Reading, Mass.: Addison-Wesley, 1992), 119, 103, 149.

72. Connolly, *The Triumph of Ethnic Progressivism*, 67, 17, 3.

Chapter 4. San Francisco: Pioneers in the Classroom

1. Catherine Ann Curry, telephone interview by author, 12 January 1998, San Francisco; and Curry, San Francisco, to author, Chicago, 6 May 2003.

2. C. A. Curry, Menlo Park, Calif., to author, Evanston, Ill., 27 March 1998, and Curry, San Francisco, to author, Chicago, 6 May 2003.

3. This figure comes from counting the number of women primary and grammar school teachers with Irish last names (390 out of a total of 804 teachers, or 49 percent) listed in the "Directory of Teachers," San Francisco Public Schools, *Annual Report of the Board of Education, San Francisco, 1910*, 52–100.

4. See J. Nolan, "St. Patrick's Daughter."

5. J. Nolan, table 14, *Ourselves Alone*, 82.

6. J. Nolan, "The National Schools and Irish Women's Mobility."

7. Caren Cotter Ellis, Santa Rosa, Calif., to author, Evanston, Ill., 16 September 1998.

8. Patrick J. Dowling, *California: The Irish Dream* (San Francisco: Golden Gate Publishers, 1988), xiv, 242; R. A. Burchell, *The San Francisco Irish, 1848-1880* (Berkeley: University of California Press, 1980), 28.

9. *Thirty-Seventh Annual Report of the Superintendent of Common Schools of the City and County of San Francisco for the Fiscal Year Ending June 30, 1890* (San Francisco: W. M. Hinton and Company, 1890), 8.

10. Catherine Ann Curry, "Shaping Young San Franciscans: Public and Catholic Schools in San Francisco, 1851–1906" (Ph.D. diss., Graduate Theological Seminary, 1987), 1.

11. Ibid., 109, 30, 31, 34, 20.

12. The sophisticated foreign-language curriculum offered by the cosmopolitan schools was aimed at keeping middle- and upper-class San Franciscans in the city's schools by providing them with an elite education formerly available only in private academies. These schools were also incentives for German and other non-English-speaking immigrants to enroll in the public schools. Ibid., 36.

13. United States Department of the Interior, Bureau of Education, *Bulletin. 1917, No. 46: The Public School System of San Francisco, California* (Washington, D.C.: Government Printing Office, 1917), 10.

14. Department of Public Schools, City and County of San Francisco, *Twenty-Seventh Annual Report of the Superintendent of Public Schools for the School Year Ending June 30, 1880* (San Francisco: W. M. Hinton and Company, 1880), 289; "Secretary's Report," *Thirty-Third Annual Report of the Superintendent of Public Schools for the School Year Ending June 30, 1886* (San Francisco: W. M. Hinton and Company, 1886), 49, 50; *Report of the Superintendent of Schools and Board of Education, San Francisco, California, for the Fiscal Years 1906–07 and 1907–08* (San Francisco: Neal Publishing Company, 1907), 7; and *Directory of Teachers and Schools, 1891; Directory of the Department of Public Schools, 1909.*

15. See James P. Walsh, "The Irish in Early San Francisco," in *The San Francisco Irish, 1850–1976*, 2d ed., ed. James P. Walsh (San Francisco: Irish Literary and Historical Society, 1979), 11; William A. Bullough, "Christopher Buckley and San

Francisco: The Man and the City," in ibid., 28; Burchell, *San Francisco Irish*, 3; P. J. Dowling, *California*, xiv.

16. John Swett, "Report of the Principal of the Girls' High and Normal School (August 1886)," "Secretary's Report," and "List of Teachers," in *Thirty-Third Annual Report . . . 1886*, 30, 49, 79–92; *Directory of the Department of the Public Schools, 1909*, 148; and San Francisco Public Schools, "List of Schools and Teachers," *Annual Report of the Board of Education, San Francisco, 1910*, 52–100.

17. *Twenty-Seventh Annual Report . . . 1880*, 60. See also C. A. Curry, "Shaping Young San Franciscans," 56, 90, and "Three Irish Women and Social Action in San Francisco: Mother Theresa Comerford, Mother Baptist Russell, and Kate Kennedy," *Journal of the West* 31 (April 1992): 66–72; Miriam Allen De Ford, "America's Marx and His Bebel: Henry George and Kate Kennedy," in *They Were San Franciscans* (Caldwell, Idaho: Caxton Printers, 1947), 144, 146; and P. J. Dowling, *California*, 241, 242.

18. *Twenty-Seventh Annual Report . . . 1880*, 43, 60, 54.

19. P. J. Dowling, "Kate Kennedy: Women's Suffragist and Educator," in *California*, 242; C. A. Curry, "Shaping Young San Franciscans," 91.

20. Eileen M. Murphy, telephone interview by author, 12 January 1998, San Francisco. See also P. J. Dowling, "Kate Kennedy," 241, 244; and De Ford, "America's Marx," 147, 151.

21. John W. Anderson, *Thirty-Seventh Annual Report . . . 1890*, 10, 11.

22. C. A. Curry, "Shaping Young San Franciscans," 92, 313.

23. De Ford, "America's Marx," 153.

24. *Thirty-Third Annual Report . . . 1886*, 79; *Annual Report of the Board of Education, San Francisco, 1910*, 57.

25. De Ford, "America's Marx," 152.

26. San Francisco Board of Education, *Directory of Teachers and Schools of the Department of Public Schools, City and County of San Francisco, June 8, 1891*.

27. Ibid.; San Francisco School Department, *Directory of the Department of Public Schools of the City and County of San Francisco, November 1, 1909* (San Francisco: Phillips and Van Orden Company, 1909); *List of Teachers, Schools, and Residences, 1909*; and San Francisco Public Schools, *Annual Report of the Board of Education, San Francisco, 1910*.

28. San Francisco School Women, "Alice Rose Power Commendation," June 1943 (photocopy). My thanks to Tom Carey, San Francisco's United Irish Cultural Center librarian, for drawing this citation to my attention.

29. Inscription (photocopy), enclosed in Urania Michaela Moran, San Francisco, to author, Evanston, Ill., 4 March 1998.

30. Urania Michaela Moran, to author, Evanston, Ill., 19 April 1998.

31. Patricia Walsh, Redwood City, Calif., to author, Evanston, Ill., 16 September 1998; and Sandy Finegan, Tiburon, Calif., to author, Evanston, Ill., 1 September 1998.

32. C. A. Curry, "Shaping Young San Franciscans," 112, 109; and "Three Irish Women and Social Action in San Francisco," 66, 67.

33. Margaret O'Sullivan (Sister M. Columba), "Annals of the Sisters of Mercy," n.d., 1, quoted in Gerald O'Sullivan, "Sister M. Columba O'Sullivan, R.I.P.," 1987 (?), (photocopy); and Neilus O'Sullivan, Mountain View, Calif., to author, Evanston, Ill., 9 November 1998.

34. Sister M. Columba O'Sullivan in G. O'Sullivan, "Sister M. Columba O'Sullivan," 1, 2.

35. Ibid. Sister Columba's immigration experience seems not to have been uncommon. According to Caren Cotter Ellis, American nuns made regular scouting expeditions to Ireland in hopes of gathering up surplus girls to fill American convents. Her great aunt Molly Cotter is a case in point. Unceremoniously "shipped off to the U.S. to become a Daughter of the Presentation Order" at the age of fifteen, Molly eventually became Sister Mary Regina and earned a degree in nursing. Despite her success in America, her brother in Ireland never forgave his father for having "virtually sold his sister into slavery." C. C. Ellis, to author, 16 September 1998.

36. G. O'Sullivan, "Sister M. Columba O'Sullivan," 2.

37. Victor L. Shrader, "Ethnicity, Religion, and Class: Progressive School Reform in San Francisco," *History of Education Quarterly* 20 (Winter 1980): 385, 386; Moses Rischin, "Introduction: The Classic Ethnics," in J. P. Walsh, *San Francisco Irish*, 5; and C. A. Curry, "Shaping Young San Franciscans," 187.

38. Swett, *Superintendent of Public Instruction, Reports (1865)*, 121, quoted in C. A. Curry, "Shaping Young San Franciscans," 43.

39. Ibid., 39.

40. *Annual Report of the Superintendent, 1880*, 16, 22, 21, 25.

41. Arnold Guyot, *Earth and Man* (1849), quoted in C. A. Curry, "Shaping Young San Franciscans," 52, 53.

42. Quoted in C. A. Curry, ibid., 250.

43. Swett, *Appendix to Journals of Senate and Assembly, Eighteenth Session* (Sacramento, 1870), 1, *Third Biennial Report of the Superintendent of Public Education*, 14, quoted in Burchell, *San Francisco Irish*, 169–170.

44. Public Schools of San Francisco, *Course of Study* (San Francisco: J. R. Brodie and Company, 1891), 11.

45. Ibid., 12, 21.

46. Department of Public Instruction, San Francisco, *Schedule of Work for the Primary and Grammar Grades, July 28, 1898*, 16.

47. Anderson, *Thirty-Seventh Annual Report . . . 1890*, 14.

48. Superintendent Anderson's fears were no doubt exacerbated by the fact that, only the year before, the Buckley machine had not only refused a teaching appointment to his predecessor John Swett's daughter, but had then fired Swett. Swett reappeared in 1891 as the new Progressive school superintendent. C. A. Curry, "Shaping Young San Franciscans," 244, 281.

49. R. H. Webster, *Annual Report of the Public Schools of the City and County of San Francisco for the School Fiscal Year Ending June 30, 1898* (San Francisco: W. M. Hinton and Company, 1898), 29, 30, 31.

50. Cecil W. Mark, "Our City School System," 7, in *Annual Report of the Superintendent of the Common Schools of San Francisco, 1899.*

51. C. A. Curry, "Shaping Young San Franciscans," 270.

52. *Twenty-Seventh Annual Report . . . 1880*, 289; "Secretary's Report," *Thirty-Third Annual Report . . . 1886*, 49, 50; *Report of the Superintendent of Schools . . . 1906–07 and 1907–08*, 7; *Directory of Teachers and Schools, 1891*; and *Directory of the Department of Public Schools, 1909.*

53. Benjamin F. Gilbert and Charles Burdick, *Washington Square, 1857–1979: The History of San Jose State University* (San Jose, Calif.: San Jose State University, 1980), 1.

54. *Directory of the Department of Public Schools, 1909*, 57, 58; *Twenty-Seventh Annual Report . . . 1880*, 29, 274-276; *Thirty-Seventh Annual Report . . . 1890*, 15, 42; *Annual Report of the Public Schools . . . 1898*, 61; *Annual Report of the Superintendent . . . 1899*, 17; R. H. Webster, "Report of the Superintendent of Common Schools," in *The Annual Report of the Public Schools of the City and County of San Francisco for the Fiscal Year Ending June 30, 1901* (San Francisco, 1901), 55; *Annual Report of the Superintendent of the Common Schools of the City and County of San Francisco for the Fiscal Year Ending June 30, 1888* (San Francisco: W. M. Hinton and Company, 1888), 104; and U. S. Department of Interior, Bureau of Education, *Bulletin. 1917, No. 46*, 228.

55. *Rules of the Board of Education and Regulations of the Public Schools of San Francisco Adopted February 25, 1885* (San Francisco: A. L. Bancroft and Company, 1885), 18.

56. *Revised Course of Study for the Public Schools, June 1892*, 197; *Course of Study, Public Schools, San Francisco, California, 1897–1898* (San Francisco: H. S. Crocker Company, 1897), 111; *Some Conditions in the Schools of San Francisco: A Report Made by the School Survey Class of the California Branch of the Association of Collegiate Alumnae, May 1st, 1914: What Kind of Education Shall San Francisco Buy in 1914–1915?*, (San Francisco: Walter N. Brunt Company, 1914), 51.

57. Anderson, *Annual Report of the Superintendent . . . 1888*, 23.

58. *Twenty-Seventh Annual Report . . . 1880*, 18, 19.

59. *Annual Report of the Superintendent . . . 1899*, 151.

60. Ibid., 13, 20, 59.

61. *Twenty-Seventh Annual Report . . . 1880*, 92, 23, 21.

62. C. A. Curry, "Shaping Young San Franciscans," 271.

63. U. S. Department of Interior, Bureau of Education, *Bulletin. 1917, No. 46*, 64, 231.

64. Anderson, *Annual Report of the Superintendent . . . 1888*, 20.

65. San Francisco History Center, San Francisco Public Library, *Partial List of Importations in [the] San Francisco School Department* (San Francisco, n.d.), 2, 3.

Chapter 5. Chicago: Paradigm Shift

1. In 1908, Parliament extended the provisions of the British Old Age Pensions Act to Ireland. Henceforward, any Irish person over age seventy who had been a resident of the United Kingdom for at least twenty years and who had an annual income of no more than £31.10s. was eligible to receive a pension of between 1s. and 5s. a week. Paupers, lunatics, convicts, and the "chronically idle" were excluded. See F. S. L. Lyons, "The Developing Crisis, 1907–1914," in *A New History of Ireland*, 6:124–125n. McGowan's kindly neighbor, like many other parents of emigrants, often lost contact with their overseas children once this scheme was put in place. Only the most dutiful continued to send money to their parents in Ireland, and daughters outnumbered sons in this group. The state took up the slack, even if only in the most minimal way.

2. Mary McGowan Clancy, Chicago, to author, Evanston, Ill., 9 November 1998.

3. All quotations about Mary Theresa Meehan McGowan in this section are from ibid. unless otherwise noted.

4. Annmarie McNeela Ricker, Chicago, to author, Evanston, Ill., 15 September 1998.

5. Mark Twain to Amelia Dunne Hookway, October 1908, cited in J. Nolan, "Saint Patrick's Daughter," 103.

6. Elmer Ellis, *Mr. Dooley's America: A Life of Finley Peter Dunne* (New York: Alfred A. Knopf, 1941), 11.

7. Ibid., 10.

8. Ibid., 15; Charles Fanning, "Introduction," in Finley Peter Dunne, *Mr. Dooley and the Chicago Irish: The Autobiography of a Nineteenth-Century Ethnic Group* (Washington, D.C.: Catholic University of America Press, 1987), xvi.

9. George Howland, "Report of the Superintendent," *Twenty-Ninth Annual Report of the Board of Education for the Year Ending June 30, 1883* (Chicago: Jameson and Morse, 1884), 61.

10. See Sr. Mary Innocenta Montay, *The History of Catholic Secondary Education in the Archdiocese of Chicago* (Washington, D.C.: Catholic University of America Press, 1953), Table I: "Catholic Secondary Schools in the Archdiocese of Chicago," xxvi; Skerrett, "The Catholic Dimension," 44; J. Seymour Curry, *Chicago: Its History and Its Builders* (Chicago: S. J. Clarke Publishing Company, 1912), 304; and Mary J. Herrick, *The Chicago Schools: A Social and Political History* (Beverly Hills, Calif.: Sage Publications, 1971), Table 3: "The Training and Salary of Chicago Public School Teachers," 404. Catholic education in Chicago is also considered

in Suellen Hoy, "Caring for Chicago's Women and Girls: The Sisters of the Good Shepherd, 1859–1916," *Journal of Urban History* 23 (March 1997): 260–294; Timothy G. Walch, "Catholic Education in Chicago: The Formative Years, 1840–1890," *Chicago History* 7 (Summer 1978): 87–97; Ellen Skerrett, "Chicago's Irish and 'Bricks and Mortar' Catholicism: A Reappraisal," *U. S. Catholic Historian* 14 (Spring 1996): 53–71 and "The Irish Parish in Chicago, 1880–1930," Cushwa Center for American Catholicism, Working Paper Series 9, no. 4 (Notre Dame, Ind.: University of Notre Dame Press, 1981); and F. Michael Perko, S.J., ed., *Enlightening the Next Generation: Catholics and Their Schools, 1830–1980* (New York: Garland, 1988).

11. *Proceedings of the Board of Education of the City of Chicago, September, 1884, to September, 1885* (Chicago, 1885), 235; Department of Public Instruction, *Thirty-Second Annual Report of the Board of Education for the Year Ending June 30, 1886* (Chicago: George K. Hazlitt and Company, 1887), 175; Chicago Board of Education, *Twenty-Sixth Annual Report, 1880–1881*, 118; "Appendix: Names of Teachers Employed," Department of Public Instruction, City of Chicago, *Twenty-Ninth Annual Report of the Board of Education for the Year Ending June 30, 1883* (Chicago: Jameson and Morse, 1884), 155; "Appendix: Names of Teachers Employed," Department of Public Instruction, City of Chicago, *Thirty-Fourth Annual Report of the Board of Education for the Year Ending June 30, 1888* (Chicago: Hack and Anderson, 1889), 215; and "Names of Teachers Employed, March 1894," Public Schools of the City of Chicago, *Thirty-Ninth Annual Report of the Board of Education for the Year Ending June 30, 1893* (Chicago: George K. Hazlitt and Company, 1894), 298.

12. Len Hilts, "The Dunnes of New Brunswick and Chicago" n.d. (photocopy), 26. I wish to thank Ellen Skerrett for bringing this source to my attention.

13. "Amelia Dunne Hookway," *The New World*, 20 November 1914.

14. "Finley Peter Dunne at Bedside of Sister," *Chicago Daily Tribune*, 13 November 1914.

15. "Hookway," *The New World*, 20 November 1914.

16. Ella Flagg Young, "In Memoriam," in "Report of the Superintendent of Schools," *Public Schools of the City of Chicago: Sixty-First Annual Report of the Board of Education for the Year Ending June 30, 1915* (Chicago, n.d.), 35.

17. *Chicago Daily Tribune*, 13 November 1914.

18. I am grateful to Mary Leonard's descendent, Mary Foerner, a recent retiree from Chicago's teaching force, for sharing her family's history and photographs with me for use in this book.

19. Margaret Haley, *Battleground: The Autobiography of Margaret A. Haley,* edited and with an introduction by Robert L. Reid (Urbana: University of Illinois Press, 1982). All quotations attributed to Haley in this chapter are from her autobiography unless otherwise noted.

20. Ibid., 3. Henry George's *Progress and Poverty; An Inquiry into the Cause of Industrial Depressions, and the Increase of Want with Increase of Wealth. The Remedy* (New York: Henry George and Co., 1887) also influenced fellow-teacher San Franciscan Kate Kennedy's thinking about the rights of teachers and of the public schools in a rapidly urbanizing United States. See De Ford, *They Were San Franciscans,* 137.

21. Haley, *Battleground,* 23, 8, 9, 14. Haley's mother was paraphrasing the words of Charles Gavan Duffy, one of the founders of the mid-nineteenth century's nationalist organization, Young Ireland. Duffy's words gained wide readership in John O'Leary's *Young Ireland: The Old and the New* (Dublin: Young Ireland Society, 1885), 13. Although Haley does not specify this source, it is very likely that her mother was influenced by O'Leary's popular work as were many other Irish Americans. See also Keith Aldritt, *W. B. Yeats: The Man and the Milieu* (New York: Clarkson Potter, 1997), 39.

22. Haley, *Battleground,* 6, 13, 15, 20, 21, 22.

23. Louise C. Wade, "Haley, Margaret Angela," in *Notable American Women, 1607–1950: A Biographical Dictionary* 2, ed. Edward T. James, Janet Wilson James, and Paul S. Boyer (Cambridge: Harvard University Press, 1971), 115.

24. Haley, *Battleground,* 17, 24.

25. See Janet Nolan, "A Patrick Henry in the Classroom," 104–117; "Haley, Margaret Angela," in *Women Building Chicago 1790–1990: A Biographical Dictionary,* ed. Rima Lunin Schultz and Adele Hast (Bloomington: Indiana University Press, 2001), 338–341; and "Irish-American Teachers and the Struggle Over American Urban Public Education, 1890–1920: A Preliminary Look," *Records of the American Catholic Historical Society of Philadelphia* 103 (Winter 1992): 13–22.

26. Haley, *Battleground,* 40.

27. Ibid., 23, 8, 9, 24.

28. Ibid., 276.

29. Ibid., 28.

30. Ibid., 29, 30, 31, 33.

31. Herrick, Appendix C, Tables 1 and 2, 405–406.

32. For the 1908 and 1910 totals, see James Sanders, *The Education of an Urban Minority: Catholics in Chicago, 1833–1965* (New York: Oxford University Press, 1977), 131. Ellen Skerrett attributes the 1920 total to Archbishop George Cardinal Mundelein in "The Catholic Dimension," 46. See also J. Nolan, "Education: Irish-American Teachers in Public Schools, 1880–1920."

33. "Temperance Workers on Reforms. Woman Suffrage, Romanism's Power, and the Public Schools Touched Upon," *Chicago Tribune,* 27 February 1891; Sanders, *Education of an Urban Minority,* 163, 166; Skerrett, "The Catholic Dimension," 44–46.

34. Sanders, *Education of an Urban Minority*, 27, 28.

35. Ibid., 28, 130.

36. Reid, "Introduction," in Haley, *Battleground*, xi.

37. Ibid.

38. Haley, *Battleground*, 24.

39. Ibid., 43.

40. Reid, "Introduction," *Battleground*, xiii, xxviii.

41. Haley, *Battleground*, 90.

42. Ibid., 270.

43. Ibid., 276.

44. The distinction between "administrative progressives" and Haley's more democratic progressivism is made in David Tyack, *The One Best System: A History of American Urban Education* (Cambridge: Harvard University Press, 1974), 126, 127, 128, 129.

45. While Young was the most influential advocate of the teacher council movement, a female Chicago high school teacher—Frances Temple—was the first to promote the idea in Chicago. Haley, *Battleground*, 113.

46. Haley, "Why Teachers Should Organize," *Addresses and Proceedings of the National Education Association*, 43rd Annual Meeting, St. Louis, Missouri, 1904, in Haley, *Battleground*, Appendix B, 286.

47. Haley, *Battleground*, 113, 114.

48. Ibid., 13.

49. Ibid., 148.

50. Reid, "Introduction," *Battleground*, xxiv.

51. Haley, *Battleground*, 35, 36, 37.

52. Ibid., 60.

53. Ibid., 3.

54. Haley's autobiography, written in segments between 1910 and 1935, was not published until 1982. Even today, no biography of Haley exists. See Reid, "Introduction," xxxii; Wayne J. Urban, *Why Teachers Organized* (Detroit: Wayne State University Press, 1982), 78; and Marvin Lazerson, "Teachers Organize: What Margaret Haley Lost," *History of Education Quarterly* 24 (Summer 1984): 261.

55. Haley, *Battleground*, 37.

56. Ibid., 8.

57. Ibid., 45.

58. Ibid., 35.

59. Ibid., 114.

60. Chicago Board of Education, *Procedings, Board of Education, 1915–1916*, 734, quoted in ibid., *Battleground*, 171.

61. Ibid., 169.

62. Ibid., 180.

63. Ibid., 181. While Haley's reference to Gompers' ethnicity may seem anti-Semitic, her lifelong opposition to British rule in Ireland makes "English" the term of opprobrium, not "Jew."

64. While opposition to having married women in Chicago classrooms had existed since at least 1879, when the Board of Education ruled that "the marriage of any female teacher should be deemed the equivalent to a tender of, and the acceptance of, her resignation," a formal marriage bar preventing wives from being city teachers was not formalized until well into the twentieth century, allowing Amelia Dunne Hookway, among many others, to continue a career even after marrying. See "Amendment to Rule in Reference to Married Teachers," *Proceedings of the Board of Education of the City of Chicago, September, 1879, to September, 1880* (Chicago, 1880), 76; and "Ask Labor to Take Jobs from Women When They Marry," *Chicago Tribune,* 18 March 1912.

65. Carl Sandburg, "Margaret Haley," *Reedy's Mirror* 24 (December 1915): 445, quoted in Reid, "Introduction," *Battleground,* xxxi; Richard Finegan in the *Chicago Times,* quoted in ibid., xxxii; and Haley, *Battleground,* 3.

66. Haley, *Battleground,* 3.

67. Richard Finegan, *Chicago Times,* quoted in Reid, "Introduction," *Battleground,* xxxii; Agnes Nestor, *Woman's Labor Leader: An Autobiography* (Rockford, Ill.: Bellevue Books, 1954), 165; C. Sandburg, "Margaret Haley," 445, quoted in Reid, "Introduction," xxxi. The reference to Haley as a "little woman" was a description of her physical size—she was only a hundred pounds—and should not be taken as a sexist statement.

Chapter 6. The End of a Golden Age

1. George S. Counts, *School and Society in Chicago* (New York: Harcourt, Brace, and Co., 1928; reprint, New York: Arno Press, 1971), 11, 12, 20, 21, 28. For more on Counts, see George W. Dixon, "George S. Counts and the Imposition Controversy," *Journal of the Midwest History of Education Society* 5 (1977): 105; and Gerald S. Gutek, "George S. Counts As an Ideologist of American Education, the 1930s," ibid., 99–104; *idem, The Educational Theory of George S. Counts* (Columbus: Ohio State University Press, 1970); and *idem, George S. Counts and American Civilization: The Educator as Social Theorist* (Macon, Ga.: Mercer University Press, 1984).

2. Counts, *School and Society,* 28, 30, 31, 43.

3. Ibid., 49, 50.

4. Ibid., 51, 53.

5. Ibid., 65, 66, 67.

6. Ibid., 63.

7. Ibid., 100.

8. John Swett, "California Superintendent of Public Instruction, *Reports*" (1865), 124, quoted in C. A. Curry, "Shaping Young San Franciscans," 85.

9. Dowling, *California*, 242, 245. According to C. A. Curry, in 1907, only 90 of the 971 teachers in San Francisco were men, one-third of whom taught in high schools. Since the mostly male high school teachers were better paid than the mostly female elementary school teachers, some of the inequality in male and female teaching salaries can be explained by rank rather than sex. On the other hand, women teaching in San Francisco's high schools in that year earned an average of $126 per month as opposed to the $140 average monthly salary paid their male colleagues. Sex as well as rank, therefore, accounts for the wage discrepancy. C. A. Curry, "Shaping Young San Franciscans," 312.

10. U. S. Department of Interior, Bureau of Education, *Bulletin. 1917*, no. 46, 224, 231.

11. Kate Rousmaniere, *City Teachers: Teaching and School Reform in Historical Perspective* (New York: Teachers College, Columbia University, 1997), 24, 25, 26, 27.

12. See John Lyons, "The Chicago Teachers' Union, Politics, and the City's Schools, 1937–1970" (Ph.D. diss., University of Illinois at Chicago, 2001), especially chapter 1: "The Great Depression and the Crisis in Chicago Public Education, 1929–1934," 1–72.

13. Haley, *Battleground*, 132.

14. Reid, "Why Teachers Should Organize," in ibid., Appendix B, 279–287.

15. George Howland, *Moral Training in the Public Schools* (Chicago: Jameson and Morse, 1882, 1889).

16. Ibid., 11, 19, 20.

17. Ibid., 33, 110, 150, 169, 170.

18. Lotus Delta Coffman, *The Social Composition of the Teaching Profession* (New York: Teachers College, Columbia University, 1911), 1.

19. Ibid., 14, 77, 71.

20. Ibid., 84, 85, 70.

21. For fertility figures, see Table 71, "Census for the United States," in U.S. Congress, Senate, *Reports of the Immigration Commission: Abstracts of Reports of the Immigration Commission with Conclusions and Recommendations and Views of the Minority* 1, 1911, 61st Cong., 3d sess., S. Doc. 747, 429; and Table 82, Niles Carpenter, *Immigrants and Their Children*, Census Monograph (New York: Arno Press, 1969), 18.

22. Mary Ledger Moffett, *The Social Background and Activities of Teachers College Students* (New York: Teachers College, Columbia University, 1929), 2, 14, 103.

23. See J. P. Walsh, "Peter C. Yorke: San Francisco's Irishman Reconsidered," in *San Francisco Irish*, 45. The Illinois Supreme Court declared the classroom use of

the King James Bible in the state's public schools unconstitutional only in 1910. Sanders, *Education of an Urban Minority*, 24.

24. Jurgen Herbst, *And Sadly Teach: Teacher Education and Professionalization in American Culture* (Madison: University of Wisconsin Press, 1989), 101.

25. Marvin Lazerson, "If All the World Were Chicago: American Education in the Twentieth Century," *History of Education Quarterly* 24 (Summer 1984): 165–179, 169.

26. Ibid., 190–191.

27. Wayne J. Urban, "Teacher Organizations in New York City, 1905–1920," in *Educating an Urban People: The New York City Experience*, ed. Diane Ravitch and Ronald K. Goodenow (New York: Teachers College Press, Columbia University, 1981), 189.

28. Grace C. Strachan, *Equal Pay for Equal Work: The Story of the Struggle for Justice Being Made by the Women Teachers of the City of New York* (New York: B. F. Buck and Company, 1910), 11, 7.

29. Urban, "Teacher Organizations," 188; K. Rousmaniere, "City Teachers," 27, 28, 35. See also Robert E. Doherty, "Tempest on the Hudson: The Struggle for 'Equal Pay for Equal Work' in the New York City Public Schools, 1907–1911." *History of Education Quarterly* 19 (Winter 1979): 413–434.

30. The discussion of the philosophy of professional ethics that follows stems from a semester spent as a research fellow at the Loyola University, Chicago, Center for Ethics in the spring of 2000. See also David T. Ozar, "An Outcomes-Centered Approach to Teaching Public-Sector Ethics," in *Teaching Ethics and Values: Program Innovation and Classroom Strategies,* ed. James Bowman and Donald Menzel, 85–99 (Albany: State University of New York Press, 1997); Ozar, "Profession and Professional Ethics," in *The Encyclopedia of Bioethics,* rev. ed., vol. 4, ed. Warren Reich (New York: Macmillan, 1995); idem, "Framework for Discussing Ethics," 1997 (photocopy), 4; and idem, "Five Approaches to Moral/Ethical Decision-Making," 1998 (photocopy) 2, 3.

31. J. Lyons, "Chicago Teachers' Union," 4, 8, 10, 11.

32. Ibid., 12, 13, 19.

33. Ibid., 20, 21.

34. Ibid., 22, 25, 26.

35. Ibid., 27, 29, 31.

36. Ibid., 36, 38, 39.

37. Ibid., 41, 43, 44, 45.

38. Paul H. Heidebrecht, "Hefferan, Helen Maley," in *Women Building Chicago 1790–1990: A Biographical Dictionary,* ed. Rima Lunin Schultz and Adele Hast (Bloomington: Indiana University Press, 2001), 371, 372, 373.

39. Ibid., 371.

40. J. Lyons, "Chicago Teachers' Union," 51.

41. Ibid., 52, 55.

Chapter 7. "The One Thing They Can't Take Away"

1. "Warm Welcome for Tully Family," Swinford, County Mayo, August 1999 (photocopy).

2. Delia McNeela Tully, "Memoir," 1999 (photocopy).

3. See Janet Nolan, "Legacy: Education and Women's Mobility in Irish Chicago and San Francisco in the Early Twentieth Century," in "New Approaches to Family History, Genealogy, and Irish Studies," *Working Papers in Irish Studies,* ed. James Doan, 1–5 (Fort Lauderdale, Fl.: Nova Southeastern University, 2002).

4. Mary DeCock, B.V.M., "Creating a College: The Foundation of Mundelein, 1929–1931," in *Mundelein Voices: The Women's College Experience, 1929–1931,* ed. Ann Harrington and Prudence Moylan (Chicago: Loyola Press, 2001), 13, 17.

5. Lorraine X. Page, "The Genealogy of Galena: Nineteenth Century Americana," 1993 (unpublished photocopy); and idem, Martinez, G., to author, Evanston, Ill., 10 August 1998.

6. Joan Enright, Orland Park, Ill., to author, Evanston, Ill., 9 July 1998.

7. Marguerite Mullen, "Michael Tully, 1895–1983," March 1977 (photocopy of unpaginated manuscript).

8. Ibid.

9. Ibid.

10. Dorothy Hastings Valeo, Lamont, Ill., to author, Evanston, Ill., 16 July 1998.

11. Mary Nolan was a graduate of the prestigious college-preparatory Classical High School in Lynn as well as the (then three-year) junior high course at Salem Normal School, later Teachers College, in 1930. Although she spent nearly a year on the unemployment rolls during that first grim year of the Great Depression, Mary became one of the first home-class teachers hired in Lynn. In fact, she was one of the first home-class teachers in the state of Massachusetts. William F. Nolan, "Memoirs to My Family," 1979 (photocopy of unpublished manuscript), 107, 22, 103, 104.

12. Ibid., 71–77, 103–104, 109–114, 156–157.

13. Ibid., 193, 194.

14. Ibid., Emphasis in the original.

15. Ibid., 194, 195.

16. The Pinkham scholarship was donated by the family of Lynn-native Lydia Pinkham, inventor of the "restorative" tonic named after her and manufactured in the city. Lawrence "Nuggets" McGinn was a graduate of Lynn Classical High School and Brown University. He was named Lynn Schools superintendent in 1958, and retired in the early 1970s. Ibid., 195n.

17. Ibid., 197.

18. Ibid., 204, 214.

19. Philip Cashman had taken a leave of absence from his teaching post at the Cobbet Ungraded to become the Superintendent of Special Education Programs in the Massachusetts Department of Education in Boston. While there was a chance that Cashman would return to his Lynn job and Nolan would again return to the ranks of the unemployed, Steve Walsh, the Lynn school attendance officer and friend of Nolan's father Harry in their General Electric days, assured him that "Once they've tasted champagne they never come back to beer." Walsh proved to be correct, and Nolan kept his job. Ibid., 217, 218.

20. Ibid., 217–220.

21. Ibid., 224, 246.

22. Ibid., 249, 250.

23. Ibid., 255, 275.

24. Ibid., 309.

25. Edward Mueller, Chicago, Ill., to author, Evanston, Ill., 13 August 1998; and Eleanor Mueller King, Chicago, Ill., to author, Evanston, Ill., 25 July 1998.

26. John O'Leary, interview by author, 12 July 1999, Dublin, Ireland.

27. Dudley Nee, Chicago, Ill., to author, Evanston, Ill., 10 July 1998.

28. Thomas J. O'Brien, Sr., Huntington Beach, Calif., to author, Evanston, Ill., 9 September 1998.

29. William King, Indianhead Park, Ill., to author, Evanston, Ill., 25 September 1998.

30. Margaret "Peg" Cunningham, Chicago, Ill., to author, Evanston, Ill., 24 August 1998.

31. Ibid.

BIBLIOGRAPHY

Ireland

National Archives Ireland

Aghaloora School, County Cavan. "Margaret Smyth and Mathew Comisky Case." ED9/4516/7732/33/1886–87.

Brown, James. "Application for Salary for a Workmistress, Castlegregory National School, County Kerry." 29 February 19/856. ED1/39, #163.

Browne, Rev. P., Castlegregory, County Kerry, to the Secretaries of National Education, Dublin, 2 September 1897. ED2/197, folio 100.

———. Castlegregory, County Kerry, to the Commissioners of National Education in Ireland, Dublin, 5 March 1901. ED9/14848.

———. Castlegregory, County Kerry, to the Secretaries of National Education, Dublin, 20 August 1912. ED9/file 23624.

"Castlegregory National School, County Kerry." ED9/file 7394.

Daly, Louis. "District Inspector's Observation Book, Caherciveen Number 2 National School, Kerry, 12 February 1907, 13 January 1908, 28 July 1908, 26 May 1910." ED9/1186/7/11.

Darman, E. T. "District Inspector's Observation Book, Caherciveen Number 2 National School, Kerry, 17 May 1917." ED9/1186/7/11.

Dee, John. "Application to the Commissioners of National Education in Ireland for Payment of Teachers' Salaries and Supply of Books, Castlegregory National School, County Kerry." 1 May 1850. ED1/39, #96.

"District Inspector's Notes: Castlegregory Girls National School, County Kerry." ED2/196, folio 26.

"District Inspector's Notes: Castlegregory Girls National School, County Kerry, 17 August 1880, 8 November 1892, 14 November 1892, 19 December 1892. ED2/197, folio 101.

Doody, J. V., Jr., "District Inspector's Observation Book, Caherciveen Number 2 National School, 10 November 1908." ED9/1186/7/11.

Driscoll, Denis F. "Queries—Application for Salary of Assistant Teacher, Castlegregory National School, County Kerry, 16 February 1865." ED1/40, #167.

Healy, Thomas. "Queries to Be Answered on Application to the Commissioners of Education for Aid Towards the Salary of the Teacher or Teachers of Castlegregory National Schools, County Kerry, 6 May 1844." ED1/38/ #122.

Johnston, Isabella F. "Roll for Cookery and Laundry Work, 1912–1913." In *District Inspector's Reports, Coorlespratten National School, Cavan.* ED9/1178/ Nos. 26 and 33.

Kane, ?. "District Inspector's Observation Book, Caherciveen Number 2 National School, Kerry, 21 December 1911. ED9/1186/7/11.

Lehane, D. "District Inspector's Observation Book, Caherciveen Number 2 National School, Kerry, 12 September 1910." ED9/1186/7/11.

Little, Robert. "Memorandum for the Secretaries to the National Commisssioners, 5 August 1913." ED9/ file 23624.

"Student Cookery Notebook." In *Miscellaneous Papers.* ED9/2008/7/22.

Welply, W. H. "District Inspector's Observation Book, Caherciveen Number 2 National School, Kerry, Teachers, 12 August 1907." ED9/1186/7/11.

Public Record Office of Northern Ireland

Guide to Educational Records. Belfast: Public Record Office of Northern Ireland, n.d.

Kelly, John. "School Record of John Kelly, School Attendance Officer." Belfast, June 1896.

Moriarty, Bishop. "Emigrant Letters." T.1767, 66.

National Library of Ireland

Board of Guardians. *Children's History Book.* Dublin: Hely's, n.d.

Commissioners of National Education in Ireland:

Biographical Sketches of Eminent British Poets Chronologically Arranged from Chaucer to Burns . . . Intended for Teachers and the Higher Classes in Schools. Dublin: Alexander Thom, 1870.

Commissioners of National Education in Ireland Manual of Needlework. Dublin: Alexander Thom and Co., 1889.

Epitome of Geographical Knowledge, Ancient and Modern, Compiled for the Use of Teachers and Advanced Classes of the National Schools of Ireland, new and rev. ed. Dublin: Alexander Thom, 1857.

Fifty-Seventh Annual Report of the Commissioners of National Education in Ireland for the Year 1890. Dublin: Alexander Thom, 1891.

Reading Book for the Use of Female Schools, Fifth Level. Dublin: Alexander Thom, 1862.

Rules and Regulations of the Commissioners of National Education in Ireland. Dublin: Alexander Thom, 1869.

Rules and Regulations of the Commissioners of National Education in Ireland, 1903. Dublin: Office of National Education, 1903.

Rules and Regulations of the National Commissioners of Education in Ireland, 1914–1915. Dublin: Alexander Thom, 1914.

The Seventy-Seventh Report of the Commissioners of National Education in Ireland, Year 1911. Dublin: Alexander Thom, 1912.

Simple Directions in Needlework and Cutting Out; Intended for the Use of National Female Schools of Ireland to Which Are Added Specimens of Work Executed by the Pupils of the Female National Model School. Dublin: Alexander Thom and Sons, 1853.

Egan, P. M. *The National Readers for Irish National Schools Fifth Book (First Stage).* Kilkenny, Ireland: P. M. Egan, 1897.

Erskine, W. *A Review of the National School System of Education: Its Evils Exposed, and Improvements Suggested.* Belfast: J. W. Boyd, 1895 (?).

Foster, Vere. *Vere Foster Copy Book of Mata Blackwood [County Down], November 24th, 1882–March 8th, 1883.* Dublin: Blackie and Son Printers, n.d.

———. *Vere Foster's Drawing Books—K.2, Drawn by J. Needham.* London and Belfast: Marcus Ward and Co., n.d.

Great Britain. Intermediate Education Board for Ireland. *Reports of Inspectors, 1909–1910. Vol. 3, Girls Schools:*

Kerin, R. C. B. "Convent of St. Louis, Carrickmacross [County Monaghan], 13 and 18 April 1910."

———. and T. Rea. "Ladies School, Dundalk [County Louth], 7 and 11 April 1910."

Maguire, Mr. "Mount Pleasant School, Ballinasloe [County Mayo], 25 February 1910."

O'Neill, J. J. and T. Rea. "Ladies Collegiate School, Carrickfergus [County Antrim], 9–10–31 May 1910."

Wright, C. E. and E. Ensor. "Brigidine Convent, Abbeyleix [Queen's County], 3 May 1910."

———. "Convent of Mercy High School, Carrick-on-Suir [County Tipperary], 4 February 1910."

———. "Presentation Convent, Bagenalstown [County Carlow], 8 March 1910."

————. "Presentation Convent, Bagenalstown [County Kilkenny], 8 March 1910."

————, E. Ensor, and J. J. O'Neill. "Loretto Convent, Balbriggan [County Dublin], 11–12 October 1909."

Joyce, P. W. *A Handbook of School Management and Methods of Teaching,* 17th ed. Dublin: Gill and Son, 1897.

————. *The Teaching of Manual Work in Schools.* Dublin: Gill, 1892.

Kenny, Louise. "A New Irish School of Housewifery." *Irish Homestead* 11 (March 25, 1905): 240–241.

O'Kane, Michael M. *Woman's Place in the World.* Dublin: M. H. Gill and Son, 1913.

Ryan, Frederick W. *School Attendance in Ireland under the Compulsory Education Act, 1892.* Dublin: E. Ponsonby, 1912.

United Kingdom. *Census for Ireland for the Year 1911: General Report, with Tables and Appendix.* Athlone, Ireland: Athlone Printing Works Co., 1913.

Wyse, Thomas. "Elementary Education in Ireland." *American Journal of Education* 2 (1862): 133–154.

Young, Thomas Urry. *The Teacher's Manual for Infant Schools and Preparatory Classes.* Dublin: M'Glashan and Gill, 1856.

Books and Articles

Akenson, Donald H. *The Irish Education Experiment: The National System of Education in the Nineteenth Century.* London: Routledge and Kegan Paul, 1970.

————. "Pre-University Education." In *A New History of Ireland,* Vol. 6, *Ireland under the Union, 1870–1921,* edited by W. E. Vaughan, 523–538. Oxford: Oxford University Press, 1996.

Aldritt, Keith. *W. B. Yeats: The Man and the Milieu.* New York: Clarkson Potter, 1997.

Atkinson, Norman. *Irish Education: A History of Educational Institutions.* Dublin: Allan Figgis, 1969.

Bourke, Joanna. *Husbandry to Housewifery: Women, Economic Change, and Housework in Ireland, 1890–1914.* Oxford: Clarendon Press, 1993.

"Census of Ireland, 1821." In Table 3, "Population, 1821–1971." In *Irish Historical Statistics,* edited by W. E. Vaughan and A. J. Fitzpatrick, 3. Dublin: Royal Irish Academy, 1978.

Daly, Mary. "Women in the Irish Free State, 1922–1939: The Interaction Between Economics and Ideology." *Journal of Women's History* 6/7 (Winter 1995): 99–116.

Dowling, Patrick. *The Hedge Schools of Ireland.* Cork: Mercier, 1968.

Fitzpatrick, David. "Emigration, 1871–1921." In *A New History of Ireland*. Vol. 6, *Ireland under the Union, 1870–1921*, edited by W. E. Vaughan, 606–652. Oxford: Oxford University Press, 1996.

———. "The Futility of History: A Failed Experiment in Irish Education." In *Ideology and the Historians,* Historical Studies 17, edited by Ciaran Brady, 168–183. Dublin: Lilliput Press, 1991.

———. *Irish Emigration, 1801–1921*. Dublin: Dundalgan Press, 1984.

———. "The Modernisation of the Irish Female." In *Rural Ireland, 1600–1900: Modernisation and Change,* edited by Patrick O'Flanagan, Paul Ferguson, and Kevin Whelan, 162–180. Cork: Cork University Press, 1987.

———. "'A Share of the Honeycomb': Education, Emigration and Irishwomen." *Continuity and Change* 1 (1986): 217–234.

———. "Women and the Great Famine." In *Gender Perspectives in Nineteenth-Century Ireland, Public and Private Spheres,* edited by Margaret Kelleher and James H. Murphy, 50–69. Dublin: Irish Academic Press, 1997.

Goldstrom, J. M. "Richard Whately and Political Economy in School Books, 1833–1880." *Irish Historical Studies* 15 (September 1966): 131–146.

———. *The Social Context of Education, 1808–1870: A Study of the Working Class Reader in England and Ireland*. Shannon: Irish University Press, 1972.

Hyland, Aine and Kenneth Milne, eds. *Irish Educational Documents*. Vol. 1, *A Selection of Extracts Relating to the History of Irish Education from the Earliest Times to 1922*. Dublin: Church of Ireland College of Education, 1987.

Jackson, Pauline. "Women in Nineteenth Century Emigration." *International Migration Review* 18 (Winter 1984): 1004–1021.

Kamm, Josephine. *Hope Deferred: Girls' Education in English History*. London: Methuen, 1965.

Lawson, John and Harold Silver. *A Social History of Education in England*. London: Methuen, 1973.

Logan, John. "Sufficient to Their Needs: Literacy and Elementary Schooling in the Nineteenth Century." In *The Origins of Popular Literacy in Ireland: Language Change and Educational Development 1700–1920,* edited by Mary Daly and David Dickson, 113–137. Dublin: Trinity College Press, 1992.

Luddy, Maria. *Women and Philanthropy in Nineteenth-Century Ireland*. Cambridge: Cambridge University Press, 1995.

Lyons, F. S. L. "The Developing Crises, 1907–1914." In *A New History of Ireland*. Vol. 6, *Ireland under the Union, 1870–1921,* edited by W. E. Vaughan, 123–144. Oxford: Oxford University Press, 1996.

McCurtain, Margaret. "Late in the Field: Catholic Sisters in Twentieth Century Ireland and the New Religious History." *Journal of Women's History* 6/7 (Winter 1995): 49–63.

McLysaght, Edward. *The Surnames of Ireland.* 2d ed. Dublin: Irish Academic Press, 1997.

MacShambrain, A. S. "Ideological Conflict and Historical Interpretation: The Problem of History in Irish Primary Education c. 1900–1930." *Irish Educational Studies* 10 (Spring 1991): 229–243.

Murphy, James H. "Chapter Six: A Religious Education, 1801–1884." 2001. (Photocopy).

Murphy, Maureen. "The Fionnuala Factor: Irish Sibling Migration at the Turn of the Century." In *Gender and Sexuality in Modern Ireland,* edited by Anthony Bradley and Maryann Gialanella Valiulis, 85–101. Amherst: University of Massachusetts Press, 1997.

Neville, Grace. "Dark Lady of the Archives: Towards an Analysis of Women and Emigration to North America in Irish Folklore." In *Chattel, Servant or Citizen: Women's Status in Church, State and Society,* edited by Mary O'Dowd and Sabine Wichert, 200–214. Belfast: Institute of Irish Studies/Queen's University Belfast Press, 1995.

Nolan, Janet. "The Great Famine and Women's Emigration from Ireland." In *The Hungry Stream: Essays on Famine and Emigration,* edited by E. Margaret Crawford, 67–75. Belfast: Institute of Irish Studies/Queen's University Belfast Press, 1997.

———. "The National Schools and Irish Women's Mobility in the Late Nineteenth and Early Twentieth Centuries." *Irish Studies Review* 18 (Spring 1997): 23–28.

Ó Buachualla, Seamus. "The Language in the Classroom." *Crane Bag* 5 (1981): 18–31.

O'Connell, T. J. *History of the Irish National Teachers' Organization, 1868–1968.* Dublin: INTO/Dakota, 1968.

O'Flynn, Grainne. "Our Age of Innocence." In *Girls Don't Do Honours: Irish Women in Education in the Nineteenth and Twentieth Centuries,* edited by Mary Cullen, 79–99. Dublin: Women's Educational Bureau, 1987.

Ó Grada, Cormac. *Ireland: A New Economic History, 1780–1939.* New York: Oxford University Press, 1994.

O'Leary, Eoin. "The Irish Teachers' Organization and the Marriage Bar for Women National Teachers, 1933–1958." *Saothar* 12 (1987): 47–52.

O'Leary, John. *Young Ireland: The Old and the New.* Dublin: Young Ireland Society, 1885.

Travers, Patrick. "Emigration and Gender: The Case of Ireland, 1922–1960." In *Chattel, Servant or Citizen: Women's Status in Church, State and Society,* edited by Mary O'Dowd and Sabine Wichert, 187–199. Belfast: Institute of Irish Studies/Queen's University Belfast Press, 1995.

Valiulis, Maryann. "Power, Gender, and Identity in the Irish Free State." *Journal of Women's History* 6/7 (Winter 1995): 117–136.

Walsh, Lorcan. "Images of Women in Nineteenth Century Schoolbooks." *Irish Educational Studies* 4 (1984): 73–87.

The United States

Memoirs (Unpublished)

Hilts, Len. "The Dunnes of New Brunswick and Chicago" (photocopy), n.d. In possession of Len Hilts, Chicago.

Lennon, Mary Crowe. "Pages of My Life" (photocopy), 30 June 1989. In possession of author, Chicago.

Mullen, Marguerite. "Michael Tully, 1895–1983" (photocopy), March 1977. In possession of author, Chicago.

Nolan, William F. "Memoirs to My Family" (photocopy), 1979. In possession of author, Chicago.

O'Sullivan, Margaret (Sister M. Columba). "Annals of the Sisters of Mercy," n.d. In Gerald O'Sullivan, "Sister M. Columba O'Sullivan, R. I. P." (photocopy), 1987 (?). In possession of the author, Chicago.

Page, Lorraine X. "The Genealogy of Galena: Nineteenth Century Americana" (photocopy), 1993. In possession of the author, Chicago.

Tully, Delia McNeela. "Memoirs" (photocopy), 1999. In possession of the author, Chicago.

Interviews

Curry, Catherine Ann. Telephone interview by author. San Francisco, 30 January 1998.

Murphy, Eileen M. Telephone interview by author. San Francisco, 12 January 1998.

O'Leary, Joan Crean. Telephone interview by author. St. Charles, Ill. 30 January 1998.

O'Leary, John. Interview by author. Dublin, Ireland. 12 July 1999.

Letters to Author

Clancy, Mary Ann. Chicago, 9 November 1998.

Conlon, Elizabeth. Chicago, 4 June 1998.

Cunningham, Margaret "Peg." Chicago, 24 August 1998.

Curry, Catherine Ann. Menlo Park, Calif., 27 March 1998.

Ellis, Caren Cotter. Santa Rosa, Calif., 6 September 1998.

Enright, Joan. Orland Park, Ill., 9 July 1998.

Finegan, Sandy. Tiburon, Calif., 1 September 1998.

Hawkins, Margaret O'Connell. Elmwood Park, Ill., 28 July 1998.

Hester, Catherine "Kay." Orland Park, Ill., 24 August 1998.

Hogan, Mary Coletta. Chicago, 30 June 1999.

Hornung, Mary McDonnell. Lamont, Ill., 16 July 1998.

King, Eleanor Mueller. Chicago, 25 July 1998.

King, William. Indianhead Park, Ill., 25 September 1998.

McNally, Ann. Chicago, 16 July 1998.

Moran, Urania Michaela. San Francisco, 4 March 1998.

Mueller, Edward. Sheboygan, Wisc., 13 August 1998.

Nee, Dudley. Chicago, 10 July 1998.

Nolan, Loretta Fisher. Lincolnwood, Ill., 9 November 1998.

O'Brien, Thomas J. Huntington Beach, Calf., 9 September 1998.

O'Sullivan, Neilus. Mountain View, Calf., 9 November 1998.

Page, Lorraine X. Chicago, 10 August 1998.

Ricker, Annmarie McNeela. Chicago, 15 September 1998.

Schmit, Maureen Sheehan. Chicago, 15 December 1998.

Sullivan, Helen. River Forest, Ill., 5 July 1998.

Valeo, Dorothy Hastings. Lamont, Ill., 16 July 1998.

Walsh, Julia Mulvaney. Chicago, 31 August 1998.

Walsh, Kate. Port Orchard, Wash., 30 July 1998.

Walsh, Patricia. Redwood City, Calf., 16 September 1998.

Boston

City of Boston. School Doc. 27. Moran, John B., Henry P. Bowditch, and Abram E. Cutter. *Thirty-Seventh Annual Report of the School Committee of the City of Boston, March 1 1880.* Boston: Rockwell and Churchill, 1881.

———. School Doc. No. 54. "City of Boston Annual Report, by the City Registrar, of the Births, Marriages, and Deaths in the City of Boston for the Year 1874." Boston: Boston Public Library, n.d.

———. School Doc. No. 104—1886. "Population of the City of Boston: An Analysis of the Population of the City of Boston, As Shown in the State Census of May, 1885." *Documents of the City of Boston for the Year 1886* 3. Boston: Rockwell and Churchill, 1887.

———. School Doc. No. 152. "Report Submitted by Thorton D. Appollonio." *Communication from the School Committee Relative to the Text-Books on Irish History in the Public Schools,* 1–3. Boston: Boston Public Library, 21 December 1906.

San Francisco

Association of Collegiate Alumni, California. *Some Conditions in the Schools of San Francisco: A Report Made by the School Survey Class of the California Branch of the Association of Collegiate Alumnae, Mary 1st, 1914: What Kind of Education Shall San Francisco Buy in 1914–1915?* San Francisco: Walter N. Brunt Company, 1914.

Department of Public Instruction, San Francisco. *Schedule of Work for the Primary and Grammar Grades, July 28, 1898.*

Department of Public Schools, City and County of San Francisco. *Twenty-Seventh Annual Report of the Superintendent of Public Schools for the School Year Ending June 30, 1880.* San Francisco: W. M. Hinton and Company, 1880.

———. "Secretary's Report." In *Thirty-Third Annual Report of the Superintendent of Public Schools for the School Year Ending June 30, 1886.* San Francisco: W. M. Hinton and Company, 1886.

———. *Thirty-Seventh Annual Report of the Superintendent of Common Schools of the City and County of San Francisco for the Fiscal Year Ending June 30, 1890.* San Francisco: W. M. Hinton and Company, 1890.

Mark, Cecil. "Our City School System." In *Annual Report of the Superintendent of the Common Schools of San Francisco, 1899.* San Francisco, n.d.

"Partial List of Importations in [the] San Francisco School Department." San Francisco, n.d.

Public Schools of San Francisco. *Course of Study.* San Francisco: J. R. Brodie and Company, 1891.

San Francisco Board of Education. *Directory of Teachers and Schools of the Department of Public Schools, City and County of San Francisco, June 8, 1891.*

———. *Rules of the Board of Education and Regulations of the Public Schools of San Francisco Adopted February 25, 1885.* San Francisco: A. L. Bancroft and Company, 1885.

San Francisco Public Schools. *Annual Report of the Board of Education, San Francisco, 1910.*

———. *Annual Report of the Public Schools of the City and County of San Francisco for the School Fiscal Year Ending June 30, 1898.* San Francisco: W. M. Hinton and Company, 1898.

———. *Annual Report of the Superintendent, 1880.*

———. *Annual Report of the Superintendent of the Common Schools of the City and County of San Francisco for the Fiscal Year Ending June 30, 1888.* San Francisco: W. M. Hinton and Company, 1888.

———. *Annual Report of the Superintendent of the Common Schools of San Francisco, 1899.*

———. *Course of Study, Public Schools, San Francisco, California, 1897–1898.* San Francisco: H. S. Crocker Company, 1897.

———. *Directory of the Department of Public Schools, 1909.*

———. "Directory of Teachers." In *Annual Report of the Board of Education, San Francisco, 1910.*

———. *Directory of Teachers and Schools, 1891.*

———. "List of Teachers, Schools, and Residences, 1909."

———. *Report of the Superintendent of Schools and Board of Education, San Francisco, California, for the Fiscal Years 1906–07 and 1907–08.* San Francisco: Neal Publishing Company, 1907.

———. *Revised Course of Study for the Public Schools, June 1892.*

San Francisco School Department. *Directory of the Department of Public Schools of the City and County of San Francisco, November 1, 1909.* San Francisco: Phillips and Van Orden Company, 1909.

San Francisco School Women. "Alice Rose Power Commendation" (photocopy), June 1943.

Webster, R. H. "Report of the Superintendent of Common Schools." In *The Annual Report of the Public Schools of the City and County of San Francisco for the Fiscal Year Ending June 30, 1901.*

Chicago

Board of Education of the City of Chicago. "Amendment to Rule in Reference to Married Teachers." In *Proceedings of the Board of Education of the City of Chicago, September, 1879, to September, 1880.*

———. *Proceedings of the Board of Education of the City of Chicago. September, 1879, to September, 1880.* Chicago, 1880.

———. *Proceedings of the Board of Education of the City of Chicago, September, 1884, to September, 1885.* Chicago, 1885.

———. *Proceedings. Board of Education, City of Chicago. June 8, 1914 to June 30, 1915.*

———. *Proceedings. Board of Education, City of Chicago. July 1928 to June 1929.*

Department of Public Instruction, City of Chicago. "Appendix: Names of Teachers Employed." In *Twenty-Ninth Annual Report of the Board of Education for the Year Ending June 30, 1883.* Chicago: Jameson and Morse, 1884.

———. "Appendix: Names of Teachers Employed." In *Thirty-Fourth Annual Report of the Board of Education for the Year Ending June 30, 1888.* Chicago: Hack and Anderson,1889.

———. *Thirty-Second Annual Report of the Board of Education for the Year Ending June 30, 1886.* Chicago: George K. Hazlitt and Company, 1887.

Howland, George. "Report of the Superintendent." In *Twenty-Ninth Annual Report of the Board of Education for the Year Ending June 30, 1883.* Chicago: Jameson and Morse, 1884.

Public Schools of the City of Chicago. "Names of Teachers Employed, March 1894." In *Thirty-Ninth Annual Report of the Board of Education for the Year Ending June 30, 1893.* Chicago: George K. Hazlitt and Company, 1894.

———. *Twenty-Sixth Annual Report of the Board of Education, 1880–1881.*

————. *Fifty-Sixth Annual Report of the Board of Education for the Year Ending June 30, 1910.* Chicago: Board of Education of the City of Chicago, 1910.

————. Young, Ella Flagg. "In Memoriam, July 21, 1915." In "Report of the Superintendent of Schools." *Sixty-First Annual Report of the Board of Education for the Year Ending June 30, 1915,* 3–37. Chicago, 1916.

Books and Articles

Barnes, Sam. "Progressivism on the Wane: The Entrenchment of the Bureaucracy, 1900–1945." In *From Common School to Magnet School: Selected Essays in the History of Boston's Schools,* edited by James L. Fraser, Henry L. Allen, and Sam Barnes, 92–107. Boston: Boston Public Library, 1979.

————. "Reform and the Struggle for Control, 1870–1900." In *From Common School to Magnet School: Selected Essays in the History of Boston's Schools,* ed. James L. Fraser, Henry L. Allen, and Sam Barnes, 76–91. Boston: Boston Public Library, 1979.

Bayor, Ronald H. and Timothy J. Meagher, eds. *The New York Irish.* Baltimore: Johns Hopkins University Press, 1996.

Beatty, Jack. *The Rascal King: The Life and Times of James Michael Curley (1874–1958): An Epic of Urban Politics and Irish America.* Reading, Mass.: Addison-Wesley, 1992.

Bullough, William A. "Christopher Buckley and San Francisco: The Man and the City." In *The San Francisco Irish, 1850–1976,* 2d ed., edited by James P. Walsh, 27–41. San Francisco: Irish Literary and Historical Society, 1979.

Burchell, R. A. *The San Francisco Irish, 1848–1880.* Berkeley: University of California Press, 1980.

Clark, Dennis. *Hibernia America: The Irish and Regional Cultures.* Westport, Conn.: Greenwood Press, 1986.

Coffman, Lotus Delta. *The Social Composition of the Teaching Profession.* New York: Teachers College, Columbia University, 1911.

Connolly, James J. "Maternalism in Context: Protestant and Catholic Women's Activism in Progressive-Era Boston." *Mid-America: An Historical Review* 81 (Summer 1999): 91–123.

————. *The Triumph of Ethnic Progressivism: Urban Political Culture in Boston, 1900–1925.* Cambridge: Harvard University Press, 1998.

Counts, George S. *School and Society in Chicago.* New York: Harcourt, Brace, and Company, 1928. Reprint, New York: Arno Press, 1971.

Curry, Catherine Ann. "Shaping Young San Franciscans: Public and Catholic Schools in San Francisco, 1851–1906." Ph.D. diss., Graduate Theological Seminary, 1987.

———. "Three Irish Women and Social Action in San Francisco: Mother Theresa Comerford, Mother Baptist Russell, and Kate Kennedy." *Journal of the West* 31 (April 1992): 66–72.

Curry, J. Seymour. *Chicago: Its History and Its Builders.* Chicago: S. J. Clarke Publishing Company, 1912.

DeCock, Mary, BVM. "Creating a College: The Foundation of Mundelein, 1929–1931." In *Mundelein Voices: The Women's College Experience, 1930–1991,* edited by Ann M. Harrington and Prudence Moylan, 3–29. Chicago: Loyola Press, 2001.

De Ford, Miriam Allen. "America's Marx and His Bebel: Henry George and Kate Kennedy." In *They Were San Franciscans,* 122–153. Caldwell, Idaho: Caxton Press, 1947.

Diner, Hasia. *Erin's Daughters in America: Irish Immigrant Women in the Nineteenth Century.* Baltimore: Johns Hopkins University Press, 1983.

Dixon, George J. "George S. Counts and the Imposition Controversy." *Journal of the Midwest History of Education Society* 5 (1977): 105.

Doherty, Robert E. "Tempest on the Hudson: The Struggle for 'Equal Pay for Equal Work' in the New York City Public Schools, 1907–1911." *History of Education Quarterly* 19 (Winter 1979): 413–434.

Dowling, Patrick J. *California: The Irish Dream.* San Francisco: Golden Gate Publishers, 1988.

Doyle, David Noel. "The Remaking of Irish America, 1845–1880." In *A New History of Ireland,* Vol. 6, *Ireland under the Union, 1870–1921,* edited by W. E. Vaughan, 725–763. Oxford: Oxford University Press, 1996.

Ellis, Elmer. *Mr. Dooley's America: A Life of Finley Peter Dunne.* New York: Alfred A. Knopf, 1941.

Emmons, David. *The Butte Irish: Class and Ethnicity in an American Mining Town, 1875–1925.* Urbana: University of Illinois Press, 1989.

Fanning, Charles, ed. "Introduction." In *Exiles of Erin: Nineteenth-Century Irish-American Fiction,* 1–17. Notre Dame, Ind.: University of Notre Dame Press, 1987.

———. "Introduction." In *Mr. Dooley and the Chicago Irish: The Autobiography of a Nineteenth-Century Ethnic Group, by Finley Peter Dunne.* Washington: Catholic University of America Press, 1987.

Fraser, James L. "Reform, Immigration, and Bureaucracy, 1820–1870." In *From Common School to Magnet School: Selected Essays in the History of Boston's Schools,* edited by James L. Fraser, Henry L. Allen, and Sam Barnes, 28–42. Boston: Boston Public Library, 1979.

———. "Who Were the Progressive Educators Anyway?: A Case Study of the Progressive Education Movement in Boston, 1905–1925." *Educational Foundations* 2 (Spring 1988): 4–30.

George, Henry. *Progress and Poverty: An Inquiry into the Cause of Industrial Depressions, and the Increase of Want with [the] Increase of Wealth: The Remedy.* New York: Henry George and Company, 1887.

Gilbert, Benjamin F. and Charles Burdick. *Washington Square, 1857–1979: The History of San Jose State University.* San Jose, Calif.: San Jose State University, 1980.

Glazier, Michael. *The Encyclopedia of the Irish in America.* Notre Dame, Ind.: University of Notre Dame Press, 1999.

Gutek, Gerald L. *The Educational Theory of George S. Counts.* Columbus: Ohio State University Press, 1970.

———. *George S. Counts and American Civilization: The Educator as Social Theorist.* Macon, Ga.: Mercer University Press, 1984.

———. "George S. Counts As an Ideologist of American Education, the 1930s." *Journal of the Midwest History of Education Society* 5 (1977): 99–104.

Haley, Margaret. *Battleground: The Autobiography of Margaret A. Haley,* edited, with an introduction, by Robert L. Reid. Urbana: University of Illinois Press, 1982.

———. "Why Teachers Should Organize." In *Addresses and Proceedings of the National Education Association, 43rd Annual Meeting, St. Louis, Missouri, 1904.*

Handlin, Oscar. *Boston's Immigrants: A Study in Acculturation, 1790–1880.* Cambridge: Harvard University Press, 1941; New York: Atheneum, 1977.

Heidebrecht, Paul H. "Hefferan, Helen Maley." In *Women Building Chicago 1790–1990: A Biographical Dictionary,* edited by Rima Lunin Schultz and Adele Hast, 371–373. Bloomington: Indiana University Press, 2001.

Herbst, Jurgen. *And Sadly Teach: Teacher Education and Professionalization in American Culture.* Madison: University of Wisconsin Press, 1989.

Herrick, Mary J. *The Chicago Schools: A Social and Political History.* Beverly Hills, Calif.: Sage Publications, 1971.

Howatt, John. "Notes on the First One Hundred Years of Chicago School History" (photocopy). Chicago, 1946.

Howland, George. *Moral Training in the Public Schools.* Chicago: Jameson and Morse, 1882, 1889.

Hoy, Suellen. "Caring for Chicago's Women and Girls: The Sisters of Good Shepherd, 1859–1916." *Journal of Urban History* 23 (March 1997): 260–294.

———. "The Journey Out: The Recruitment and Emigration of Irish Religious Women to the United States, 1812–1914." *Journal of Women's History* 6/7 (Winter/Spring 1995): 64–98.

Jordan, Donald, ed. *The Bay Area Irish.* Forthcoming.

Kaufman, Polly Welts. *Boston Women and School Politics, 1872–1905.* New York: Garland, 1994.

Kenny, Kevin. *The American Irish: A History.* New York: Longman/Pearson, 2000.

————. *Making Sense of the Molly Maguires.* New York: Oxford University Press, 1998.

Lazerson, Marvin. *Origins of the Urban School: Public Education in Massachusetts, 1870–1915.* Cambridge: Harvard University Press, 1971.

————. "Teachers Organize: What Margaret Haley Lost." *History of Education Quarterly* 24 (Summer 1984): 261–270.

Lyons, John. "The Chicago Teachers' Union, Politics, and the City's Schools, 1937–1970." Ph.D. diss., University of Illinois at Chicago, 2001.

McCaffrey, Lawrence J. *The Irish Diaspora in America.* Bloomington: Indiana University Press, 1976.

————. *Textures of Irish America.* Syracuse, N.Y.: Syracuse University Press, 1992.

Mageean, Deirdre. "Making Sense and Providing Structure: Irish-American Women in the Parish Neighborhood." In *Peasant Maids—City Women: From the European Countryside to Urban America*, edited by Christiane Harzig, 77–97. Ithaca, N.Y.: Cornell University Press, 1997.

————. "To Be Matched or to Move: Irish Women's Prospects in Munster." In *Peasant Maids—City Women: From the European Countryside to Urban America*, edited by Christiane Harzig, 57–76. Ithaca, N.Y.: Cornell University Press, 1997.

Meagher, Timothy J. *Inventing Irish America: Generation, Class, and Ethnic Identity in a New England City, 1880–1928.* Notre Dame, Ind.: University of Notre Dame Press, 2001.

Miller, Kerby. *Emigrants and Exiles: Ireland and the Irish Exodus to North America.* New York: Oxford University Press, 1985.

Moffett, Mary Ledger. *The Social Background and Activities of Teachers College Students.* New York: Teachers College, Columbia University, 1929.

Montay, Sister Mary Innocenta. *The History of Catholic Secondary Education in the Archdiocese of Chicago.* Washington, D.C.: Catholic University of America Press, 1953.

Murphy, Marjorie. *Blackboard Unions: The AFT and the NEA, 1900–1980.* Ithaca, N.Y.: Cornell University Press, 1990.

Nester, Agnes. *Woman's Labor Leader: An Autobiography.* Rockford, Ill.: Bellevue Books, 1954.

Nolan, Janet. "Education: Irish-American Teachers in Public Schools, 1880–1920." In *The Encyclopedia of the Irish in America*, edited by Michael Glazier, 236–239. Notre Dame, Ind.: University of Notre Dame Press, 1999.

————. "Haley, Margaret Angela." In *Women Building Chicago 1790–1990: A Biographical Dictionary*, edited by Rima Lunin Schultz and Adele Hast, 338–341. Bloomington: Indiana University Press, 2001.

————. "Irish-American Teachers and the Struggle Over American Urban Public Education, 1890–1920: A Preliminary Look." *Records of the American Catholic Historical Society of Philadelphia* 103 (Winter 1992): 13–22.

———. "Legacy: Education and Women's Mobility in Irish Chicago and San Francisco in the Early Twentieth Century." In "New Approaches to Family History, Genealogy, and Irish Studies," *Working Papers in Irish Studies*, edited by James Doan, 1–5. Fort Lauderdale, Fla.: Nova Southeastern University, 2002.

———. *Ourselves Alone: Women's Emigration from Ireland, 1885–1920*. Lexington: University of Kentucky Press, 1989.

———. "Patrick Henry in the Classroom: Margaret Haley and the Chicago Teachers' Federation." *Eire-Ireland* 30 (Summer 1995): 104–117.

———. "Pioneers in the Classroom: The Irish in San Francisco's Schools." In *The Bay Area Irish*, edited by Donald Jordan. Forthcoming.

———. "St. Patrick's Daughter: Amelia Dunne Hookway and Chicago's Public Schools." In *At the Crossroads: Old Saint Patrick's and the Chicago Irish*, edited by Ellen Skerrett with a foreword by Mayor Richard M. Daley, 103–117. Chicago: Loyola Press, 1997.

Ozar, David T. "Five Approaches to Moral/Ethical Decision-Making" (photocopy), 1999. In author's possession, Chicago.

———. "Framework for Discussing Ethics" (photocopy), 1997. In author's possession, Chicago.

———. "An Outcomes-Centered Approach to Teaching Public-Sector Ethics." In *Teaching Ethics and Values: Program Innovation and Classroom Strategies*, edited by James Bowman and Donald Menzel, 85–99. Albany: State University of New York Press, 1997.

———. "Profession and Professional Ethics." In *The Encyclopedia of Bioethics* 4, rev. ed., edited by Warren Reich. New York: Macmillan, 1995.

Perko, F. Michael, S. J., ed. *Enlightening the Next Generation: Catholics and Their Schools, 1830–1980*. New York: Garland, 1988.

Perlmann, Joel. *Ethnic Differences: Schooling and Social Structure among the Irish, Italians, Jews, and Blacks in an American City, 1880–1935*. New York: Cambridge University Press, 1988.

Rischin, Moses. "Introduction: The Classic Ethnics." In *The San Francisco Irish, 1850–1976*, 2d ed., edited by James P. Walsh, 1–6. San Francisco: Irish Literary and Historical Society, 1979.

Rousmaniere, Kate. *City Teachers: Teaching and School Reform in Historical Perspective*. New York: Teachers College, Columbia University Press, 1997.

Rury, John L. "Urban Structure and School Participation: Immigrant Women in 1900." *Social Science History* 8 (Summer 1984): 219–241.

Sanders, James W. "Boston Catholics and the School Question, 1825–1907." In *From Common School to Magnet School: Selected Essays in the History of Boston's Schools*, edited by James L. Fraser, Henry L. Allen, and Sam Barnes, 43–91. Boston: Boston Public Library, 1979.

———. *The Education of an Urban Minority: Catholics in Chicago, 1833–1965*. New York: Oxford University Press, 1977.

Schiltz, Mary Pieroni. "The Dunne School Board: Reform in Chicago, 1905–1908. Ph.D. diss., Loyola University Chicago, 1993.

Schultz, Nancy Lusignan. *Fire and Roses: The Burning of the Charlestown Convent, 1834.* Boston: Northeastern University Press, 2000.

Schultz, Stanley K. *The Culture Factory: Boston Public Schools, 1789–1860.* New York: Oxford University Press, 1973.

Shrader, Victor L. "Ethnicity, Religion, and Class: Progressive School Reform in San Francisco." *History of Education Quarterly* 20 (Winter 1980): 385–401.

Skerrett, Ellen, ed. *At the Crossroads: Old Saint Patrick's and the Chicago Irish.* With a foreward by Mayor Richard M. Daley. Chicago: Loyola Press, 1997.

———. "The Catholic Dimension." In *The Irish in Chicago,* edited by Lawrence J. McCaffrey et al., 22–60. Urbana: University of Illinois Press, 1987.

———. "Chicago's Irish and 'Bricks and Mortar' Catholicism: A Reappraisal." *U.S. Catholic Historian* 14 (Spring 1996): 53–71.

———. "The Irish Parish in Chicago, 1880–1930." Cushwa Center for American Catholicism, Working Paper Series 9, No. 2. Notre Dame, Ind.: University of Notre Dame Press, Spring 1981.

Smith, Timothy. "Immigrant Social Aspirations and American Education, 1880–1930." *American Quarterly* 21 (Fall 1969): 523–543.

Strachan, Grace. *Equal Pay for Equal Work: The Story of the Struggle for Justice Being Made by Women Teachers of the City of New York.* New York: B. F. Buck and Company, 1910.

Tyack, David. *The One Best System: A History of American Urban Education.* Cambridge: Harvard University Press, 1974.

Urban, Wayne J. "Teacher Organizations in New York City, 1905–1920." In *Educating an Urban People: The New York City Experience,* edited by Diane Ravitch and Ronald K. Goodenow, 187–205. New York: Teachers College Press, Columbia University, 1981.

———. *Why Teachers Organized.* Detroit: Wayne State University Press, 1982.

U.S. Department of the Interior. Bureau of Education. 1917. *The Public School System of San Francisco, California.* Bulletin No. 46. Washington, D.C.: Government Printing Office, 1917.

U.S. Congress. Senate. 1911. "Census for the United States." In *Reports of the Immigration Commission: Abstracts of Reports of the Immigration Commission with Conclusions and Recommendations and Views of the Minority.* Vol. 1, S. Doc. 747, 429. 61st Cong., 3d sess.

Wade, Louise C. "Haley, Margaret Angela." In *Notable American Women, 1607–1950: A Biographical Dictionary* 2, edited by Edward T. James, Janet Wilson James, and Paul S. Boyer, 115–117. Cambridge: Harvard University Press, 1971.

Walch, Timothy G. "Catholic Education in Chicago: The Formative Years, 1840–1890." *Chicago History* 7 (Summer 1978): 87–97.

————. "Catholic School Books and American Values: The Nineteenth Century Experience." *Religious Education* 73 (September/October 1978): 582–591.

Walsh, James P. "The Irish in Early San Francisco." In *The San Francisco Irish, 1850–1976*, 2d ed., edited by James P. Walsh, 9–25. San Francisco: Irish Literary and Historical Society, 1979.

————. "Peter C. Yorke: San Francisco's Irishman Reconsidered." In *The San Francisco Irish, 1850–1976*, 2d ed., edited by James P. Walsh, 42–57. San Francisco: Irish Literary and Historical Society, 1979.

INDEX

AFL (American Federation of Labor): endorsement of public education, 95; pro-war stance, 1917, 100. *See also* CTF; Fitzpatrick, John
AFT (American Federation of Teachers): policies, 118–120; role in Chicago school politics, 100, 117. *See also* CTF
agriculture, Ireland, post-Famine changes, 23, 27, 41
Americanization in public schools, 4, 52, 74–75, 106, 112

backlash against Irish-American teachers, 53–58, 73, 91–92, 112, 123. *See also* Blake, John; Blake, Mary Elizabeth; Boston public schools; Coffey, Sr. Mary Justitia; Duff, Julia Harrington; Haley, Margaret; Kennedy, Kate
Blake, John, 46, 56
Blake, Mary Elizabeth (Mrs. John Blake): anti-Irish prejudice, 46, 48; Boston school committee campaign, 46
Boston: anti-Irish prejudice, 46–47, 53–58, 60, 62; impact of industrialization and urbanization on public schools, 52; impact of Irish immigration on schools, 49–51, 53–54, 57, 62; Irish-American

teachers, 2, 5, 44–45, 58–59; as regional center, 2, 4–5
Boston public schools: attendance 51, 54; average class size, 51; curriculum, 49, 52–53; girls' high school, number of Irish-American students, 58–59; grammar and high school enrollment, 51, 58–59; health conditions, 50, 61; history of, 48–49, 52–53; Irish history text, 47; kindergartens, 57; length of school year, 52; primary school enrollment, 50; student composition, 54; school texts, 55–56, 58; typical years of education, 51, 60
Boston school committee: anti-Catholic and anti-Irish nativism of, 44, 46–47, 53–54, 56–57, 60–61; Catholic members, 43; first Irish Catholic male and female members, 43, 46–48, 56; Public School Association, 44–46, 61; women members, 43, 46, 57–58. *See also* Blake, John; Blake, Mary Elizabeth; Duff, Julia Harrington

California state board of education: first equal-pay-for-equal-work law in U.S., 69; pensions, 69; tenure (life certificates), 69–70. *See also* Kennedy, Kate; Power, Alice Rose

Casey, Hannah (Mrs. Sylvester Cotter),
66; Clare McGrath Cotter
(daughter-in-law) and Caren
Cotter Ellis (granddaughter), 66
Catholic education: in Boston, 6,
43–44, 54–55, 58; in Chicago, 6,
91–92, 112; in San Francisco, 67,
71–72. *See also* Fenwick,
Benjamin; Williams, John
Catholic Order of Foresters, 91. *See
also* Haley, Margaret
CFL (Chicago Federation of Labor).
See AFL; CTF
Chicago, as regional center, 2, 4–5
Chicago board of education, 90, 91,
93, 97. *See also* strikes, Chicago
Chicago public schools: conflict and
competition with parochial
schools, 91–92; numbers of Irish-
American high and normal school
students, 92–93; numbers of Irish-
American teachers and attempts to
limit their numbers, 92–93, 109,
112, 123; origins and growth of
school system, 91–93, 103–106
Chicago schools (Scammon, West
Division, Central Park, Howland,
and Hendricks), 86–87, 90
Coffey, Sr. Mary Justitia: first
president, Mundelein College
(Chicago), 123; principal, St.
Mary's High School (Chicago),
123; teacher training success, 123
Coffman, Lotus Delta, author, *The
Social Composition of Teaching,*
110–112
Comerford, Mother Theresa, 71
Commissioners of National Education
in Ireland. *See* national schools,
Ireland
Counts, George S., author, *School and
Society in Chicago,* 103–105
Coyle, Julia (Mrs. Edward Mueller,
Sr.), 135; Eleanor Mueller King
(daughter) and Edward Mueller, Jr.
(son), 135

CTF (Chicago Teachers Federation):
advocacy of teachers' councils, 96,
99–100, 105, 108; affiliation with
AFT, 100, 104, 117–119; alliance
with CFL/AFL, 90, 95, 99–100;
campaigns for equal pay, tenure,
pensions for women teachers, 95,
100–101, 105, 113, 115; legislative
lobbying, 94; origins, 90, 93;
program, 90, 93–94, 96, 99, 102,
108; withdrawal from AFT/AFL,
100. *See also* Goggin, Catherine;
Haley, Margaret
CTU (Chicago Teachers Union, Local
Number One of AFT), 120

Depression, the: impact on economic
displacement of men, 126, 133,
135; impact on teacher gender
balance, 133, 135; impact on
teacher hiring, xii, 117, 123, 126,
133; impact on teacher professionalism, 118, 124; stock market
crash, ix, 117–118, 124, 126. *See
also* marriage bar
Donovan, Mary Ann (Mrs. Harry J.
Nolan), ix, xi, 127, 132; John,
Harry, James, Joseph, William,
Edward Nolan (sons), x, 127;
Mary (Mrs. John Mahoney),
Kathleen, and Helen (Mrs.
Herbert Need) Nolan (daughters),
ix, xi, 127; emigration to U.S., ix;
influence on children's careers,
xxii; Skibbereen national school
pupil teacher, ix, xii. *See also*
Nolan, William Francis
Duff, Julia Harrington (Mrs. John),
43–48, 57, 60–63, 98, 107; John
Duff, M.D. (husband), 43–44, 46;
John Jr., Paul, and Mae Duff (chil-
dren), 44. *See also* Boston school
committee; women's suffrage and
feminism
Dunne, Amelia (Mrs. William Hookway), 85–88, 92, 101, 107, 113,

133; Ellen Finley Dunne (mother), 85, 87, 102; Peter Finley Dunne (brother), 85–88; Kate, Mary, and Charlotte Dunne (sisters), 86–87

Ellis Island Immigration Museum, 1, 6–7

emigration from Ireland, ix, xi, 2–3, 5, 24, 27, 40–42

Famine, the: impact on Irish economy, 2–3; impact on Irish emigration, 2–3, 5, 27–28; impact on Kate Kennedy, 68; impact on national schools, 13; impact on women, 2–3, 5, 28. *See also* agriculture, Ireland, post-Famine changes

Fenwick, Benjamin, bishop of Boston: accommodation with Protestants, 54–56; attitude toward public schools, 54, 58

Fitzgerald, John "Honey Fitz," 44, 63

Fitzpatrick, John, 95, 100. *See also* AFL; CTF; Haley, Margaret

Fleming, Maryanne (Mrs. Dudley Nee), 136; Dudley Nee (son), 136

Fleming, Mary Huvane, 71; Patricia Walsh (daughter), 71

gender: discrimination against women teachers, 62–63, 66, 77–79; fathers encouraging daughters to become educated, 65–66; girls more apt to stay in school, 14, 86, 124, 126–127, 132, 135–136; impact on Irish-American social mobility, x, 1, 45, 66; mothers urging sons to become teachers, 124, 126–127, 132, 135–136. *See also* teaching, impact on Irish and Irish-American social mobility; teachers (U.S.)

Goggin, Catherine: anti-Irish prejudice directed against, 98; death, 101; first CTF president, 90, 100, 101. *See also* CTF; Haley, Margaret

Grady, Kate, 124–125; John Grady (brother), Margaret Grady (niece), and Lorraine Page (greatniece), 125

Haley, Margaret, 88–92, 94–96, 103, 116, 118, 122; alliance with CFL, 95, 100; *Battleground*, 98, 101–102; founding member and business manager, CTF, 90, 94–95, 97–102, 105, 107–109, 116; influence of mother and father, 88–90, 96–97, 102, 124. *See also* Catholic Order of Foresters; CTF; NEA; women's suffrage and feminism

Harper, William Rainey, 96–97, 99

Harper Commission. See Harper, William Rainey

Harrington, Catherine (Mrs. James Curry), 65, 72; Viola and John (children), 65. *See also* O'Donnell, Patrick

Hastings, John Joseph (married Mary Ann Hurley), 126; John Hastings, Jr., Betty Hastings O'Connor, and Dorothy Hastings Valeo (children), 126

hedge schools, 11–13, 18

Hefferan, Helen Maley, 119–120

Hogan, Kate, co-founder IAWT, 113–114. *See also* Strachan, Grace; New York City

Howland, George, author, *Moral Training in the Public Schools*, 86, 109–110

Hunt, Ann (Mrs. Patrick King), 136; William and Daniel King (sons), 136

IAWT (Interborough Association of Women Teachers). *See* Hogan, Kate

immigration: to Boston, xi, 49–50; to Ellis Island, 1, 6–7; impact on Boston public schools, 50–51, 54, 56. *See also* emigration from Ireland

INTO (Irish National Teachers Union), 37–38

Irish: in Boston, 49–51, 53–54, 57, 62; in Chicago, 103; in San Francisco, 66, 68, 71, 73, 80

Kennedy, Kate, 68–69, 77, 107, 113–114; Alice Kennedy and Lizzie Kennedy Burke (sisters), 68–69, 73. *See also* San Francisco public schools

Kildare Place Society (Society for Promoting the Education of the Poor in Ireland), 12

Know-Nothings, 53, 54, 68

labor union attitude toward public schools. *See* AFL; AFT; CFL; CTF; Fitzpatrick, John

Lennon, Mary Crowe, 40–42

Leonard, Mary (Mrs. Nicholas Dunne), 88; Catherine Dunne (daughter), Mary Dunne (Mrs. James Bancroft, granddaughter), Edward, Frances, and Mary Angela (Mrs. John Hillan) Bancroft (great-grandchildren), Margaret Mary Hillan (Mrs. Frank Foerner, great-great granddaughter), and Mary Foerner (great-great-great granddaughter), 88

Loeb, Jacob, 99–100, 118, 120

Loeb Rule / Loeb Commission. *See* Loeb, Jacob

Lynn, Massachusetts: history, ix, 134; public schools, ix, 126–127, 132–133; teacher examinations, 130–133. *See also* Nolan, William Francis

Lyons, Mary (Mrs. Dennis O'Brien), 136; Thomas O'Brien (son), 136

McGovern, Judith Comisky, 71

McNeela, Delia (Mrs. Michael Tully), 121–122, 125; Irene Tully Ryan

(daughter), 122, 125. *See also* Tully, Michael

marriage bar: in Ireland, 37, 148n39; in U.S., xi, xii, 107. *See also* national schools, Ireland, teachers

Meehan, Mary Theresa (Mrs. John McGowan), 81–84, 102; Mary Ann McGowan Clancy (daughter), 81, 83–84

Meehan, Norah (Nonie, Mrs. Michael McNeela), 81, 84–85, 102; Annemarie McNeela Ricker (daughter), 89

Martin, Mary Ellen (Ella, Mrs. William Moakley), x, xi; Louise Moakley Bennett and Laura Moakley Harvey (daughters), x, xi. *See also* Moakley, Janet

Martin, William, and Annie Power Martin (widow), xi

Mitchell, Delia (Mrs. Patrick Dowd), 125; Joan Dowd Enright (daughter), 125

Moakley, Janet (Mrs. William Francis Nolan), ix–xi, 128–129, 134–135. *See also* Nolan, William Francis; Martin, Mary Ellen

Moffett, Mary Ledger, author, *The Social Background and Activities of Teachers' College Students,* 111–112

Moran, Urania Cloney, 71; Urania Moran Garner (daughter), 71; Urania Michaela Moran (grand-niece), 71

Mundelein, George Cardinal, 93, 123

Mundelein College. *See* Coffey, Sr. Mary Justitia

national schools, Ireland
—Commissioners of National Education in Ireland, 10, 12–13, 25–27; sectarianism in school administration, 12, 25–27, 38; usurpation of local school control, 25–27, 30

—curriculum: British history and literature, 17, 29–30; cookery, 20–22; geography, 17, 19, 29–30; impact on spread of English language, 28; Irish history and Irish language in classroom, 28, 40–41; laundering, 20, 22; needlework, 16, 20–22; political economy, 10; texts, 10–13, 17, 19–20

—district inspectors' reports, 28, 30, 33; impact on teacher hiring and firing, 36

—history of: attendance, 14–16; first state-supported primary education in United Kingdom, 3, 12; Kildare Place Society (Society for Promoting the Education of the Poor in Ireland), 12; parliamentary studies of, 11–12; proliferation after the Famine, 9, 14–15

—impact on emigration, 2, 4–5, 7, 27–28, 40–42

—school managers, 13–14, 25–27, 30, 32, 40

—schools: Aghaloora, Cavan, 25–27, 30, 39; Ballinrobe Convent, Mayo, 41; Caherciveen, Kerry, 33; Callow, Foxford, Mayo, 125; Castlegregory, Kerry, 9–10, 13–14, 22–24, 27, 33; Clonakilty, Cork, 136; Cloonfarna, Mayo, 136; Coolpora, Galway, 125; Gortnacor, Donegal, 135; Kilasser, Mayo, 81; Knockreagh, Kerry, 136; Roundstone, Galway, 136; Swinford, Mayo, 121; Tankerstown, Tipperary, 137

—teachers: Hannah Crowley, 23–24; Honoria Crowley, 23–24; Joanna Crowley, 22; W. Erskine, 34; Mr. and Mrs. Mansfield, 37–38; Mary Morris, 36, 38; Michael O'Shea, 40; Mrs. O'Sullivan, 39; Margaret Smyth, 25–27; classroom duties, 31–32, 34–35; evaluations and promotions, 25–27, 32–39; infringements on private and public lives, 34–35; rules and regulations: 20, 34–36, 39; salaries, gender inequities in, 31, 36–37

—teacher training: Lancastrian system of Andrew Bell and Joseph Lancaster, 30; Marlborough Street Model School curriculum, 31–32; model schools, 12; pupil-teachers, ix, xii, 31; training manuals, 16–17, 29, 34–35, 37

—See also marriage bar; Welply, W. H.

NEA (National Education Association), 93–94, 96, 109, 115. See also Haley, Margaret

Nester, Agnes, 102

New York City: numbers of Irish-American teachers, 2; teacher unions, 113. See also Hogan, Kate; Strachan, Grace

Nolan, William Francis, ix, x, xi, 126–129, 131–135; Brian Moakley Nolan, Janet Ann Nolan, and Nancy Kathleen Transue (children), xii. See also Moakley, Janet; teacher training (U.S.), examinations

normal schools. See teacher training (U.S.)

O'Brien, Hugh, 56

O'Brien, Sara, 52

O'Donnell, Patrick, 65–66; Genevieve, Regina, and Mary O'Donnell (daughters), 65–66, 70; Catherine Ann Curry (granddaughter), 72. See also Harrington, Catherine

O'Leary, Bridget Mulloy, 24; John O'Leary (son), 135

O'Leary, Nora (Mrs. John Crean), 24, 27; Joan Crean O'Leary (daughter), 24

O'Sullivan, Margaret (Sr. M. Columba), 72–73; Neilus O'Sullivan (grandnephew), 72

Otis Law, impact on teacher hiring, Chicago, 104

"payless paydays," cause of Chicago teacher unrest, 118, 124. *See also* strikes, Chicago

PEA (Public Education Association). *See* Hefferan, Helen Maley

Penal Laws, 11, 13

Power, Alice Rose, 107; commendation, 70–71; school text author and member, San Francisco board of education and California state board of education, 70

professional ethics, 108–110, 114–117, 119–120. *See also* strikes, Chicago

progressivism in education, 47, 96; impact on female suffrage in school board elections, 57

Providence, Rhode Island, number of Irish-American public school teachers, 2

PSA (Public School Association), 44–46, 61

Russell, Mother Mary Baptist, 71–72

Ryan, Helen (Mrs. Michael Brown), 136–137; Margaret (Peg) Brown Cunningham (daughter), 137

Salem (Massachusetts) Teachers College, entry requirements and curriculum, ix, x, 128–132

San Francisco: history of, 67; as regional center, 4–5

San Francisco board of education, reaction to Irish-American teachers, 73–77. *See also* Swett, John

San Francisco public schools: anti-Irish prejudice, 72–73, 75; cosmopolitan schools, 67–68; enrollments and numbers of schools, 67; history of, 67; number of Irish-American students in high and normal schools, 76–77; number of Irish-American teachers, 2, 68, 70, 78; as regional center, 4, 5. *See also* Kennedy, Kate

San Francisco schools (Greenwich Primary, North Cosmopolitan Grammar, Kate Kennedy School, South Cosmopolitan Grammar, Croker Grammar, Burke/Delmar, Whittier Primary, Pacific Heights Grammar, Grant Grammar, Edison Grammar, and Washington Irving), 68–70

"Seven Sisters," working-class educational alternatives to elite women's colleges, 2, 44

Skibbereen, County Cork, national schools, ix, xii. *See also* Donovan, Mary Ann

Society for Promoting the Education of the Poor in Ireland (Kildare Place Society), 12

Starkie, W. J. M., 29, 38–39

Stincen, Alice and Emma, 70

Strachan, Grace, 113–114. *See also* Hogan, Kate; New York City

strikes, Chicago, 90–91, 93, 97, 108, 113, 117–119. *See also* professional ethics

Swett, John: "Americanization" in texts, 73–74; change of heart toward Irish-American teachers, 73, 75; superintendent, San Francisco public schools, and superintendent of public instruction, California, 72–73. *See also* San Francisco board of education, reaction to Irish-American teachers

teachers (U.S.): benefits, 62–63, 78; class composition, 8, 43, 45, 58–59, 62–63, 78, 104, 109–112;

feminization of, 77, 79, 97–99, 105–106; politics in hiring, 43, 45, 47, 56–57, 63, 103–104; professional autonomy, 47, 62–63, 79–80, 105–108, 112–113, 117–118; salaries, 37, 61, 69, 90, 95, 99, 113–114, 117. *See also* gender, discrimination against women teachers

teachers' councils, 96, 99, 100, 105, 108. *See also* Young, Ella Flagg

teacher training (U.S.): attempts to re-strict Irish-American entry, 43–44, 58–60; curriculum, 76–77, 103; examinations, 68, 130–132; increase in entrance and gradu-ation requirements, 45, 47, 59, 60–61, 76, 93, 107; numbers of Irish-Americans enrolled, 44, 58, 59, 76–77, 92–93, 112–113; origins of normal schools, 58–59, 68, 76–78; school committee oversight, 45, 47, 76. *See also* Nolan, William Francis

teaching, impact on Irish and Irish-American social mobility, 28, 30, 40–42, 58–59, 63, 65–73, 79–80, 106–107. *See also* gender, impact on Irish-American social mobility

Tully, Michael, 122, 125–126. *See also* McNeela, Delia

Twain, Mark, 85

Watertown, Massachusetts, schools, x, xi, 134

Welply, W. H., 36–38

Williams, John, archbishop: accom-modation with Protestants, 55; attitudes toward Boston public schools, 58

women's suffrage and feminism, 45, 91, 97–99, 102. *See also* Duff, Julia Harrington; Haley, Margaret

Young, Ella Flagg, 86–87, 93, 96, 101, 104, 108. *See also* teachers' councils

JANET NOLAN is professor of history at Loyola University Chicago.